Nick Kaldas was born in Egypt in 1957 and moved with his family to Australia in 1969. He served in the NSW Police Force for 35 years, the last ten as the Deputy Commissioner. His career was mainly in major and organised crime investigations and counter terrorism. He led the investigation into the murder of John Newman MP, and as the Commander of the Homicide Squad and the Gangs Squad for some years, he oversaw many murder investigations, including the murders committed by Sef Gonzales.

Nick also held a number of significant international roles, including Deputy Chief Police Adviser with the Coalition Forces in Iraq in 2004, overseeing the rebuilding of the Iraqi police and security forces; Chief of Investigations in the UN Special Tribunal for Lebanon in 2009–10, investigating the assassination of former prime minister Rafic Hariri and a number of other assassinations; and Chief of Investigations of the UN/OPCW investigation into the use of chemical weapons in 2016.

Nick served as Chair and Commissioner in the Royal Commission into Defence and Veteran Suicide, 2021–24.

BEHIND THE BADGE

Nick Kaldas

with Roger Joyce

ABC
BOOKS

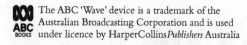 The ABC 'Wave' device is a trademark of the
Australian Broadcasting Corporation and is used
under licence by HarperCollins*Publishers* Australia

HarperCollins*Publishers*
Australia • Brazil • Canada • France • Germany • Holland • India
Italy • Japan • Mexico • New Zealand • Poland • Spain • Sweden
Switzerland • United Kingdom • United States of America

HarperCollins acknowledges the Traditional Custodians
of the lands upon which we live and work, and pays respect
to Elders past and present.

First published on Gadigal Country in Australia in 2025
by HarperCollins*Publishers* Australia Pty Limited
ABN 36 009 913 517
harpercollins.com.au

A catalogue record for this book is available from the National Library of Australia

ISBN 978 0 7333 4212 7 (paperback)
ISBN 978 1 4607 1417 1 (ebook)

Cover design by Louisa Maggio, HarperCollins Design Studio
Cover images: Nick Kaldas © Tim Bauer / Fairfax Media; background image
by istockphoto.com
Typeset in Sabon LT Std by Kirby Jones

Printed and bound by CPI Group (UK) Ltd, Croydon, CR0 4YY

To my family, who have been with me along this journey and without whom I am certain I could not have prospered.

And to the men and women of the NSW Police Force, past and present. I shall always be grateful for my time working alongside you and leading you. Our work has been my raison d'être for most of my life; it is a great and noble cause, and I shall always be proud to have worn that uniform.

CONTENTS

FOREWORD
By Malcolm Turnbull

During my time as Prime Minister of Australia, the dominant security concern was terrorism. The Australian Defence Force was supporting a US-led coalition to defeat the so-called Islamic State or ISIS (or Da'esh) in Iraq and Syria.

At home, our police and security agencies were devoting enormous resources to preventing terrorist actions. The fact that there were so few terrorist attacks in Australia is a tribute to the professionalism of the men and women in the Australian Security Intelligence Organisation, the Australian Federal Police and the State and Territory police services in particular.

Every prime minister is acutely aware of Cicero's famous line 'Salus populi suprema lex' – the security of the people, of the nation, is the highest responsibility of the government. Coming into office I was very concerned that the anxiety about terrorism was leading to conduct and rhetoric by government that was only likely to make the problem worse. Worse still, much – sometimes most – of the media were ramping up hostility towards Islam and Muslims generally.

All of this seemed to me to be playing into the hands of the terrorists. ISIS was predicting they would be shortly sweeping across Europe to stable their horses in the Vatican. And our leaders, or too many of them, were acting as though they took this seriously. Many young Muslim men became increasingly alienated from society at large and were more susceptible to propaganda from the extremists.

All of this led me to call Nick Kaldas, who had lunch with me at our home in January 2016. I knew a fair bit about him. He was the Deputy Commissioner of the NSW Police, one of the largest police forces in the world. His life story is the very epitome of modern, multicultural Australia. Born in Egypt, fluent in Arabic and French, he understood the culture, the politics, the mind of the Arab world whether it was in Cairo, Beirut, Baghdad or, indeed, the suburbs of Sydney. There was nobody senior in the Australian security community who understood the complex Australian Middle Eastern communities in the way Nick did. While Nick is a Coptic Christian, like ten per cent of Egyptians, he was deeply respected by the Muslim communities.

Our agenda was terrorism and Nick explained that the core of the problem in Australia lay in the disconnection and alienation of young Muslims, both from their parents (who they felt were stuck in the old ways) and the society at large (which they felt was anti Muslim). This, he explained, made them very vulnerable to radicals and terrorists.

After all, he said, the ISIS pitch is simply: *the Australians hate you. You will never be accepted, you can never get ahead or win respect. The government, the media, the police hate you for who you are. So join us, the Islamic State, we are your real family.*

He explained to me that counter-terrorism policy was only focused on the final kinetic action – how to stop it and how to punish those who are planning or doing it. It was focused only on the end, and we had to get to where it starts in the community instead.

As for political rhetoric, we agreed that far too much of it was reactive and counterproductive – indeed so much so that on one occasion I told the radio shock jock Alan Jones that I thought he was doing the terrorists' work with his anti-Muslim rants.

Nick's advice was enormously helpful to me. He described how police and other agencies should work with the community, supporting those who speak out against extremism or recant their extremist views. He stressed the importance of providing alternatives to arrest and of working with parents to help them divert their young people from an extremist path.

Nick was on the point of leaving the NSW Police and travelling to The Hague to head up the United Nations investigation into the use of chemical weapons in Syria, but we stayed in touch, often exchanging emails on these important issues from Amman, Jordan, or wherever he was based at the time.

This book is the life story of a very remarkable Australian. His police career in Australia would make for a book in itself, but when you add to that his youth spent in Egypt and Lebanon and then later in life his international missions in the Middle East, you have an Australian career unlike any other I have known.

There are dark passages in Nick's life, as I suppose there are in most lives. Nick sets out the history of the now discredited

Operation Prospect, which was supposed to investigate how he, and many others, were bugged by NSW Police Internal Affairs without any demonstrated justification but which failed to do so and instead targeted the complainants. It almost certainly prevented him becoming Commissioner of Police in NSW – it certainly caused him years of unnecessary pain and anguish – but it did not beat him, nor did it hold back his career which, spread over the international stage, was far more influential (and interesting) than that of a police commissioner. That said, the bugging saga he describes is a reminder that security agencies, especially those that operate in secret, must be held accountable and comply with the law.

Six months before Nick and I met for lunch, I had given a speech on this theme on the 800th anniversary of Magna Carta. I recalled Robert Menzies' speech to introduce national security legislation to the House of Representatives in 1939. His warning then should never be forgotten: 'The greatest tragedy that could overcome a country would be for it to fight a successful war in defence of liberty and lose its own liberty in the process.'

Smoking with the Enemy

2017

Smoke from the big expensive Cohiba cigars curled in the air around us. I'd sunk deep into a luxurious lounge, and the only thing between me and one of the most feared men in the Middle East was an elegant coffee table laden with French cakes, tiny cups of Arabic coffee and a massive ashtray.

My companion was a man so powerful he could make people disappear in a heartbeat – including me, if he felt like it. And I was on *his* turf.

In the Syrian regime, there was a committee made up of all the generals in charge of intelligence. The head of this committee ran the military intelligence services, which included air-force and army intelligence, as well as the ruthless mukhabarat, allegedly responsible for arresting, torturing and executing enemies of the government.

Syria's mukhabarat is the most feared and fearsome of intelligence organisations. For decades, citizens and visitors had been warned not to stand out in Syria, not to flash money around or use their mobile phones in public for fear of being suspected of being a spy. Now, with the civil war in full flight, there were informers everywhere. Stories abounded of people who'd been tortured and disappeared.

Even for a high-ranking United Nations (UN) official like me, the head of the mukhabarat was next to impossible to contact, let alone meet. I was the director of the internal oversight function of the United Nations Relief and Works Agency (UNRWA), which provides all aid to over five and a half million Palestine refugees spread across five countries, one of which was Syria. And our staff, myself included, were being forced to apply for visas each time they entered the country, which was against international protocols, since we travelled on UN diplomatic passports. Some of my investigators were being refused visas, which was beginning to hamper our work there. We'd tried a number of diplomatic channels, but all efforts had failed.

Knowing Arabic culture as I did, I'd felt certain that the head general was someone who could click his fingers and get things done. But would he meet with me? It was something others had warned couldn't, perhaps shouldn't, be attempted.

I'd made contact with the general through a senior UN official with an Egyptian background, who I knew had a good relationship with the Syrian regime. Amazingly, he had agreed to see me in his compound.

My protection team had asked if I really *needed* to go in. As a senior UN official, I wasn't someone the mukhabarat could kidnap without causing an international incident. Still, I was on heightened alert as I made my way to the general's secret headquarters for the first time.

It was midsummer, and the streets of Damascus were crowded despite the shimmering heat. Everything was abnormally normal. The frontline of the siege being waged by the government against the rebels in Ghouta and other places was just a few kilometres away. The sounds of mortars and gunfire were occasional reminders of the fighting, especially at night. But most people in Damascus were just trying to get on with living their lives.

I had my bodyguard with me, and we drove around the area three times before we finally found the unmarked gate into the compound. It was so large that it seemed to take up a suburb. We then had to go through a number of checkpoints, but the guards appeared to be expecting us, otherwise we wouldn't have got far.

I was met by the general's aide on the marble steps leading into the main building, where I parted company with my bodyguard, who had to wait outside. As I was escorted through a maze of rooms and past another couple of checkpoints, I tried to memorise the way out, conscious that I might need an escape route if it all went south. As a former undercover police officer, I'd been trained to always look for an exit.

In my suit pocket was a mobile phone with my bodyguard's number dialled up ready to go. But if anything happened, he was now too far away to be of any real help.

I'd carried a gun for decades in my job as a police officer. On many days it could have meant the difference between life and death – mine and my team's. Feeling the firearm on my hip had always given me some comfort. But now I was unarmed, except for my powers of negotiation.

Finally, we reached the general's office, deep inside the belly of the building. It was tastefully decorated, and the general and his staff were urbane and sophisticated, dressed in fine suits.

I suspected the general knew my history. I had previously led investigations into his government's use of chemical weapons in the civil war, and into the assassination of former Lebanese prime minister Rafic Hariri, to which Syria had been linked. Yet the general was surprisingly warm and welcoming.

My years of living and working in the Middle East had taught me that in situations like this, it is imperative to start with general chitchat and only discuss business once a rapport has been built. The general asked me about my background and where I grew up, and I gave him a cut-down version of my story. I explained that I was Egyptian born and bred, which he would have immediately picked up from my accent in Arabic, and that I had migrated to Australia where I had served for 35 years in the police force. I then explained my role as the director of Internal Oversight Services at UNRWA.

Eventually we got to my request for our investigators to be granted visas. I went to some lengths to point out the fact that we were investigating allegations of misbehaviour or corruption within the agency, and not the actions of the Syrian regime.

In the end I met with the general several times, and he obliged me in everything I asked him for. My staff got their visas.

It was not until the very last meeting that he dropped into the conversation the fact that he knew all about my investigations into Hariri's death and the chemical weapons. He got a kick out of breaking this news to me, laughing raucously. I think he'd agreed to meet me because he was keen to size me up. He got what he wanted, and *I* got what *I* wanted: access for my staff to Syria. I have to admit, it was difficult to dislike him up close.

It really was one of life's surreal scenes. There I was, in this secret compound in the heart of the Syrian regime: me, a kid from Cairo, via Marrickville, sitting there smoking a Cuban cigar, shooting the breeze with the head honcho of the mukhabarat.

CHAPTER 1

Wearing the Uniform

1981

I believe policing is a calling.

Later in my police career I was often invited to speak to graduating classes. I used to say this to the student cops:

'You'll never have to die wondering about whether you'll make a difference; you will make a difference every day. You will go towards danger when everybody else is heading in the other direction.'

I think most people who join the force do so because they're passionate about helping people, about making a difference. A friend of mine, Mike Julian, who was once a deputy commissioner in the NYPD, maintains that all of us in the police force were bullied at some point in our lives, or saw others being bullied and couldn't stop it. So we join because subconsciously we want to stick up for those who can't stick up for themselves, as perhaps we couldn't back then. And maybe he's right; I've certainly experienced my fair share of bullies.

As kids, my siblings and I were told, if we were ever in strife, to look for someone in uniform – a fireman, a bus conductor. As a police officer, you know that each time you put on that uniform, you're going to make someone's life better. But on my first day of training in 1981, I didn't realise just how much wearing that uniform meant.

At the NSW Police Academy in Redfern, the crown sergeant, Bruce Gould (the father of legendary rugby league personality Phil Gould), looked us new recruits up and down and then, for some reason, came and stood right behind me.

'You don't mind if I touch you, do you?' he said.

Given this was my first day, I wasn't about to object. 'No, sergeant,' I said.

He took his index finger and ran it from the back of my shirt collar and up my neck to my head. 'I don't want to see *any* hair flopping over my finger.'

I thought, *Sheesh!*, because my hair was indeed flopping over the sergeant's finger. Before that I'd actually thought it was quite short.

'Can everybody see this?' the crown sergeant asked. Everyone else leaned back to look at New Recruit Kaldas's hairline. 'There's an Italian barbershop across the road. You need to go there at lunchtime.' He was speaking to me but meant just about everybody.

As instructed, we all lined up at Guido's barbershop that lunchtime, and we continued to do so about once a week, to satisfy the academy's requirements. It was a first lesson in just how much was expected of a new police officer.

* * *

I'd got a job in insurance straight out of school. Eventually, though, I thought, *I'm going to have to get a career.* Despite the great people I worked with, and the amazing social life, I just wasn't going to be doing this job for the rest of my life. I wanted to do something that meant more to me. I wanted a job I could be passionate about.

In the back of my mind there was this niggling thing about wanting to join the police – maybe thanks to my fictional childhood heroes Arsène Lupin (a French 'gentleman thief' in literature and cartoons) and Batman – but I didn't think I was tall enough. Still, I saw that they were advertising for recruits in the newspaper. So I took a day off and I went into the police headquarters on College Street in Sydney.

I was 23, so I was too old for a cadetship, but you could join up until the age of 50. They used to talk about 'real-world experience' and how those who'd joined as cadets probably missed out on that. I'd already had a few years out in this 'real world'. I don't think I was immature, though I probably wasn't as worldly-wise as I thought I was.

As a part of the process, you were vetted. Officers knocked on the doors of all your neighbours and you had to nominate referees, who would be subject to a very thorough background check.

A uniformed sergeant came and knocked on my next-door neighbour's door first, but there was no response.

My mum, seeing a policeman through the one-way peephole, came out. 'Is everything all right?' she asked.

'Are you Mrs Kaldas?' the sergeant asked.

'That's me.'

The sergeant explained who he was and what he was doing, so my mum invited him in.

When I'd first told my mum I wanted to become a cop, she was horrified. 'No, you're not doing it, absolutely not. I'm going to disown you, you're not doing it. It's too dangerous, you'll get killed!'

This was a discussion we had again a few times, much later.

Now, she was sitting in front of someone who was looking for the smallest reason as to why my application should be rejected. He asked her if she was happy that I wanted to join the police.

She could have put the kibosh on my policing career right then and there, but she swallowed her apprehensions because she knew being a cop was my dream. There was no way she was going to say no.

Right up until the day she died, she told me that she should have sat down with that sergeant and made up stories about what a bad person and a terrible son I was, then I would never have got the job and put her through years of worry. That was my mum's idea of humour.

After they'd measured me and carried out all their character checks, there was nothing more to do. I just had to wait.

Some weeks later, I got home from work one day and *the letter* had arrived. With only my mother there – who would have preferred for my application to be rejected – I opened the envelope. It said I'd been accepted and that I would need to turn up at Redfern Police Academy to start my career in the NSW Police Force.

My mother's enthusiasm was tempered by her misgivings, but I was elated. My only thought was: *This is it, this is my future, and it begins now.*

CHAPTER 2

A Country in Crisis

1957–1969

I was born in 1957, in a neighbourhood in Cairo. My parents named me Naguib after my grandfather, who'd been knighted by King Farouk for his contribution to architecture. He'd been responsible for most of the significant buildings in his hometown of Asyut, 365 kilometres south of Cairo.

My dad, Samy, was born in Asyut in 1918. His mother, Evelyn, raised 13 children, two of whom sadly died before the age of two.

Through my profession, I've met some brave people – but in many ways I think my dad was the most courageous man I ever knew. Because he was one of the younger children, he didn't inherit much. But he became a self-made man. He toughed it out, worked hard and didn't tolerate bad behaviour from anyone.

He'd made his fortune through agriculture by the time he was 30, ending up with hundreds if not thousands of feddans (Egyptian acres). He also had aunties, distant relatives whose husbands had died, and he would manage their operations for an agreed financial arrangement. He had hundreds of people working for him, and they farmed chamomile, cotton, tomatoes and all sorts of vegetables, and the produce was both sold within Egypt and exported. He earned an excellent name for the quality of his product and the efficiency of his food-chain logistics, which he oversaw at every point. My father's boast was that cucumbers that were cut from his land and loaded onto a van in Asyut would be in a Milanese market within 24 hours.

There was a famous local criminal active in Asyut and the mountains in that part of Upper Egypt who went by the name of El Khut. He and his gang were brigands; he'd killed people and was wanted by the police. While everyone feared him, he was also thought of as a bit of a Robin Hood figure, because he stood up for locals against the authorities. My father wasn't happy with a few things El Khut had done, so he sent word saying he wanted to meet. Everyone was horrified and warned my father not to do it. The story goes that my dad met with El Khut, looked him in the eye and told him that he didn't want him carrying out any of his shady business on his patch. Apparently El Khut acquiesced, and they shook hands on it.

My father had been a weightlifter and had 'arms as big as some men's legs', as people would say. So whether he charmed El Khut or intimidated him, I'm not quite sure. But I don't think anyone had stood up to El Khut in this way before, and he must have respected the guts my father had in doing this. My dad feared no man: a character trait I hope he passed on to me.

* * *

My father met my mother, Soheir, when he went to pay condolences to her family after her father passed away. Her father had been a doctor in Malawi, a much smaller city to the north of Asyut, also on the Nile, and their families were related by marriage somehow.

My father was in his thirties. He'd lived the high life for a while and was a very eligible bachelor with a lot of money. And in Egypt, if you're not married by that age, people want to know what's wrong with you.

My mum had an older sister, and tradition has it that the older sister should be the one to marry first. Relatives and friends told him, 'No, you can't think about Soheir, you must court her older sister,' but my father was adamant. He only had eyes for Soheir. He won the argument, and they eventually got married.

Dad just idolised Mum and showered her with gifts. Every time he went to Paris or London on a business trip – and he travelled a great deal – he'd return with furs or the finest haute couture fashions for her. And though my father ruled the roost, when my mother put her foot down, she inevitably got what she wanted, even if it took a little time.

We were very well-to-do and had a really good life. We lived on a huge piece of land, a couple of acres right in the heart of Asyut, with cows and lots of date-palm trees.

We lived in a beautiful Roman-style apartment complex with the finest stonework there was. There were two apartments upstairs and two downstairs; I remember the majestic carved wooden staircase that linked them. The right upstairs apartment was for my widowed grandmother, Evelyn, who spoiled me rotten. I was constantly accused of being her favourite by my sister, Dallal, who is four years older than I am, because I was the only grandson named after Naguib, my grandfather.

Like most people who did well in Egypt, we had a cook, a maid and a driver. We always had a couple of cars, including a big Ford; Dad loved that car.

My father sometimes got attention from various ladies at black-tie dinners and the like. My mum did her best not to get jealous, but she had no reason to worry: he was absolutely devoted to her, and she to him. Even though she would outlive him by many years, not for one second did my mum think about going on a date with anyone else, let alone getting married again. For Soheir, there was only *her* Samy.

* * *

Faith was an important thing in my family. We were all baptised Coptic Orthodox in a predominantly Muslim country. We went to church reasonably regularly and we tried to live a Christian life. My dad told us that it wasn't just about going to church on Sunday but also about what you did Monday to Saturday.

In my teenage years, I toyed with the idea of becoming a monk and spending the rest of my life serving God, but it was a fleeting impulse, and in the end it just wasn't me. However, the notion of service has obviously stuck with me. To do good work, hold decent values and live by your beliefs: these were things instilled in me by both my father and my mother.

My father really cared about the Coptic Orthodox people and our plight. Christians struggle in Egypt and most of the Middle East. Today some people think of the Middle East as being Muslim, if not extremist Muslim. But it is, of course, considered the Holy Land to Christians as well, and we often forget that a lot of people in Lebanon, Egypt and other Middle Eastern countries are Christian.

* * *

Growing up in the Middle East, I had a great awareness of politics, even at the age of five or six. I would be in the room with my parents, uncles, aunties and family friends, and everyone would be passionately discussing what was happening between America and the Arabs. It is very different from Australia where kids – indeed, most Australians – aren't so interested. But every Arab kid can tell you about the political parties in their country and what's happening, because an interest in politics seems to be in their DNA.

While we were living an idyllic lifestyle in Asyut, great change was underway in the rest of the country. King Farouk had been overthrown five years before I was born, and the country was now the Republic of Egypt. The revolution of 1952 had been driven by a group of army officers led by General Muhammad Naguib and Colonel Gamal Abdel Nasser. Nasser was to become an agent of radical change in that corner of the Arab world, steering his country through the Suez Crisis of 1956 and denouncing Western imperialism along the way. He became the second president of Egypt in 1954, a position he held until his death in 1970.

Nasser was incredibly popular in the Arab world: he 'lifted up the heads' of Arabs and encouraged them not to be subservient to the West.

After the toppling of King Farouk, it took Nasser a few years to swing the country to the left. I think it was his contempt for the imperialist West that caused him to veer towards the Soviet Union, and Premier Nikita Khrushchev welcomed Nasser with open arms. Nasser had Soviet advisers in most government departments, and they got their claws into the country.

* * *

We moved from Asyut to Cairo when I was six. It was just easier for my father workwise. Not long after that, my brother, Alaa, was born.

We settled in Heliopolis, part of Greater Cairo, busy and bustling compared with languid Asyut. In the early 1960s the population of Asyut was 127,000, while the population of Cairo was 3.6 million and growing rapidly.

Our apartment was on the seventh floor of a semi-circular building. I would play soccer in the hallways between the apartments with the other kids on our floor; it would get really loud and sometimes one of the parents would scream at us to stop and we would have to calm down for a while. But there wasn't really anywhere else for us to go. Cairo was and is one of the most built-up cities in the world and there wasn't a lot of green space. So we made do with what we had.

I went to a fabulous school, St George College. The principal was a Greek man named George Macredis. He had the unbelievable talent of knowing each one of us – hundreds and hundreds of students – by our first name. I remember thinking, *Isn't it good for someone to be able to call people by their first name, making them feel like they're important, that they've been noticed, singled out, that each individual has worth!*

Later, in the police, I would work under a chief superintendent called John Anderson. He'd come in early, 6.30 in the morning, and he would always stop and chat to each of the cleaners for a couple of minutes; like Macredis, he knew each of them by their first name. He was a big wheel, and yet there he was, displaying a personal interest in a class of workers who were often overlooked.

That kind of personal interest would always be important to me, no matter what rank I moved up to. Right from my days at St George College, it was an attribute that I wanted to cultivate, and I did.

* * *

Throughout my childhood, and certainly during our years in Cairo, every summer was spent at an apartment in the sun-drenched coastal city of Alexandria, three hours north of Cairo on the Mediterranean. A couple of aunties would be there with their children; each family would take a room and we kids would just have mats on the floor as beds. My father would go back and forth because of his work, but my mum, siblings, cousins and I would be there the entire two or three months. The summers were warm; we'd go to the beach every day and to the outdoor cinema at night. Movie magic under the stars and those long, hot summer days on the seashore became the happiest memories of my childhood.

I remember seeing *The Sound of Music* something like five times; I still know it back to front. I also recall some Egyptian movies in Arabic, in which the hero was a police officer or detective. My parents would take me to all the James Bond movies; the gadgets and the cars really struck a chord with me. I'd think, *He's got a gun, he's a figure of power and he does all this brave, courageous stuff, doing right by people. That'd be cool.*

It was also around this time that I discovered the books of Maurice Leblanc, the creator of the fictional gentleman thief and sometime detective Arsène Lupin. Recently reborn on French TV, Lupin was the central character of 24 books, notable for solving a case that even the great Sherlock Holmes couldn't unravel.

As a ten-year-old, I loved the world of this jewel thief who worked on the wrong side of the law yet had his own moral code that compelled him to act for good. His investigative skills and ability to work his way around problems resonated with me.

I had also started collecting Batman comic books. For me, Batman was the ultimate detective. He was the only superhero without any superpowers; he just relied on his wits and his brain. That impressed me at that early age.

I was interested in how all these characters would go about finding things out in order to help others, and how they would stick up for those who couldn't help themselves.

* * *

Up until the late 1950s there were many Greeks and Italians in Egypt, and often they owned restaurants or sweet shops. The jewel in the crown, for me, was the most famous Cairo dessert bar Café Groppi. Groppi was an institution, having been there since the early 1900s, and it was one of my favourite places for gelato, Italian pastries and a dessert called rum baba, a sponge cake soaked in rum and syrup.

Groppi was very opulent and the waiters wore bow ties and aprons, not unusual in Cairo. Despite coming under attack during Nasser's push for Arab nationalism, it's still there today, in what used to be called Soliman Pasha Square, now Talaat Harb Square.

* * *

One day in the early 1960s, my father and the rest of Egypt awoke to hear President Nasser proclaim the nationalisation of farming land. The president decreed that landowners could only keep 100 acres per person within a family. The government would be taking the rest, remunerating owners with government bonds, which had next to no real value, and allegedly distributing the land they'd appropriated among the peasant class.

It was a big hit for my father and a lot of our family. Many families had their wealth wiped out overnight, and some people suicided because of it. Eventually the government cut the amount of land you could own even further.

Even so, we did well for quite a few more years, but by the late 1960s, the nationalisation drive was in full swing. My dad had shifted entirely to exporting agricultural produce to Europe.

Then the Nasser Government also nationalised *this* business. My dad was essentially told he could continue to export produce, utilising his name and reputation in the European markets, but would be working for the government, which would pay him a hundred pounds or so a month.

For my father, this was a tipping point. He had a lot to say about how wrong it was. He was vocal because he was fearless.

Then came the infamous committee hearings, investigating anyone with a whiff of capitalism. Part of the Sovietisation of Egypt was that we now had a secret police force, the mukhabarat. (Sadly, mukhabarats can be found in quite a number of countries throughout the Middle East.) People were disappearing, being dragged out of bed in the middle of the night. The committees singled out wealthy capitalists and demanded of them: 'Why should *you* have all this money?' My dad knew his name was on a blacklist somewhere.

My father had worked his butt off for everything we had, yet he was dragged before these committees and grilled, sometimes in televised hearings. For most people, only their wealth went against them, but my father had three strikes next to his name. He was a capitalist, a Christian, and the son of a man with a title. They had got rid of the Egyptian monarchy, and now they wanted to erase the memory of everything that was aligned with it.

My parents did their best to shield my siblings and me from the family's predicament, so I wasn't aware how bad it was at the time, but I could sense that my parents were stressed.

Then I began to overhear my father say things like: 'We're going to have to get out.'

I don't think it dawned on me how much my father was up against. I just didn't think there was any possibility that anyone could defeat him. He'd always looked after us and he had an answer for everything.

My father began to plot. There was a discussion about going to Canada, but the feeling was that it was probably too cold. Of course, America was suggested, but I think

23

my parents recognised that we'd be joining a long line of 'huddled masses' waiting to get there. So my father settled on Australia, even though he and my mother didn't really know anyone there or anything about the place.

It didn't need to be said that whatever my siblings and I overheard in our parents' conversations was not to be shared outside the home.

* * *

The Six-Day War came in 1967. Tensions had been building for a few years and finally exploded into conflict, with a group of Arab States including Egypt, Syria and Jordan declaring war on Israel. Israel struck first, using the element of surprise, and gained a sweeping victory that resulted in the capture of significant territories: the Gaza Strip, the Golan Heights, the Old City of Jerusalem, the West Bank and the Sinai Peninsula. (Apart from the Sinai Peninsula, all these lands remain in Israeli hands to this day and are the source of much contention.)

I was only ten at the time. We had to black out the windows so the light didn't guide the Israeli bombers. There were certain times of the day when we couldn't go out, times when we could hear the bombing raids.

Our apartment building in Cairo had two doormen; one had a son, Badr, who would only have been 17 or 18. Still, he got conscripted, went to war and was killed. When we went to pay our respects, his father was inconsolable.

I used to sit avidly listening to all the discussions my father had with my uncles and visiting friends. I was deeply concerned about what was going to happen to us. Were we going to get bombed? Was everything going to be all right? What was going to happen to the country? I didn't really understand what would happen if we lost the war. Would the Israelis invade and turn us into a Jewish state?

My sister, Dallal, recalls that I slept a lot during that time – trying to escape the night raids, the noise, the way everyone was reacting.

We did lose the war, and the mood of the country slumped. Egyptian casualties numbered over 11,000. For my father, I think the defeat to Israel was the final straw. He always said that if he had to pick one thing that convinced him we had to leave the country, it was that he just couldn't see a future for us in the chaos after the war. He talked it through with his brothers and sisters and closest friends, but really his mind had already been made up.

Even so, things were far from a done deal. The first crucial stage in the process was to get exit visas for all of us. The Egyptian Government had now made it incredibly difficult to get into the country, but it was also much, much harder to get out.

At first the authorities told my father *he* could go but not his family. Later on, they decided all the rest of the family could go, but *he* couldn't. Finally they granted a two-week holiday visa to all of us, but only as far as Lebanon, just an hour away by plane. Secretly, my father began planning a new life for us – in Australia.

Mum and Dad sat the three of us down and told us that we couldn't discuss with anyone what we were really doing. Even though the ruse was that we were going on a family holiday, it felt very different from preparing for any other holiday we'd ever been on.

We hadn't really told anyone that we weren't coming back, but my father had quietly begun to sell things. We kept our apartment and all the furniture; we couldn't just sell everything because that would have made it too obvious what we were doing.

I left most of my toy cars – around 200 of them. My mother said, 'You can't take them all, just pick 20.' She did, however, get my Batman comic books bound into a single volume for me to take.

There were goodbyes to a few of those in whom we'd confided, but for safety's sake not everyone. Right at the eleventh hour we told the family, and naturally some of them were pretty upset. But they understood, because a lot of them either had kids who had already left or were in fact thinking of leaving themselves.

The leaving was awful. At the airport some of my aunties were in tears. Auntie Betty, my father's sister, grabbed hold of me and implored me not to forget her, insisting that every night before I went to bed, I would recite her name again and again: 'Auntie Betty, Auntie Betty, Auntie Betty!'

While we were meant to look like a family going on holiday, I could see that everyone was apprehensive. What if someone somewhere changed their mind at the last minute about letting us leave? I don't think I really understood at the time what could have happened to my father if he had been arrested trying to flee the country. It's not as though he would have got a fair trial.

I remember sitting on the plane waiting for it to take off. I didn't let anyone know it, but deep down I didn't want to go. I didn't really understand why we had to. I was saying goodbye to my friends, a school I dearly loved, idyllic nights under the stars in Alexandria and those afternoons hanging out at Café Groppi.

It was equally disconcerting to contemplate our future. What on earth was going to happen to us over there, on the other side of the world?

While I sat there consumed with all this, the plane hurtled down the runway, rose up above the sprawling city of Cairo, banked over the Nile Delta and took us away from Egypt.

CHAPTER 3

Refugees

1969–1979

It was the middle of summer when we arrived in Beirut, at the eastern end of the Mediterranean. The city once called 'the Paris of the Middle East' lived up to its name: physically stunning, with the shimmering ocean on one side and snowcapped mountains, rising to over 2000 metres, in the near distance on the other. My father had organised an apartment for us in a neighbourhood called Hamra, a corner of the city to which Arabic poets, writers and thinkers once gravitated. To this day, Hamra's Rue Jeanne d'Arc is a thriving thoroughfare lined with bookshops and fabulous restaurants.

On the day we arrived and moved into our apartment, I walked in on my father with his suitcase open. He beckoned me over. 'Come here,' he said. 'I know you're worried. I couldn't say anything before, but look …'

He opened the suitcase and carefully manoeuvred a false bottom. He pulled aside the original torn lining to reveal a coloured plastic sheet underneath.

I wasn't prepared for what I saw when he removed the plastic. It covered a hidden layer of banknotes. There must have been tens of thousands of Egyptian pounds. He had quietly liquidated most of our assets and managed to smuggle the cash out of the country. My father explained that the money in the case was our future. He looked me straight in the eye, with his hands on my shoulders, and told me that we were going to be fine.

There were streetside stalls in Beirut where you could get money changed into different currencies. Bit by bit, so as not to attract attention, he would go out with some cash and change Egyptian pounds into American dollars.

Had the authorities at Cairo airport stopped my father and found the secret compartment in the case, I don't know what would have happened to him. He had known he had to get the money out and would never have asked anybody else to take that risk for him. He never said a word about it to anyone apart from my mum. Not until I walked in on him.

I can't imagine the relief he must have felt when he finally got through the airport security in Cairo, still in possession of all the money we had in the world. I don't know how he didn't collapse as the pent-up stress and anxiety ebbed out of him.

His courage touches me to this day, and I know he did it for us.

* * *

There was no work for my father in Beirut and no school for us, so our time was spent having a good look around and basically being tourists – which was exactly what we were meant to be. Acting like all the other southern Europeans holidaying there, every evening we would go out, heading towards favourite local eateries or in search of an ice cream on the famous Corniche.

I don't recall that we cooked much at all. I just remember the street stalls, which sold pretty much anything. They specialised in shawarma, that popular street food of every Middle Eastern country: spit-roasted lamb served in Lebanese bread, often with hummus, pickles and chilli, dripping all over your chin and hand. You'll find it in any souk. I also remember jallab, a drink unique to Lebanon made with date molasses and rosewater with pine nuts on top. It was just delicious.

We were in Beirut for two or three months, frequently attending the Australian Embassy – finalising the process my father had started secretly in Cairo. There was a family in Adelaide who were friends of my father's family and they were very happy to sponsor our visas. We had to have medical examinations, take an English language test and do numerous other things to satisfy the Australian authorities. I had the mumps at the time, which we kept secret, thinking it might in some way mean the cancellation of our plans.

* * *

Finally, we got our visas and flew out of Beirut. We travelled via Greece to Sydney, where we planned to stay for a little while before heading to Adelaide.

It's a long way to Australia. I remember the flight here was a hard slog.

The plane was full of migrating Lebanese and a lot of them couldn't speak, read or write English. Once the cabin crew discovered my father's fluency in English, they asked if he could fill out the immigration cards of everybody on the plane who couldn't speak the language of the country they planned to call their home.

I remember my father, glasses on and pen in hand, hunched over his tray table, with the overhead light on and all the passports stacked up beside him, opened at the appropriate page. Alongside him was a queue of people giving him their details as he filled in one form after another.

I often wonder what happened to all those people, and what sort of lives they made for themselves in Australia.

* * *

We came into Sydney first thing in the morning and were greeted by the extraordinary temperature. I say extraordinary, because we'd come from the warmth of the Middle East summer, only to be met by the cold of a Southern Hemisphere winter. Our first impression was that Sydney was nowhere near as busy as Cairo.

The five of us disembarked with nothing but the luggage we could carry: not quite just the clothes on our backs, but almost. Due to a foot-and-mouth disease outbreak in the UK, we'd been told before we arrived that our shoes would be confiscated and we'd have to buy new ones at the airport. So, there we were, rugged up against the cold and all in new footwear.

There were hawkers waiting at the airport, anticipating newly arrived migrants and trying to get us into their cars. One guy was Italian and spoke a bit of Arabic because he'd spent part of his childhood in Egypt. This guy's sales pitch was that he was a migrant too and he would look after us. We all got into his car and he took us to meet his cousin, who was a real estate agent. My father was in his office for quite some time, while we sat in the car wondering what was happening.

What was happening was that the Italian hawker and his cousin were putting the hard word on my father. His plan had been to stay in a hotel to begin with. But they were telling him that he needed to buy a house, to sign up there and then, and give them all his cash in exchange. We were literally fresh from the airport, our bags still in the boot! It was nothing but a standover job.

My father was physically imposing, and he told our conman driver that he wasn't buying anything and we just wanted to go to a hotel. When the guy saw that his get-rich-quick scam wasn't going to fly, he got cranky. He took us to a hotel as requested – only it was the infamous 'People's Palace' in the city, a Salvation Army hostel for the homeless. The façade of the building still stands in Pitt Street.

The People's Palace had an open-dormitory set-up, males in one section and females in the other, with bunk beds, a shared bathroom, and a lot of roommates you wouldn't want to hang out with. The heating was non-existent, so it was freezing. We were safe and we had a roof over our heads, but it was terrible.

I wish I could find that Italian hawker now, and it wouldn't be to thank him for his generous welcome. After a day or so, my dad could see we needed somewhere new to stay. We had one contact in Sydney: Heshmat Sharata, a man who had gone to university with one of my uncles and whom my dad had known in years gone by.

All we had was an address for him in the eastern suburb of Randwick, so on a Saturday, we found our way there and knocked on the door. Nobody was home. My father slipped a note under the door that said: *It's Samy Kaldas, I'm here with the family. We're staying at the People's Palace in the city. Please contact us.*

We didn't hear from him. We went back on Sunday; again, nothing. It felt like a very long weekend.

When it got to Monday, my mum and sister told my father that we had made a terrible mistake. If this was what Australia was like, we needed to go back to Egypt and throw ourselves at the mercy of Nasser.

Dad stood firm and said we weren't going anywhere. And anyway, he hadn't bought return tickets.

That evening, Heshmat finally turned up at the People's Palace. He'd only just seen our note because he'd been out of town for the weekend with his family.

'What on earth are you doing here?' he cried. 'This is accommodation for Sydney's homeless people!'

As if we hadn't already worked that out.

'Don't worry,' he continued, 'I'll get you out of here. What are your plans?'

My father told Heshmat about our sponsors in Adelaide.

Heshmat said, 'Don't go to Adelaide, there won't be much work there. There are more opportunities in Sydney, stay here. I'll help you get an apartment.'

The next day, Heshmat took time off from his job and drove my father out to a couple of places in Marrickville, in Sydney's Inner West. In the late 1960s a large number of Greeks, Italians, Yugoslavs and Lebanese and a smattering of Egyptians were settling there.

My father and Heshmat found a two-bedroom apartment for rent on George Street, and my father took it on the spot. Next they went to a store where my father bought five mattresses and about a dozen blankets. And we were off.

Heshmat told my father to get a newspaper called the *Sydney Morning Herald* on Tuesdays, the day they advertised all the jobs that were available. I remember Dad with the newspaper, circling job after job, making call after call in the hope of employment.

Within a couple of weeks he'd got a job on a factory floor at Standard Telephones and Cables in nearby Redfern. Gone were the fine suits, replaced by khaki pants, work gloves and hard-toed shoes. That was a big enough change, but what really made an impact on me was when he said it was the first time in his life he'd ever worked for anyone other than himself. He'd been his own boss, with hundreds of staff and labourers, but now all of a sudden he was taking orders.

I think he struggled with that. Even so, he swallowed his pride and did it.

* * *

Egypt to Australia, Cairo to Marrickville. Our new home was very, very different from anything we were used to. I had to watch myself when I stepped off the kerb, as cars drove on the opposite side of the road. I was used to the big American car models, but Ford Falcons and Holden Commodores were the go here.

At least Sydney was a lot tidier than Cairo, which impressed me. Another plus was my discovery of peanut butter; that was a revelation!

Almost as soon as we arrived in Marrickville, Dad bought a brand-new Falcon station wagon – that was where the cash in the case came in handy. It was silver with a red interior, bench seats front and back, a stick shift, and that new-car smell that they used to have. We thought it was just fantastic.

My parents enrolled me in a Catholic school, De La Salle College Marrickville, just up the road. For a 12-year-old from Egypt, school in Australia was difficult, but I really enjoyed De La Salle. I spoke fluent Arabic, French and English when I arrived here, so language wasn't a problem. History was my favourite subject, and I also quite liked English.

Just after I came through the doors, the world stopped to watch man land on the moon. It brought the whole school to a halt; everyone was in one huge room, glued to the TV. I can't believe those guys came back alive: I'm told that the phone I use today has way more memory in it than they had in the computers they were relying on to land that module on the moon's surface.

There were some good kids at De La Salle whom I was friendly with, a lot of Lebanese and Italians and some Aussies. We played cricket – or, I should say, they tried to teach me cricket, but I just didn't get it. I didn't like it then, and my view hasn't changed over the years. Rugby league I did enjoy, and still love watching it. To this day I have a soft spot for the local team, the Newtown Bluebags, who later became the Jets.

My sister, now 17, did not want to go back to school, and after much arguing she convinced my father she should go out to work. With his help, she quickly found a job in the office of Standard Telephones and Cables.

My mother didn't go to work straight away, as she had to look after my brother, Alaa, who wasn't quite old enough to go to school. But eventually she got a clerical job with Central District Ambulance, even though her English wasn't good at that stage. She ended up staying there for 35 years.

When my brother started school, I remember he was worried because he couldn't speak much English. But kids learn languages really easily; he'd already picked up bits and pieces from television, and within a short space of time he was speaking pretty well. We used to walk to and from school together every day.

Life in Marrickville fell into a nice routine. As family members we respectively went to school or work and, like the good Copts we were, on Sundays we went to church. The Coptic Orthodox community had bought a really old run-down church in Sydenham, formerly the Tempe Park Methodist Church. It was painted and done up and in 1968 it was consecrated as St Mary and St Mina, the first Coptic Orthodox church in Australia. There was one priest to cater for the Coptic Orthodox community throughout the whole country, Father Mina Nemattalla. We became very involved with the church and we met a lot of people through it.

Another Egyptian Coptic Orthodox family moved into the apartment upstairs from us. My father really hit it off with the husband, one of the biggest, burliest men I've ever met. He was a champion boxer, married to an Armenian woman. He often gave me unsolicited advice about how to fight, in case I got into a scrap with other kids.

After a few years, my parents had saved enough money to put a deposit down on a house in Pendle Hill, out west. Ours was a brand-new house, on a brand-new street, in a brand-new suburb. In Marrickville everything had been just around the corner, but in Pendle Hill you had to walk a long way to the shops.

Most of our neighbours were Anglo-Saxons. It took me a little while to realise that migrants were picked on here. At my new school, Greystanes High, there was a bit of bullying and I got into a few fights. More often than not, I came out the other side of these scraps okay.

After a while things settled down, though the other kids still had trouble with my name. A friend called Lance said that he couldn't pronounce 'Naguib' (it's pronounced 'Nageeb', with a hard g) so he had decided to call me Nick instead. He explained how in the long run it would make it easier for me. The other kids followed suit. For a long time after that, other kids would be yelling, 'Nick, Nick!' across the playground and it would take me a minute to register that they meant me.

By this stage my sister was receiving marriage proposals from Egyptian men at church. On Saturday mornings over a period of 12 months, a string of guys in suits would turn up at our house, seeking my father's permission to marry her, as was customary in Egyptian culture back then. Dallal would go out and have a coffee with them, but she just kept saying no.

Finally, my father told her that this couldn't go on; she would have to say yes to *someone*. Of course, the reason why she didn't want to marry any of them was because she was already in love with someone else. Out of the blue, she told my parents that there was an Australian guy she was working with that she wanted them to meet because she wanted to go out with him.

My father had formed a negative view of Australian men. Many of the Aussies he worked with on the shop floor went to the pub after work on payday and got drunk, spending most of their wage packet. They were sometimes unpleasant or violent towards their wives, and because of this, my father was vehemently against the idea that his daughter would go out with an Aussie. 'He'll go to the pub on payday and get drunk. He's going to beat you up, and I can't have that,' he told her.

There was nothing more to be said on the matter. Today we'd call that a 'hard no'.

After many months, my sister was close to giving up and marrying an Egyptian, but my mum could see she would spend the rest of her life unhappy. Once my mother changed sides, my father had no chance. He finally agreed to meet the guy.

So, one Saturday, we were visited by a very blond six-foot-three Australian named Bruce, in his best suit and tie. He was an engineer, and about as un-Egyptian as you could get. He passed the initial inspection, but next my father said he needed to meet his parents.

So, a week later, his parents came over. Bruce and his dad both had suits on, Bruce's mum had a blue rinse, and they were just salt-of-the-earth Aussie folk.

All up, Bruce was a decent guy. He hardly drank, never smoked, never swore and was a real gentleman. So, he passed the final test, they got married and I got a new suit for the wedding.

Some 50 years later, they are still a loving, happily married couple, now with five grandkids.

My little brother, Alaa, was always the brains of the family. He was dux of his school in Year 12 and was accepted to study medicine at the University of Sydney. He did well academically, as I knew he would. He graduated, got married and began to practice, with a view to specialising in paediatrics.

But fate intervened. Our Patriarch at the time, His Holiness Pope Shenouda, visited Sydney. I'm guessing he'd worked out that 60-year-old priests from Egypt, who did not speak English well and could not relate to the younger generation, were not good for the long-term survival of our church in Australia. So he asked to meet about a dozen youth from the church, mostly doctors, with the odd lawyer thrown in. My brother was one of them. The Pope told them, 'This is your calling, your church needs you.' All of them gave up their careers and joined the church, including Alaa.

In the Orthodox faith, you can be married and be a parish priest, but you cannot be promoted to Bishop or any other level. If you join as a monk, and take the vow of celibacy, you can be promoted and can eventually be the Patriarch or Pope. Alaa chose marriage over becoming the next Pope. He is still a parish priest and does amazing work for the church and our community. He is also an active researcher in the philosophy of mind and cognitive science, and he recently completed his PhD about the same time as his son completed his.

* * *

My father left Standard Telephones and Cables after a while and worked at a few other jobs, including as a courier. But he wanted to start his own business.

He did his homework and figured out that some parts of the Western Suburbs were full of newly married couples, usually living in apartments without their own washing machines. These apartment-dwellers needed somewhere to do their washing, and laundromats were all the go in the 1970s.

Ever the astute businessman, he worked out that one of the largest concentrations of apartments where there was no existing laundromat or dry-cleaner was in the suburb of Flemington. So, he went to Flemington, found a vacant shop and rented it, then he and I painted and tiled it and basically did it up. It wasn't run-down, but we brought it up to scratch. He bought everything he needed: four or five washing machines, three dryers and all the dry-cleaning paraphernalia required.

His predictions were accurate and the business took off, so he would travel to and from Pendle Hill to the laundromat every day, including weekends.

Then, in his mid-50s, Dad suddenly had a heart attack. He was in a bad way. He was going to be hospitalised for quite some time, so we had to work out what we were going to do with the laundromat.

I had just begun Year 11, but I knew the business because I'd been working with him on weekends and sometimes after school. So I pulled out of classes, put my education on hold, and ran the family business while Dad was in hospital for a few months. We had one or two staff, but someone had to be in charge, and that was me.

It's fairly hard labour; you're not lifting huge things, but you're on the go all day long. You're putting on loads of washing, making sure you don't mix up different people's undies, and then you're lifting that wet washing and putting it into the dryers, then folding it all up and putting it into bags. On top of that you're doing ironing, and of course you're dealing with people all day too. So even though I was young and fit, I was worn out by the end of a working day.

My dad had treatment and was put on medication and all went well. They told him to lose weight and exercise – things Egyptians don't do – and not to stress himself with work, which was also unlikely to happen. He eventually got better and slowly eased back into work, and when he did, he said to me, 'I want you to go back to school. You can't just pull out in Year 11, I won't have it. I want you to go to university.'

Having run a business and made decisions, seven days a week for several months, I struggled with the idea of sitting in class again. I told him, 'I don't want to go back to school.'

He said, 'You must do the HSC [Higher School Certificate]. I don't care what you do after that, but you've got to sit the HSC.'

So we reached an agreement. Back then, you could do Years 11 and 12 compressed into one year at Granville TAFE. The deal was that I would work with him and help him out until the end of the year, then the following year, when he was fully back on his feet, I would go to Granville TAFE and get my HSC.

Those were long days as I struggled to fit two years into one, and my parents supported me through them. My heart was not in studying; I didn't do super-well, but I passed.

* * *

I did my HSC in 1975. After that I decided to get a job. My dad wanted me to go to university, but after slogging through my HSC, the idea of more studying just didn't appeal.

41

I really didn't know what I wanted to do, but I thought it would be nice to work in an office. So I went for a job at City Mutual Insurance and landed it.

While I hadn't ended up at university, I think my dad was happy I'd got a stable, well-paying job. He just wanted all of us to earn a decent wage. I've inherited that from him, and now I drive my own kids nuts by demanding they get some kind of qualification, so they can take home a good salary.

For a few years, everything was great. I was earning reasonable money. There was no reason to move out of home. By then we'd moved from Pendle Hill to Flemington, just up the street from where the laundromat was, so my dad could walk to work. The social life at City Mutual was fantastic, and I had a group of close friends I'd gone to school with who remain my closest friends. I was pottering along, not seriously thinking about the future. But deep down I knew I did not want to do insurance or superannuation for the rest of my life.

I celebrated my 21st birthday in September 1978. We rented a small hall up the road and invited a few dozen people. I felt blessed to be surrounded by my family and close friends. I still have some of the great presents the Egyptian family friends gave me, such as cufflinks and fountain pens.

Life was good.

Then, three months later, our world was rocked.

* * *

It was a Sunday. I'd gone to a party the day before at a mate's place and crashed there for the night. I'd got an early train home and was walking up the quiet suburban street when I saw my brother-in-law Bruce's car parked outside our house. It was 9 am, maybe earlier, so it was very strange for him to be there.

I let myself in. Bruce was the first one to grab me.

'Your dad has passed away.'

It was completely unexpected. I was devastated.

Mum said he had just gone peacefully in his sleep. She hadn't attempted to resuscitate him, as she didn't know he'd died until she woke up and he didn't. She felt it was a blessing that he hadn't suffered.

Still, I felt an enormous sense of guilt. I should have been there; perhaps I could have done something?

In my mind my dad was ten feet tall and bulletproof. When he got sick for the first time with his heart attack, no one had ever thought of him as being vulnerable in that way. He was our rock. He was our safety net. He was my dad.

Whatever happened, I could go to him and talk about it and we would fix things together. Occasionally we'd argue, like any father and son, but it was never anything too serious.

Now, all of a sudden, he wasn't there.

His funeral, held at St Anthony and St Paul's Coptic Orthodox Church in Guildford, was huge, a testament to how respected and well liked he was. Seemingly the entire Egyptian community of Australia came, as did all of our neighbours and in-laws, my colleagues from City Mutual and the guys I went to school with. All the superintendents who worked with my mum at Central District Ambulance came too. Father Mina oversaw the service.

One of the saddest legacies of my father's premature death was that he missed out on the life that my siblings and I have had since. He never got to meet my children, his grandkids, which saddens me no end.

I think he might have been surprised at the path I took, and maybe even the success I've had. I can only hope he's looking down and feels proud of me.

CHAPTER 4

Samoans and Samurai Swords

1981–1984

It was a couple of years after my dad's death that I decided to become a cop. Once I'd been accepted into the police, the next step was a 12-week course at the NSW Police Academy in the inner-city suburb of Redfern. Ethnic members of the police force were truly a minority then; I was the only member of my class who looked anything other than Anglo.

So, on a bright, sunny Monday morning, I turned up nice and early and walked through the sandstone archway of the old academy. I felt somewhat apprehensive but very excited and optimistic about what the future held for me. It was what I had always wanted and my dream was coming true. I met my fellow recruits and they were a great bunch of guys and gals, most of whom are still good friends today, some 44 years later.

Back then, the academy took in a new recruit class every month, usually with 100 to 150 in each group. We were told that for some reason, our group was the smallest

45

since the Second World War, possibly ever. Something to do with a shortage of funds. There were only 24 of us. When we marched we were described as a pimple on the parade ground. When you graduate, there is always an honour guard to carry the flags; they had to quadruple the numbers of *our* guard to make it look like there were a decent number of us populating the parade ground.

In the first few weeks, some who couldn't hack the fitness regime dropped out. As a group, we had to run three and a half kilometres, and a 100-metre sprint, within a certain time. We had to do push-ups, pull-ups, sit-ups, burpees, and run up and down nearby Breakfast Hill, so called because if you'd already eaten, it was guaranteed to come back up.

We all did our best, but sometimes it felt like we were never going to be good enough for the instructors. The legendary Brian 'Chicka' Moore ran the physical training team. He'd played rugby league for Australia and been named in the NSW Police Team of the Century, so what chance did we have? He looked fitter when he was torturing us than he had when he was playing football.

The abuse we used to get from the drill sergeant, Morrie Green, particularly about our marching, was extraordinary. None of us had ever marched before. Sergeant Green was a Vietnam veteran, and he and his team gave us hell. By today's standards, some of it was certainly politically incorrect. But they were just trying to whip us into shape. We were frequently told, 'If you can't take it here, then how are you going to take it out there in the streets?' Some of this behaviour and language would not be acceptable today, but I always felt reasonably comfortable because whenever a sergeant tore strips off one of us, for whatever reason, my classmates always gave the victim a pat on the back later, and told them not to worry about it. I found that loyalty and camaraderie from my peers was the antidote to coping with racists and horrible individuals I encountered, both out of and sometimes in the job.

It was tough love mixed with good fun, and I devoured it. I valued the discipline and the structure; I felt like this was where I belonged.

Long-retired Sergeant Morrie Green is now a good friend. He likes to remind me that I've been one of his greatest successes.

Academically, I knew myself well enough to realise that if I applied myself, I would do well. We learned about the fundamentals of the law, your powers as an officer and what happens in court. We had dry runs of court procedure and report writing; we'd have to bang out a ridiculous number of words a minute.

After 12 gruelling weeks, our class graduated on 5 March 1982. Before we left, they'd worked out who was going where. Sydney was divided up into a number of districts, which in turn were made up by a number of divisions. I was going to 8 Division, which comprised four stations that covered the Inner West suburbs of Annandale, Balmain, Leichhardt and Glebe. My station would be Balmain, a long way from the southern suburb of Carlton where I now lived. A lot of probationary constables got placed somewhere close to home, but I was happy I didn't. The last thing I wanted while going to the supermarket for milk was to run into someone I'd arrested the day before.

* * *

Right on the waterfront, Balmain had been a working-class shipbuilding and docking area from the earliest decades of white settlement. By the early 1980s, it was well on its way to becoming the gentrified neighbourhood that it is today, but it wasn't quite there yet. Corners of the suburb were still raw. Some of the pubs you wouldn't go into unless you were looking for a fight. Even being a cop wouldn't stop people: they didn't want cops coming into their pubs, so they'd pick you out and start a fight *because* you were a cop.

The Federated Ship Painters and Dockers Union was still a powerful force in the area, even though the Costigan Royal Commission, which had begun in 1980, was looking into its affiliation with criminal activities. It might have sounded like a legitimate workers' union, but in reality it was an organised crime group, big on 'hoisting' – stealing things off ships and trucks – and fencing the gear in pubs and other local hangouts. There were parts of Balmain and the surrounding suburbs where you really had to be on your toes. The large social housing areas of nearby Glebe were home to some famous crime families, hard crooks who had been around for decades.

* * *

One of the things that had attracted me to the job was the general duties. Every day I'd go to work with no idea of what was going to come up. Just like some sort of crime jukebox, it could be break-and-enters, assaults, domestic violence, pub brawls, stranded pets, lost kids or car thefts. I really enjoyed the variety.

I also liked the immediacy that came with uniform work. Detectives might investigate something that goes on for weeks, months or even years. The things you deal with in uniform are often resolved there and then – if not on the spot, then certainly within the day. Everything that happened has to be logged on an occurrence pad, and the bosses would come around once or twice a day to check them.

On a daily basis, you'd get rostered either to be out on the road or on duty in the station. Everyone preferred to be out on the road, but being in the station gave you time to catch up on paperwork. You'd get a rocket up your backside from a sergeant if you didn't return or destroy exhibits you'd seized within a certain timeframe; there were strict rules about what you could and couldn't do with them. You'd get a week to respond to a communication before someone somewhere got cranky, and then you'd know about it.

When I started in the police, office technology was in its infancy. We didn't have fax machines or photocopiers. If you wanted to check anything you had to pick up the landline phone and ring the head station, where they had one computer to verify car registrations, insurance and licences. As a young constable in Balmain, I was sometimes put on the switchboard at the front desk, a really old switchboard with plug-in cords. On occasion, I'd cut people off by mistake or put a call through to the wrong person, but on the whole it was good fun.

One of my first shifts on the switchboard I'll never forget. It was about 2 am on an average weeknight. Nothing was happening when all of a sudden a woman came running into the station, yelling that there was a brawl around the corner. A guy in his pyjamas was waving a samurai sword, and she was afraid people were going to get killed.

Another constable and I sprinted out of the station, rushing towards who knew what. There was no time to think about how to deal with a man wielding a feudal Japanese weapon. Although the textbooks I'd read were full of different scenarios I might encounter, none of them mentioned *this* particular situation.

We had firearms, of course; at the academy we'd spent a lot of time doing drills and learning to handle them safely. In those days we carried a Smith & Wesson .38 revolver, handcuffs, a spare round of bullets and a rubber baton, just small enough to fit into a secret pocket on the right-hand side of our uniform. Today they talk about non-lethal force – Tasers, capsicum spray – but those weapons didn't exist back then. You only had one tactical option if things got hairy: shoot.

These were my thoughts as I was running the hundred metres towards the incident.

Expecting blood and horror, what we came across was a stand-off between neighbours over a domestic dispute. It had escalated, and one resident had had enough, gone inside and come back out brandishing a Japanese ceremonial steel sword not much short of a metre long, looking to chop up the other guy.

He soon calmed down and pulled his head in after we arrived on the scene. No one was charged. We told the would-be samurai to take the sword, get inside his home and behave himself.

That was just two or three days into the job.

As we trudged back to the station and I returned to my job on the switchboard, I reflected on how this was everything I'd hoped joining the police force would be. If I had any doubts about my career choice – and I didn't – this first-hand experience of literal cut-and-thrust confirmed to me that I had made the right choice, and that my mother actually might have been justified in her anxieties.

* * *

Both at the station and out in the field, the camaraderie was really something to treasure. There were a few guys at Balmain who thought outside the square, and I learned a lot from them. One of the ones who stands out most in my memory is a crusty sergeant named Warren Skinner, one of the finest street cops I've ever had the pleasure of working with.

He had a unique way of accounting for the homeless population of Balmain, Glebe, Leichhardt and Annandale. There was a form called a P79A, on which you recorded information for the Coroner about a deceased person. We'd frequently be notified about a deceased homeless person found lying in a canal somewhere, and we'd have a hell of a time finding out who he or she really was, who their next of kin might be and where to bury them, all of which had to go on this P79A form.

So, Warren would often spot a homeless person while patrolling and holler: 'Hello, mate, come here. Hey, what's your full name? When were you born? Who are your relatives? Where have you lived?' He would pre-emptively fill in the P79A form, even though the person was obviously not dead yet. Twelve months later, we would come across the body of that same poor soul, and Warren, in his brusque and practical way, would say, 'Yeah, I've already got all his details.'

Warren wasn't particularly fond of detectives, and often when someone rang up and asked to be put through to the detectives at the station, Warren would tell them: 'There are no detectives here, son – the last detective was killed by Moriarty in 1879. I'll put you through to the plainclothes police.'

What a wit. He would often laugh at his own jokes in a very distinctive way, leading to the nickname 'Muttley', after the sneaky laughing dog in the *Wacky Races* cartoon.

I used to love watching these seasoned guys in action and soaking it all up when I was on a job with them. It was all about how they carried themselves, how they handled a menacing individual. These cops were fearless, knew their job and took pride in their appearance.

They also taught me about 'community policing'. We didn't call it that, though; there wasn't a name for it, and nobody patted us on the back for it. But it was about walking around your area and engaging with those who worked and lived on your patch.

In Annandale, Glebe, Leichhardt and Balmain, you knew all the shopkeepers and enjoyed chatting to them on a daily basis. As a result, they felt comfortable passing on information. If you wanted to get a car fixed, you knew the panel beater. If you wanted to get a haircut, you knew the barber. Even though you didn't live in the area, you got to know everyone, and they were all incredibly friendly and supportive of the police.

This was one of the biggest lessons I learned from watching the seasoned guys in our division, who could talk to everyone, good or bad. They taught me so much about human nature. If you're talking to a bank manager, you're going to talk to them in a certain way. But if you're grooming a bloke you know is a knockabout crook (or, as the Canadian police call them, a 'rounder') to provide you with information, then that calls for something else.

I learned most of my communication skills in those first few years of serving, pitching what I was saying specifically to the person in front of me at his or her level. I learned to talk to people on all rungs of society – including the lowest.

Some of the people you dealt with were not very sophisticated. Some people you could sense might be willing to talk to you. I learned that if you just gave them the time, listened and talked to them like human beings, showed them some empathy if they were in crisis, you'd usually win them over.

* * *

I had to work for a year as a probationary constable. Towards the end of the probation period, you had to go back and do another six weeks at the academy, then take your final exams. By the end of your probationary period, you pretty much knew whether you would make it in the police or not. Some didn't.

If you thought the exams would be the hardest part of all, you'd be wrong. No, the hardest part was that at the end of your probation period, you had to have maintained – or, better still, improved – your fitness level. Not sure I'll ever be as fit as I was then. I was very skinny, and they actually told me I'd have to beef up a bit when I applied to join. That's hilarious now.

After I graduated, I was posted to the sub-station of Annandale and did a couple of years there, sometimes moving back to Balmain as required. As at Balmain, some of the senior guys in Annandale became role models, and their loyalty and tenacity were inspiring. Their wit was something else.

Terry Rose was a former Western Suburbs Magpies rugby league player, and he had a habit of putting in intelligence reports that revealed what he really thought. He once wrote that someone who'd lied to him 'handles the truth carelessly'! Often these reports would be sent back – 'Needs more work' – but they were very entertaining.

* * *

I'd joined the force wanting to make a difference. And among everything else in those early years, there were many days when I thought I did.

In the 1980s, banks used to get robbed often. They didn't have security guards, they didn't have screens, they didn't have much at all. After a robbery had happened, you'd often have to sit the staff and customers down in the police station and get statements from all of them.

I learned a bit about victim care, being sympathetic to those who had been through a traumatic experience. The first thing you had to do was calm them down, because they'd never been through anything like this before. You would get them a cup of tea and let them know that everything would be all right, and that they were now safe.

Later you'd often get a thank-you card from someone you'd helped, saying: 'We appreciate what you did.' It meant a lot.

Sometimes knowing you'd saved someone from harm was all the thanks you needed. Once we were called out to a home in Leichhardt. A guy had bashed his wife, and she had significant injuries. To make things worse, there were two kids in the house. We took a notebook statement from her, which she signed. It was enough to allow us to arrest him. Even so, he gave us plenty of lip, then there was some push and shove. We took him away in the van and locked him up. He was refused bail, which gave her a chance to grab the kids and get away.

There were a number of domestics I attended that could have turned violent, but even if you and your partner were the first ones through the door, you knew the cavalry were on the way. No matter what, you needed to count on your fellow officers to be there for you. Together, you would be going through some of the most traumatic events life could throw at you, and, together, you would actually do some good on a daily basis.

Even so, there was always a gap of two or three minutes before you heard the sirens of help approaching.

I was very conscious of that gap one night after a call-out to the Empire Hotel at the end of Johnston Street, Annandale. A large group of Pacific Islanders were at war with another group, going at it hammer and tongs. The brawl had spilled out onto the street. No cars could get through, as the street was blocked by blokes punching on.

My partner and I waded into the middle, where one guy was getting absolutely flogged, to try to get him out of there. It was our patch and we'd been the first ones there. Other police cars had been called, but there was a period when it was just the two of us.

We were tackling 19 or 20 guys who all looked as though they were easy picks for the front row of Samoa's first-fifteen rugby team. Fortunately, as a probationer, I was pretty fit. And luckily, back-up arrived almost instantly. Then it was as simple as separating everyone and pulling out a couple of ringleaders to be carted off to the station for interviewing.

I don't believe I ever really feared anything. Part of that I got from my dad, but I'm also fairly focused in a crisis. The adrenaline is pumping. You know you've got a thing to do and you go out and do it. You know you're on the side of right, you know you're going to do something good: save someone from getting his skull kicked in. That idea of being in the right gives you the courage to go into what is an insane situation that you certainly wouldn't go into otherwise. It's a form of professional permission that allows you to walk into a pub mêlée to help someone, because that's what society has asked you to do – and expects of you.

* * *

The standard arrangement was that you had to do three years in General Duties, and after that you could look at specialising in whatever field took your fancy: detectives, water police, helicopters, dogs, horses, surveillance, whatever you wanted to have a go at.

My eyes were opened in those first three years. I saw the seamier side of life, I saw evil, and I hadn't really seen any of that before. I became more streetwise, there's no doubt about that. I didn't think I'd led a sheltered life, but perhaps in some ways I had.

All roles in the police force are important, but some of us yearn for something a little more testing. Uniformed, general-duty police do react to incidents and stop crime from happening. But detectives do the longer-term work, usually investigating more serious crimes like murder, and seeing them through to successful prosecution in court. Usually, if the detective's job gets done right, it ends in a conviction. I'd known all along, from the minute I joined the cops, that I wanted to be a detective one day.

This really hit home when I attended one of my first murders in Leichhardt. An Italian organised crime figure named Bruno Nesci had been gunned down in the street.

It wasn't the first dead body I'd seen. In my first couple of weeks as a probationary constable, they took a group of us to Glebe morgue to watch a couple of autopsies. One of the biggest and fittest guys in our class fainted halfway through, and a couple of us had to hold him up.

A lot of it is about how your senses respond, in particular to the dead-body smell. The sight of some of the deceased I saw in my first few years – especially the homeless people Warren Skinner used to interrogate – stays with you. I learned a trick of the trade: to carry a folded handkerchief sprayed with aftershave and put it to my nose.

In Leichhardt, we turned up and identified all the witnesses whose statements needed taking. Shortly afterwards, the detectives appeared and took over, securing the crime scene and keeping the public at a distance.

While going about my duties that day, I watched these guys in action. How they remained focused, how they got to the heart of the matter, how they took in what people were saying but kept an open mind, how they understood the law, and, perhaps most importantly, how they thought a long way ahead, to make sure evidence was obtained in a way that was going to be admissible in court down the track.

Towards the end of those compulsory three years, I talked to some of the senior detectives and they said they'd observed me at work. They'd seen that I'd cultivated a couple of informants, which impressed them. I was encouraged to apply for 'plainclothes': criminal investigation.

CHAPTER 5

The Lost Art of Tugging Coats

1984–1987

To get to the detectives from uniform might only have meant climbing one flight of stairs in most police stations, but to make that leap in your career was anything but easy.

Two things had to happen if you were to make the shift. One, you had to *really* want to do it, because it is an onerous process; and two, *they* had to want *you*.

The detectives in 8 Division knew us uniformed police pretty well, as we were together every day. We went on jobs together, we encountered each other in the meal room. They stayed away from anyone they thought was lazy, anyone who didn't get on with others, anyone who wasn't a team player. Conversely, they kept their eyes open for anyone who showed promise and was prepared to have a bit of a go, and they encouraged them.

I'm not sure I was in that category, but the 8 Division Chief of Detectives, Stan Owens, liked something he saw and encouraged me to apply. (These days the chief of detectives is called a 'crime manager', a term all the old-timers object to.

A friend of mine used to defiantly yell out: 'I'm not a crime *manager*, I'm a crime *solver*!')

First you had to put in a written application, stressing what you had to offer. I thought it would help my case if I said that I spoke Arabic and a smattering of French. Sydney's population was becoming more diverse. If you fast-forward to today, about a third of the population of NSW has one or two parents born overseas and/or that speaks a language other than English at home.

Then you had to do an interview, which was called 'the bull ring'. You got put through your paces by three senior detectives, as well as your district's detective inspector (DI), who decided whether you were any good or not. If they decided you weren't, then that was the end of it. It wasn't just about the answers you gave, it was also about how you handled yourself, what your confidence levels were like as a constable talking to three chief inspectors and the district's DI, especially when they started grilling you on the minutiae of the *Crimes Act*. If you passed that application process, there was then a small volume of relevant legislation and procedures that you had to memorise and be examined on.

The bull-ring interview took place in the F District office in nearby Enmore. I did a lot of preparation. I bought a brand-new blue pinstripe suit from David Jones, and I thought about what they were likely to ask me.

I knew the three chief inspectors by reputation; they were all hardened detectives with decades of experience. We were part of F District, and our DI was the formidable Bill Benden, a great guy but widely feared, not least because he was physically imposing: six-foot-five and heavyset.

When the day of the interview arrived, I walked in, and his first words were: 'Are you the prick that speaks ten languages?'

I didn't know how to respond, so I just said, 'Yes, sir.'

His opening salvo probably wouldn't fly today, but it was just his sense of humour, and it certainly broke the ice.

The rest of the interview went well. He and his panel ran through their questions: Who are you? Where have you been? What have you done? Are you married? And a whole lot of questions about legislation and procedure. I answered to the best of my ability. Satisfied with my responses, Bill Benden gave me his approval and then I was off to the exam.

Fortunately I acquitted myself well and passed. Two or three weeks later I was transferred to the detectives' office at Balmain.

* * *

I couldn't immediately call myself a detective; that would take about two years of training. There were two sets of formal courses I had to pass. And there was a reasonably high failure rate.

After about ten months, you took the first formal course, which was four weeks, full-time, in a classroom in the city. It was called the Potential Crime Investigators' Course. This was where you learned the law, the Acts of Parliament, how to handle informants: all theoretical. You were schooled in forensics issues, the court system, issues around prosecution. You had to know the 'ingredients', as they called them, of each offence. For example, if you were going to lock someone up for breaking, entering and stealing, you had to have the proofs of breaking, entering and stealing with an intent to deprive the owner permanently of their property. If the accused was from next door and had borrowed the property with an intention of giving it back, you wouldn't have proved your case. So, you learned about the defences that people use in court and how to counter them.

The second course took place around the two-year mark. It was the Detectives Training Course. Until then you are only a 'plainclothes constable'. When you passed this final course, and only then, you were 'designated' as a detective.

I arrived in plainclothes at Balmain wearing my new suit, and I was quickly paired up with a senior detective who would teach me the ropes. In my case, it was Owen (Jeff) 'Doc' Halliday. A huge figure in my development as a cop.

Seven or eight years older than me, Doc was a big strapping second-rower who'd played rugby league with the Canterbury Bulldogs in the 1970s and 1980s. He had worked as a homicide detective for many years and knew every legendary detective in NSW. It was Doc who'd extradited contract killer Christopher Dale Flannery, AKA Mr Rent-a-Kill, from Melbourne to Sydney in 1981, and investigated many of the hardest jail murders. He was fearless.

It was actually *Doc* who picked *me*, not the other way round. He asked: 'Would you be happy to work with me?'

I said I'd be very happy to – I was already in awe of him – so he went to the Chief of Detectives and said: 'I want Nick to work with me.'

It was as simple as that. The chief paired us up and we would remain partners for three or four years. (These days the term 'partner' causes confusion, so instead they're called 'workmates'.)

Detectives work in pairs for a number of reasons. First, it's much safer, because it means you've got back-up. Second, you need proof of everything that happens in the course of your work because it's going to come under scrutiny later on, and two memories are better than one. Third, when appearing before a court, if you have corroboration, then it works better. For these three reasons and many others, detectives always work in pairs.

You always learn from your first senior partner, so those who have a partner who isn't so good will often pick up their bad habits. But I was lucky: Doc taught me all the skills I'd need for a solid criminal investigative career. I felt that those who were given shortcuts, and who went straight into major crime squads without doing a few years of investigating basic matters like break-and-enters and assaults, missed out on valuable experience that would have better prepared them for the more serious cases.

Doc didn't just teach me about criminal investigation but also about leadership and human nature. If you did something wrong, you knew he was going to hold you to account. He had a sense of fairness that you don't see all that often, a deep belief that *If it's not right, it's not right. I'm not going to walk past it, I'm going to stop and do something.*

There were jobs that Doc and I went to where someone tried to bully or heavy us by saying, 'I know so-and-so', some high-ranking cop, implying that there'd be some sort of trouble for us when 'so-and-so' found out. Doc would never wear that. No matter what the threat, he was going to do what he thought was right, be that carrying on with an investigation or locking up someone whom 'so-and-so' didn't want locked up.

Sometimes I saw him clash with those in the senior ranks because he was so principled. On the things that mattered, he wouldn't bend. It was one of the biggest lessons I learned from him: you've got to do what you think is right – even if it's going to be unpopular, even if it's going to cause you pain. It was something that chimed with the strong moral compass I'd had since I was a boy.

The likes of Warren Skinner had shown me the basics, but Doc was the one who taught me all about the art of interviewing witnesses and crooks – understanding their motivations, and how to get the real story out of them. It was about dealing with them in a way that was appropriate, but so that you actually got something from them that would be beneficial to your investigation.

Watching Doc at work, I gleaned how to treat informants fairly, so that ultimately you'd have a clear conscience, knowing that you had done the right thing by them – and hopefully they'd then do the right thing by you. Sometimes you had to take a hard line and tell people you didn't believe them; other times – particularly when they were innocent witnesses or victims of crime – you needed the sensitivity to help them but still carry out the job demanded of you.

The ability to build a rapport, to relate to a person and to have that person relate to you so that they open up – whether they be a witness, victim or offender – is essential to the job. You need to know how to ask the right questions, in the right way, absorb the answers and then ask more questions.

Much later in life I used to lecture intermittently on the Detectives Training Course; most senior detectives do this at some stage as a way of giving back. Today it's standard practice to record all interviews and receive a copy of the transcript. What I'd say in the lectures was this:

> What you want to see on the transcript of the interview is you asking a question, then a big chunk of text from the person you're interviewing. Then there should be another one or two lines from you, and another big chunk from them. What you *don't* want to see is you doing all the talking and the person you're interviewing giving minimal responses. If that's the case, you're not going to get what you want.

You've got to make the person feel comfortable and safe, and that you're on their side. The art of interrogation is about getting *them* to tell the story and then probing, trying to get more out of them than they would naturally give you.

* * *

One of the things police are good at is giving people nicknames. We had a fellow in the office who was accused of never going home when there was a light on, hence his nickname: 'the Moth'. Someone who would only appear after all the work was done was called 'Blisters', and so on.

Doc also had a very dry sense of humour. Sometimes when we were interviewing a suspect who was obviously lying to us, Doc would say, 'You'd better put your thinking cap on, son,' and give the guy a few minutes to reflect. The 'thinking cap' became a thing in our office.

One of the cases Doc and I worked on also caused a lot of amusement. It involved a pigeon owner and another guy who was standing over him. In the right circles, racing pigeons can be quite valuable. One night, the standover man went round and spirited away all the owner's pigeons. Doc and I got the job of tracking them down. It turned out that this was no isolated incident: pigeons were being stolen all over the place. It seemed there was a thriving underground trade.

'The Pigeon Brief' went on for weeks. In the end we locked up the standover man. He was a bully, threatening all kinds of whatever. We went to court; the battle was hard fought, but we won in the end.

My strongest memory of that case, however, is the jokes in the office: 'Haven't you got anything better to do? You're chasing birds and whatever else.' 'The Pigeon Brief' certainly didn't rival John Grisham's *The Pelican Brief*, but it provided everyone in the office with endless entertainment and bird gags at our expense.

* * *

Building on what I'd started in uniform, I was becoming better at cultivating informants. I had one in particular who tipped me off about a bank job in Norton Street, Leichhardt. It was a big deal for a plainclothes constable to have an informant with access to that level of information.

We did everything we could to plan to foil the robbery. The Special Weapons and Operations Squad deployed covertly. We had a helicopter hovering unheard thousands of feet up, and detectives everywhere around the area.

We all dug in. We sat there literally all day, until the bank closed.

Nothing happened.

I was shattered. I'd instigated all this and now, nothing.

I went back to my informant. He said, 'I don't know what happened. They got cold feet.'

Doc was very supportive, and told me, 'Nicky, don't worry about it. This shit happens.' (Doc is probably the only bloke I've ever worked with who called me Nicky, right up until the day he died.)

I'll always remember that all the guys from the Armed Hold-Up Squad slapped me on the back, trying to encourage me. In particular, the squad leader, Bernie Wood, cheered me up with his acknowledgement and support.

Even though I was deflated, even though I thought I'd let everyone down, I remember feeling like part of the team. It was good for me to hear the senior people, the guys I looked up to, say the things they did. For a junior constable, it was flattering to be recognised in that way.

There was nothing I could have done to have got a better result on the Norton Street job. The information was good; it was just that someone, somewhere, changed their mind.

Many years later, Doc was diagnosed with motor neurone disease and passed away after a long illness. I was humbled to be asked by his family to read a eulogy at his well-attended funeral. It was heartbreaking to see him pass so early, but his memory and legacy, especially in all those he mentored, will always live on.

* * *

The 1980s were perhaps the most notorious decade in the history of the NSW Police Force. There've been several TV shows – *Blue Murder, Blue Murder: Killer Cop* and two instalments of the *Underbelly* series – that have focused on 'colourful' Sydney detectives from that time. Back in the 1980s, I was just a couple of degrees of separation from some of these famous and infamous figures.

The most infamous of them all was Roger Caleb Rogerson. By the start of the 1980s he'd become one of the most decorated of cops, but he had been there and done it all, frequently fabricating confessions as we later found out, and mixing with corrupt detectives and figures from the world of organised crime.

For me, probably the most unforgivable thing was his involvement in the 1984 attempted murder of Detective Sergeant Mick Drury, a dear friend of mine. For a police officer to stoop to attempting to kill another officer to please a crook is simply unbelievable. Just two years after I joined the detectives, he was sacked from the force for misconduct.

Following criminal convictions for perverting the course of justice and lying to the Police Integrity Commission, Rogerson and a fellow ex-cop, Glen McNamara, stood trial in 2016 for the murder of 20-year-old Jamie Gao in a drug deal gone wrong. Both were sentenced to life. Rogerson died in jail in January 2024.

In the first half of the 1980s, though, Rogerson was an idol to all of us. Every once in a while, he and his colleagues would come into the Bridge Hotel at Rozelle and a few of us from Balmain would have a beer with them. When he walked into a room, his charisma was undeniable. We simply did not know what he had been up to.

In the pub I'd also see seasoned veterans from the legendary Homicide and Armed Hold-Up Squads, two of the pre-eminent squads of the force. I was in awe of these blokes. They were in the news, they shot criminals, they solved major crimes using their skills and gut feelings, they saved a lot of innocent victims, and they held to account those who'd committed murders and armed robberies.

I think we've lost some of those old-fashioned police skills; the current generation resort to electronic surveillance too quickly and too often. They call that old-school police work 'the lost art of tugging coats', in the words of one of my old bosses, former chief superintendent Rod Harvey. Back in the day, when detectives and crooks used to wear overcoats and suit jackets every day – that's how long ago we're talking – a detective would see someone they knew to be 'a person of interest', and 'tug on their coat' and ask them what they were up to.

Of course, most crooks don't wear coats these days, and perhaps police don't tug as much. The whole process is so much more formal now. You can't have informants unless they're registered and approved at three levels. After that, every contact you have with them has to be approved in advance. Even if you meet them accidentally, you've got to put a form in, explaining: 'I ran into so-and-so, and we discussed X, Y and Z.' That goes to your supervisor, their supervisor, their supervisor's supervisor, and everybody approves it on a computer system.

Back in the 1980s there were people in the police doing the wrong thing. That's undeniable. We needed to sort that out. During the Wood Royal Commission in the mid-1990s, irrefutable evidence emerged of some serious systemic corruption in the NSW Police. But my view remains that the vast majority of police at the time were honest, hard-working men and women who were doing their best.

And the tragedy of it is that everybody got tarred with the same brush. It took years for the people of NSW to trust the police again.

CHAPTER 6

Playing 'Mr Big'

1987–1988

There's no doubt that drugs and crime go hand-in-hand today like never before. Drugs are either the reason people are in the prison system – for possession, dealing or trafficking – or the reason people commit the crimes: they're under the influence of drugs and/or need money for more drugs. If you had to pick one type of criminality that drives all the others, it's drug crime.

There wouldn't be a problem if society didn't have an addiction to drugs and, like it or not, we always have. Ancient civilisations used them. Going back at least 100 years, 'medications' that doctors wouldn't dream of prescribing today were sold freely over pharmacy counters. There was the heroin epidemic in the 1960s and 1970s, then it was the cocaine boom of the 1980s, heroin again in the 1990s, and today it's the scourge of methamphetamine.

Up until now, the focus of law enforcement has been on investigating and locking up those who sell drugs. Over the past couple of decades, I haven't seen enough nuanced thinking from our politicians on this issue. It's all about the 'announceables', as the politicians call them: getting a headline on page three of the *Daily Telegraph*.

I think more could and should have been done to tackle the underlying problem of demand, like setting up social services and programs that deal effectively with people's problems, so that hopefully they don't gravitate towards drugs in the first place. By the time it becomes a police issue, the horse has often long bolted.

* * *

Certainly, in the 1980s, even the most common crimes like break-and-enters, robberies and assaults were often committed by heroin users who were so badly addicted that they'd resorted to crime to fund their drug habit. In NSW, there was a general recognition, academically and otherwise, that something had to be done.

In 1986, the State Drug Crime Commission (SDCC) was established. Today all the States have a similar investigative body, but NSW was the first. The commission was chaired by three commissioners who had coercive powers: they would hold hearings and could force people to answer their questions, as in a royal commission. They also had the power to issue their own search warrants and to take out telephone-intercept and bugging-device warrants.

In the mid- to late 1980s, organised crime groupings emerged that were heavily involved in the drug trade. One was Lebanese organised crime. Coupled with that, there was a growing problem with Romanians fleeing the brutal regime of President Nicolae Ceauşescu. At one point, the Romanian

President released tens of thousands of criminals from prison and a lot of them also ended up in Sydney. When the NSW Government set up the SDCC, they formally tasked it with investigating and dismantling both these groups.

After a thorough background check, a handful of police were brought in to be the investigative arm. I was one of them. In mid-1987 I was asked to join the SDCC intermittently, to assist with the investigations focused on Lebanese crime groups. I had been chosen for the operation because I looked the part and could speak Arabic. In those days I think communities simply did not expect Arabs to be police officers, because Arabs never think of other Arabs as cops.

I was not attached formally to the SDCC until the very end of 1987, so until then I continued working at Balmain. I wasn't a full-time undercover guy; they would call me in if the job fitted me. I'd come out of the office, do the job, and then go back to being a detective. I had to navigate moving between my real life and my high-status undercover life.

The SDCC was secretive, which meant I wasn't allowed to tell my colleagues at Balmain what I was doing. I didn't feel good about that. There's a tradition in the cops that you trust your colleagues and tell each other things, good and bad.

When you finished one of these jobs, you might go back to your regular police station and the guys there would have no idea what you'd been through or the pressure you'd been under. They would say things like: 'Well, you've had a holiday, now you can get back to the real work.' They'd put shit on you for having been offline doing stuff they had no idea about, and you could never sit down and tell them the nature of the work or the risks involved.

I had to tell Doc, though. He was happy for me to be moving up to serious crime, but he had history with some of the senior staff at the SDCC. He told me: 'Just be careful.'

The first job I did for the SDCC was in connection with a Lebanese crook called Boutros Fagher. He was running a drug supermarket for the high end of the market, and to our frustration, he was also incredibly surveillance-aware. He would drive around in his car for an hour or more to make sure no one was tailing him before he went to a meeting. He wouldn't talk on the phone in case it was bugged. He lived with his in-laws and his house was occupied 24/7, so none of the surveillance guys could get inside and plant any listening devices. No one had contemplated an undercover operation, because Fagher wouldn't deal with anyone unless he knew them well or they came from the same part of Lebanon as he had.

The Australian Bureau of Criminal Intelligence, as it was known then, had written a report to the NSW Police, telling them Fagher had to be one of the major suppliers in Sydney, but they almost certainly wouldn't get him.

Then someone thought of a way in. The SDCC had an informant who was North African, a really bad crook, who was looking at deportation and a bunch of other issues because of the offences he'd committed. We used this to get him to turn on our Lebanese drug baron and help us set him up. Our African informant started the ball rolling on a huge deal, negotiating the purchase of hash oil – not just small amounts but big jerry cans of the stuff.

Now, Fagher knew that this North African informant didn't have the wherewithal to buy that much oil, so the informant had to tell him he was buying on behalf of a higher-level criminal: me. I was the Mr Big, the ultimate customer. On the day the initial discussion was to take place, they wanted me to simply sit in the car outside Fagher's house and sort of wave at him. I was basically a prop. Because I hadn't had any formal training in being an undercover operative, or any experience in drug work at this level, I wasn't to be directly involved in the discussions. But if Fagher did happen to come over to my car, I could speak to him in Arabic and pass myself off as the money behind the deal.

I wasn't daunted, but neither did I want to stuff up. I knew if I got it right, it would lead to bigger and better things.

The informant and I parked outside the house. At this stage I was dressed casually and had an average car, a Corolla.

The informant went in, and that was when things started to go off script. He came back out and told me: 'He's not going to do anything unless you come into the house and meet him.'

I thought, *Okay, those aren't my instructions, and God only knows what might happen to me in there.* But I went with it. The choice had basically been taken out of my hands. If I was who I was pretending to be, I had no reason *not* to go inside. So I went in and adopted my best drug-dealing demeanour, friendly but firm.

I could see Fagher was sizing me up, so I was very conscious of my body language. We chatted in Arabic, which seemed to put him at ease. We talked about where we each came from. There was no point in denying where I was from, because we could pick each other's accents a mile away, so I told him I came from a Christian area of Egypt. This also gave him some reassurance, as he too was from a Christian background.

My act worked. I won him over. He felt that I was someone he could relate to and trust.

After that meeting, it struck me and my supervisors that if I was masquerading as an upper-level drug dealer, I was not going to be getting around in shredded Wranglers, nor sitting around in a Toyota. So I bought some nice suits and we made an arrangement with a licensed dealer to borrow some very expensive watches and a bunch of gold jewellery. I also got a car upgrade. The other cops at the SDCC used to joke that I wouldn't get out of bed for anything less than a kilo of heroin, which had a street value of $100,000 to $150,000.

You usually have an assumed name; mine was Michael. I chose this name very deliberately: if someone recognised me and yelled, 'Nick!', and I reflexively reacted, I could get away with it by saying I thought he said, 'Mick'.

Creating a false identity was a lot easier back then. There was no social media or internet, so if a crook did a basic check on you, there wasn't much they could find out about you.

I stayed at the Hilton Hotel in the city while undercover, and if I was going to do anything socially, I went out to Juliana's, the hotel nightclub. In the final stages of the investigation, all the discussions between Fagher and me would take place in the Hilton; he even came up to my hotel room on one occasion.

It reached the point where he felt comfortable around me. He always wanted to puff himself up telling me about all the bad things he'd done, and I had to let him do that. By then he had shut out the North African informant and was dealing with me directly.

By this stage he knew I had the means to buy really expensive things. I had organised to buy kilos and kilos of hash oil, and he also agreed to supply me with heroin.

It was time for the sharp end of the operation: the 'lock-up day'.

We had his house surrounded by a large number of police. We weren't sure who else might be inside the place, so we needed a sizeable force in case of a violent retaliation and to make sure that no one was able to get away through some backyard or laneway.

Inside the house, Fagher and I did a deal for a 'large commercial quantity' of oil, according to the legislation. He handed over the gear: a number of very large, coloured jars full of sticky sweet stuff. He had stashed the money I'd given him inside the house.

He wanted to have a smoke, so he took a spoonful of my hash oil to put on a rolly cigarette. We walked out of his house together.

During an operation like this, there's usually a pre-arranged signal that you give to the waiting team when it's time to arrest the target – something that can't be mistaken, like patting your head or scratching your left ear. On this occasion, the rest of the team couldn't see me, but they were listening in, so the signal had to be verbal.

I used the code word we'd agreed on, then moved out of the way. The others jumped on him, making the arrest while he was still holding the spoon.

He was shattered. He had thought he was beyond the reach of the law.

He hadn't let me meet his suppliers, but we knew who they were. They were also being watched. At exactly the same time, at three or four other locations in southwest Sydney, it was 'Go, go, go', and they were arrested too and search warrants were executed on their homes, yielding more drugs.

In NSW the legislation states that an offer to supply carries the same penalty as *actual* supply. We locked him up for offering to supply heroin as well as actually supplying the hash oil.

I was told by my superiors: 'You've obviously got a talent for this. We didn't think we'd ever get this guy with surveillance, let alone an undercover operative.' I received my first Commissioner's Commendation for the role.

We all realised that having an undercover operative from an ethnic background was a potent tool against organised crime.

CHAPTER 7

He's in Jewellery

1988

'Mate, they're going through the house now. They can't find the money where you said it was.' I could hear the tension in my workmate's voice.

'It was definitely there in the bedroom,' I told him. 'I saw it being put there.'

My SDCC workmates and I were a tight-knit group. We had faith in each other and we had each other's backs. But this just looked bad. Tens of thousands of dollars in small bills seemed to have vanished into thin air.

This was a controlled undercover drug sting. The house was under surveillance. No one had gone in or out. I started to worry I might be blamed for the missing money.

I was frantically going over and over it in my mind. 'It's in there,' I said. 'Look harder.'

The hours ticked by and still the search team had found nothing.

* * *

In late 1987 I'd formally transferred from Balmain Detectives to the SDCC, working nine to five and mostly wearing a suit, unless I had a job on. You don't fish in the same pond twice. If I'd just had a job in Sydney's harbourside suburb of Double Bay, then my next job might be one hour south in the city of Wollongong. Which was exactly where my workmates were right now, searching for the cash I'd left there.

Early that Sunday morning, wired up with a recording device, I had driven to meet the target of our operation at his modest home north of Wollongong. He had been involved in serious drug dealing and had been named during the Woodward Royal Commission into Drug Trafficking in the late 1970s. At one point he had fled back to Lebanon to avoid arrest, but he had subsequently returned.

He had been led to believe that I was a man named (once again) Michael, a wealthy jeweller from Sydney and a drug supplier on a large scale, looking for a purchase to sell for a profit. We had met through an informant who also did not know who I was. We usually spoke in Arabic, as this made him more comfortable, and bolstered my credibility.

After a number of meetings, he had come to trust me and was happy to do business with me. We had arranged the deal days earlier, face-to-face, at a secretly recorded meeting. The plan was for me to drop the money at his house, then we would drive to a secret location in the bush, where I would take possession of the drugs and be off.

He had worked out a code earlier: 'Ring me up and say, "The watch is ready, when do you want me to bring it to you?" If I answer, I'll tell you to come on a particular day to deliver the watch. If someone else answers then tell them that you've repaired a watch for me and ask when I'll be at home so that you can bring it to me. Then I'll ring you back. That's it, no more no less.'

So the guys wired me up, and early that Sunday morning I drove to meet him as agreed in a residential street. In the back seat of the car I had a black briefcase stuffed with wads of cash.

I reached the meeting place and spotted him waiting for me. He walked up to the car and got in. He directed me to drive a little further up the street. Then he said, 'Stop the car,' and when I did, he invited me to come into his house for a cup of coffee.

Once inside, I handed him the bag, saying, 'The money is all in there. Check it.'

But he said, 'I don't want to check it. I trust you.'

He handed the cash to his wife and she went into the bedroom with it.

Together we went into the modest kitchen and had a coffee, exchanged pleasantries in Arabic and chatted about future drug deals. He promised that the marijuana he was selling was a 'good deal' to make money on.

After more chitchat, he said, 'It's time to go and pick up the drugs.'

We got into my car and drove off to get the bags of drugs. I followed his instructions to head to the Bulli Pass in the direction of Appin. It was June and there was heavy rain. But there was little traffic because it was still early morning.

He told me he had men set up to watch the deal take place.

'We come and pick it up and chuck it in the car and you go and that's it. If there is anything different they won't let anyone come near, they'll shoot them,' he said.

I took this with a grain of salt.

* * *

We were so close, but then things started to go wrong. As I was nearing the top of the Bulli Pass, my car broke down. It was supposed to be brand-new; that was the story I'd told him.

Cursing, I managed to turn it around and roll it down the hill so I could try to clutch-start it.

It didn't work. I pulled over just before a hairpin bend.

He was trying to calm me down: 'Take it easy. Give it a rest. There's plenty of time.' But then, expressing his own frustration: 'Well, why doesn't it fuckin' start?'

As we sat there, I could see the undercover surveillance teams were doing sweeping drive-bys in the distance, trying to see what was up and ascertain whether I was in danger. I had no way of communicating with them. The wire I was wearing was only taping our conversation inside the car.

As we sat there, both cursing the car, all of a sudden a white Commodore approached from the opposite direction, did a fast U-turn and pulled up behind me.

By this time I was sweating bullets. I looked in the rear-vision mirror. 'Who's that?' I asked. 'There's someone behind us.'

The man replied, 'Don't worry, I told him to come and pick me up.'

It was his son. Unbeknown to me, he had been following behind us at his father's direction.

The three of us tried unsuccessfully to start the car. His son drove off and came back with a can of WD-40. Finally, we got the car started and the man and I continued the drive.

Once on the Appin Road, we drove for some distance before he directed me to pull over at a particular spot, and we got out of the car. His son pulled up behind us.

There was no sign of the men he'd warned me would be waiting. As I'd suspected, there was no one but his son involved.

By this time the rain was pounding down. It was so heavy you could barely see. The man disappeared into the bush and came back with several large hessian sacks. He did another couple of trips, then he and his son loaded the bags into the boot of my car.

I checked them. The drugs were inside. A great deal of marijuana.

So we shook hands and I got into my car and tried to drive away. But again the undercover car I was driving had other ideas. It refused to start.

The son pushed the car while I clutch-started it. This time it worked.

I gave the signal to indicate the deal had been done, then watched in my rear-view mirror as the surveillance teams screamed into action, surrounding the son's car, pulling the two surprised men out and arresting them. The signal launched a series of simultaneous raids. Teams of police swarmed all over the man's house, and 135 police from the SDCC and the Wollongong Drug Law Enforcement Bureau started banging down the doors of 27 other properties, including several shops and petrol stations.

But 'Operation Kefek' – cheekily named after the Lebanese for 'How are you?' – was in danger of going off the rails.

Search teams tipped the contents of the house upside down, looking for the cash I'd handed over in the deal.

They couldn't find any of it. Tens of thousands of dollars. Not one note.

The man's wife was denying she had ever met a man named Michael, and said she knew nothing about any cash.

After nearly four hours with no sign of the cash, our chief superintendent, John Anderson, pulled out the search team. He brought in a fresh team of officers and said: 'Do it all again as if nothing has been done before.'

Finally, one of those officers went outside and saw two wheelie bins in the backyard. It was the only place they hadn't looked.

He tipped the wheelie bins upside down and emptied their contents onto the ground. Rummaging around, the officer found bags of garbage. Inside those bags, upside down under some leftover tabbouleh salad, was the slightly soggy cash. I was relieved to hear it was all there.

Back at Wollongong Police Station, the man was being interviewed by police. An officer was trying to convince him to talk.

The officer said to him, 'The game's up! The man you know as Michael – who bought the grass from you – is an undercover police officer.'

He simply refused to believe it. 'Nah, nah, he's a jeweller,' he said. 'He's in jewellery, he was going to sell me some watches.'

He kept that line up even after he was shown the bags of drugs and the money. It took a while for him to accept that it was actually true. He didn't take it well.

Ultimately there were six arrests and 96 bags of Indian hemp were seized.

* * *

Some months after the operation, one of my SDCC workmates received a call from an informant who asked to see us. He advised us that there was a lot of anger towards me, and that he felt there would be some sort of contract taken out on me. I made sure a record of the information was put into the system.

One day I received a phone call. 'Are you Nick Kaldas?' the man on the other end asked.

'Yes.'

'I need to talk to you. I'm from the Internal Affairs Department at the Australian Tax Office.'

Shit, I thought, *they're going to have a go at my tax returns.*

I was wrong.

I met with two investigators from the Australian Tax Office (ATO). One of them said, 'One of that man's sons was working in the tax office and he's accessed not just your personal records but your entire family's as well.'

I was stunned. So now they knew where I and everyone close to me lived and worked? I supplied a statement, and any records that were relevant.

The ATO investigators swooped on the son and he was charged with around 130 counts of illegally accessing information. He fought it all the way.

Even with the son arrested, I didn't feel like my family and I were safe. What if they hired contract killers? I went to the SDCC to see if they could do anything to help protect me, but there was nothing formal in place to support an undercover operative like me.

By the time the son's court case came up, I had left the SDCC. There had been a restructure, and I was transferred to the newly established Drug Enforcement Agency (DEA), along with all the other investigators at the SDCC. I was assigned to one of four task forces, but no one in my hierarchy there had been involved in the SDCC, nor knew about my work there. When the dust settled and the son finally had his day before the magistrate, I had to go back and give evidence – again putting me in the group's crosshairs. But by then, the unit and the team that did the job with me had scattered to the four winds, and despite my requests, there was no support for me or my family.

I promised myself that if I ever got into a position to try to fix all that, I would. Undercover operatives who come under threat need to be supported and protected.

* * *

It's undeniable that undercover police back then got a raw deal. Some undercover cops fell by the wayside, simply because they lost that identity of being a cop, or they weren't able to separate their two lives. And none of us had any training; there was no undercover course or manual in existence at that stage.

Whether it's undercover work, or the UN assignments I did later, when you come back to your normal world you have to make a decision about how much you tell your loved ones and others around you. My position has always been that I don't tell them much. Not because I'm secretive, but because I can't expect them to understand what I've been through. Like most operational police, I also worried about being seen as a 'wanker', big-noting myself. Cops have an absolute aversion to people who go to parties and talk things up: 'I went to this murder and I saw this body.' Telling gory stories is only an attempt to glorify themselves.

It's not what we do as cops. It's a case of: *Stop being a prima donna, just shut up, don't gloat and don't carry on.*

There would always be dangers you hadn't anticipated. Later in my time at the SDCC, I negotiated through a Romanian informant to buy a couple of kilos of cocaine from a Portuguese dealer called Victor Andrade-Pereira. It took some weeks to get to that point, and samples were supplied.

Andrade-Pereira was staying in a hotel in Kings Cross. On the night the deal was to take place, the informant came out and told me I would be searched once I went inside.

I had to make a snap decision about whether to call things off. There was a risk of a rip-off, as I was carrying a significant amount of money, and I was alone and would be out of sight and hearing of other police.

But I wasn't going to give up. I decided to go in, but as I was wired, I quickly told those who were listening in that I'd have to take everything off. They got the message.

I ripped off the wire and went in, but Andrade-Pereira never searched me. I think he was intimidated because I was quite a bit taller than him and adopted a somewhat aggressive persona, suited to my dealer role.

I bought the cocaine and we walked out of the hotel together; me with my bag of drugs, him swinging his bag of money. The cops were waiting at reception and swooped on him. We later raided his home and found more kilos of high-grade cocaine.

That was one of the times when the risks paid off. The senior investigators and I were later commended by the trial judge, Justice Levine.

CHAPTER 8

Crime Doesn't Pay?

1989–1993

Around the same time that I became a cop, I started going out with a young woman called Allison. She worked at City Mutual after I'd left, but I'd kept in touch with some of the guys there and that was how Allison and I met. We would be on and off for some time and eventually we split up properly. We didn't see each other for about five years, only to reunite when I was in my early thirties. In 1989, we got married.

It was also around this time that I moved to the DEA. The focus of the SDCC had been widening, and in 1990 it would become the NSW Crime Commission (NSWCC) and be given a much broader mandate. In 1989, while this change was in progress, the DEA was established to take over the SDCC's old role: taking on drug traffickers and attempting to decrease the availability of illicit drugs, while still working closely with the NSWCC.

A lot of guys moved across from the old drug squad and other crime squads. It was a competitive selection process: anyone with a patchy record was rejected. But I made it.

As in my early days at the SDCC, I wasn't a full-time undercover operative. My full-time job, or day job, with Task Force Three of the DEA was as an investigator, a detective senior constable plugging away at regular cases. But every now and then a job would come up in other task forces and I would go off and do some undercover work at their request, then return to being a detective again.

I was tasked with being the case officer in a team to investigate allegations of large-scale drug importations of cocaine from Los Angeles by an Eastern Suburbs butcher of New Zealand origin. It was a painstaking operation, in which we had to try and piece together all the trips he'd done, as well as the trips that were done by a number of 'mules' that he used to bring drugs in. We intercepted one of his female couriers coming back into the country and she had a significant amount of cocaine secretly strapped to her waist. Ultimately, she and another courier confessed and gave evidence against the butcher. It was a hotly contested trial. He was convicted, given a lengthy sentence and, on the conclusion of his jail term, deported back to New Zealand. It was a unique case in that most of the drugs he was convicted for importing, we did not actually seize.

The trial was presided over by Judge Bill Hosking QC, who later wrote a book entitled *Justice Denied* about his experiences in the law and made favourable mention of my role in that case.

* * *

My undercover work, meanwhile, was as challenging as ever.

In another operation, I was introduced by an informant to a Turkish drug dealer who operated around the Eastern

Suburbs. He was very well connected, ran a modelling agency, and operated in high-level cocaine circles. It took a relatively long period of lunches and dinners, but we got to a point where he trusted me and offered me a kilo of cocaine. Again, the shared ethnic background was helpful.

We agreed to meet at a flash Italian restaurant in Surry Hills in the inner city. The plan was that when his courier arrived with the drugs, we would walk across the road to a petrol station, do the deal and get back to lunch.

We sat down in the restaurant and ordered entrées. The courier arrived and the three of us retired to the toilet in the petrol station to do the exchange. I gave the signal and my team came in with some noise and arrested them, and pretended to arrest me as well. I did not get to eat my main meal!

At Surry Hills Police Station, the offender refused to say anything, demanding to talk to me. He simply refused to believe that I was a police officer, and that all our incriminating discussions had been recorded.

The interview team said to me, 'He won't believe you're a cop,' so I agreed to talk to him. I walked into the interview room, and told him I really was a police officer and the game was up. He looked absolutely shattered. We had hit it off; he was good company and quite worldly, but I never lost sight of who I was and why I was there.

I never enjoyed those moments, but I also recognised we were stopping a significant amount of drugs from entering the market. And personally, I knew that I had done my job well enough for him to refuse to believe I was a police officer.

* * *

At the DEA, as at the SDCC, you couldn't predict what was going to happen from one day to the next. If you were on a major operation, and time-sensitive information came in from telephone intercepts or informants, it was *go, go, go*. There were never regular hours. There was also a fair bit of travel across the state. I wasn't spending that much time at home.

On one occasion my task force was investigating a syndicate who had set up a meth lab, essentially a cooking room for the drugs. We didn't know the location so the two main suspects were to be followed around to work out where the lab was. I had just come back from a court matter, wearing a suit, and my superintendent said, 'We're short on the ground, get changed and just go out for a couple of hours to help with the follow.'

I paired up with a workmate, and we headed out. I got home four crazy days later. A number of our colleagues were also following these guys in other cars. As the crooks drove around Sydney, we followed, not knowing where they were heading but sticking with them. We took turns in being the lead car, and we ended up in Tweed Heads, on the border with Queensland.

My partner and I were in the lead position, following the targets. It was dark by then, and we didn't know the area at all. They turned into a street and we hung back for a minute or so. We turned into the street, and realised it was a dead end. They had done a U-turn and had their headlights on us.

We found out later from telephone intercepts and other sources that they were armed and suspected they were being followed by other crooks who were planning to rob them so were getting ready to 'take out' anyone on their tail. We did our best to act lost, not look at them, did a U-turn and got out of there quick smart. Some days later, we brought the operation to finality, raided the lab and arrested the targets, seizing a great deal of drugs.

As exciting as it was, my responsibilities at home were changing. Allison and I were expecting our first baby, so I wanted more of a nine-to-five job. So, in 1991, I decided that time was up for me at the DEA. Allison and I were supposed to go to birthing classes together, but being busy with an operation and other work commitments, I only attended some of the classes.

I was at the birth of our first child later that year. Men often talk about how witnessing their child's birth is one of the most important moments in their life, and that was true for me.

I've been there for all three of my children's births – two daughters, Simone and Laura, then a son, Luke. Being there when a little human being is born, holding them in your arms, is an amazing, moving experience that deeply affected me each time.

As a new husband and father, I was looking for greater predictability in my working hours. Yet, since my very first day on the job, and maybe even before that, there were two areas of policing that had always appealed to me: the Armed Hold-Up and Homicide Squads. I still felt that sense of awe I'd had for them back in my early days as a detective.

It was not lost on me that requesting a move to the Armed Hold-Up Squad might not help me achieve my aim of more regular hours! However, that was what I decided to do.

I applied for a transfer to the North West Crime Squad at Parramatta. I had an interview with the head of the Major

Crime Squad, and my transfer was accepted. I indicated a preference for Armed Hold-Ups.

The Armed Hold-Up Squad weren't cliquey, but they were certainly choosy about who came in. I had spoken to a few people and they'd said, 'The boss of the squad is Jack Ferguson and it is his decision.'

Jack Ferguson was a legendary armed robbery detective. A former 'graded' rugby league player for the North Sydney Bears (regrettably now defunct), he had the build of Dwayne 'The Rock' Johnson or Vin Diesel. He was renowned for looking after his squad.

I met with him and I felt we hit it off. I had recommendations from a number of people he knew well. Jack thought they could use me and was happy to have me on board.

Jack Ferguson's invitation that day came with a warning. If the guys in the squad started putting shit on me within a few weeks of my arrival, he said, then everything was going to be fine. However, if they ignored me, I was going to have to look at whether it was working out or not.

* * *

Luckily, it only took about three days before the team ripped into me, in a good-hearted way. They were one of the most cohesive groups I've ever worked in, filled with people who genuinely cared about each other. There was a community spirit across all the crime squads, but certainly within the Hold-Ups. We would work bloody hard, but we'd also play hard.

And as it turned out, the Armed Hold-Up Squad did give me that predictability I was after. I knew that my roster – ten days on, four days off – was set in stone, which meant that every couple of weeks I would have a long weekend when I could spend time with the family and mow the lawn. There was no shift work, but I did a lot of hours, there's no doubt about it. Sometimes we'd work through the night and into the next day if we were on an investigation.

Another bonus was that Parramatta was a lot closer to home than Balmain. Allison and I had recently moved from Carlton to Castle Hill, just north of Parramatta, and built a new home.

In the late 1980s, NSW Police was split into four regions; the North West Region I was part of covered not just northwest Sydney, but the whole of northwest NSW. When they split the state up, we seemed to get all the areas that came with more than their fair share of trouble. Someone kindly put a kink in the map, so we got Cabramatta, the hotbed of Asian organised crime, thrown in for good measure. What a twist of fate! Had Cabramatta been included in the South West Region, one of the state's biggest ever murder investigations wouldn't have been my problem, or occupied so much of my life in the years to come.

* * *

There is an argument that armed robberies – as opposed to homicides – are glamorised in films and on TV. Hollywood would have us believe it's not acceptable to kill but it *is* acceptable to hold up banks or pull off daring heists. Especially if the robberies are cleverly planned and executed by a bunch of likeable rascals led by charmers like George Clooney or Michael Caine.

In reality, armed robbers generally aren't that sophisticated or good-looking. When I was doing drug work in the SDCC and the DEA, a lot of the older guys there would say that all the armed robbers were former drug dealers who weren't smart enough to cut it. They'd resorted to blunt, violent crimes because they couldn't deal with the nuances of avoiding surveillance and all the other things that drug dealers have to do. Armed robbery is far simpler.

You don't start your criminal career doing armed robberies, though. These were hardened crooks who had served their apprenticeship carrying out lesser crimes. If a life of petty crime is the criminal's equivalent of a bachelor's degree, then armed robbery is their master's.

Any business that dealt in cash was a potential victim: banks and other financial institutions, and the cash-in-transit (CIT) industry, responsible for the armoured vans that carried the money. There would be cash constantly coming and going from banks, clubs and other places.

In the Hold-Ups we carried out our investigations to identify who the robbers were and the job they intended to do, then meticulously planned our raid to make arrests. Before each operation we'd have a planning meeting and walk through all the variations, working out who was going to be where. Then, on the day, we'd all get together, get briefed – or 'brief up', as we put it – get our guns, don protective vests, get into the cars and drive out to the job.

That sense of being on the hunt, as a group, was extraordinary. You felt you were part of a great team doing great things and holding bad guys to account.

About a third of our work in the Hold-Ups was proactive – cultivating informants, collecting information, trying to find out what was going to happen in order to either prevent it from taking place or to be there when things went down. Surveillance also played a part. The rest of it was mopping up after the event and trying to catch the bad guys after a robbery had occurred.

The CIT companies all had huge warehouses – 'counting houses' – filled with people (mainly women) sitting there using machines to count money and then bundling it up. These were literally buildings full of money, so you can see the attraction for robbers. They had incredible security measures in place, underfloor sensors and alarms everywhere, but every now and then you'd get teams of crooks who had designs on a setup like that, just like the plot of every heist film you've ever seen, from *The Italian Job* to *Ocean's Eleven*.

One time we got information about an overseas gang who had rented a factory unit a couple of doors up from a counting house in Smithfield, in southwest Sydney. Word was that the gang were planning to tunnel into the counting house from their rented property. The sensors in the counting house had started to flicker on and off after hours.

Each night for around a week, after the counting house shut down and the lights were switched off, we put a shift of cops in there. We waited and watched, but nothing came of it. We decided something must have scared the gang off, because they suddenly hightailed it back to South Africa.

Another case took place in a shopping centre out Greystanes way, 25 kilometres west of Sydney's CBD. We received information about a crooked employee who was passing on information to the Rebels Motorcycle Club. An informant contacted the CIT company to warn them that one of the armoured vans collecting takings from the shopping centre, and carrying very large amounts of cash, was going to be robbed. To this day we don't know who the informant was, but he wanted zero contact with the police. We had to take what second-hand information we could get, with the armoured van people relaying questions and answers between us and the informant. So we only had a rough idea about who was involved, what they were planning and when. We believed they were a gang of four.

It was a three- to four-week investigation, full-time for most of the team, backing up police from the surveillance branch, following the gang's every move. We drove unmarked cars and were all in plainclothes. We used old-school binoculars, but we also filmed them with cameras, big old VHS jobs, which were state-of-the-art for those days.

The week before we thought the job was going to happen, the gang did a dry run in the shopping centre. We were watching them from a distance the whole time. Our cameras tracked the movements of the armoured van and the four men following by car.

On the day of the actual robbery, we had everything thoroughly planned out. As well as all of us, waiting in different places around the shopping centre, we had police helicopters hovering nearby out of earshot, and a team from the Special Weapons and Operations Section (SWOS) in the vicinity on standby.

On cue, the bad guys turned up. Then the targeted van arrived. We had to make a quick decision: would we grab the gang before they went into the shopping centre? The problem with doing that was that the chances of getting a conviction for a serious crime would be severely decreased, if not completely wiped out. They could say – even if they had weapons on them – that they weren't planning on doing anything, which would mean we could only charge them with minor firearms offences. But if we let them go through with the robbery, we might have a gunfight on our hands.

Making a judgement call in the moment is tough. You can only base your decision on all your years of experience. And again, it comes down to having thought through everything in advance.

Although I was only a senior constable, I was one of the planners; it's always a tense moment, with the gravity of the decision to be made weighing heavily on all involved.

The decision was made to let the gang go into the shopping centre. Two of them stayed outside while the other two went into a bottle shop, presumably intending to wait for the armoured van guys to come in to collect the takings, at which point the gang would ambush them and force them back to the van so the gang could empty it.

We waited for them to hold up the bottle shop, then eight of us, all armed, burst in. We took out the two guys who were inside the shop and the SWOS back-up team grabbed the two crooks who were waiting outside the centre.

The moment we crashed into the shop, one of the two idiots inside dropped his weapon and tried to play innocent. He started walking from one aisle to another pretending to be a customer, telling me: 'Thank God you're here, Sergeant, there's been an armed robbery.'

Rolling my eyes, I said, 'Come here, old mate.'

All four pleaded guilty in the end and were convicted and received various sentences. Two of them were sworn members of the Rebels and the other two were hangers-on.

We worked out that one of the employees in the armoured van company was related to one of the armed robbers. We confronted him and dragged him in for interview after interview, but he wouldn't bend. Ultimately, he got sacked but not charged. There was no doubt in my mind that he was involved, but we just couldn't prove it.

Leaving him aside, we got all the bad guys. No one was hurt, and the money – we're talking a figure that was in the millions – was saved.

It was a great result, one where the good guys triumphed.

* * *

The Orange airport robbery was another significant job. At the time it was believed to have been the largest successful armed-car robbery in NSW's history.

At 6.40 am on Monday 22 February 1993, two masked men wielding shotguns leaped from a stolen white Commodore station wagon and held up an armoured van outside the terminal at Orange Regional Airport, which lies 10 kilometres outside the Orange city centre. The men made off with $1.46 million in unmarked bills – $50 and $100 notes – destined for the Reserve Bank's central cash repository in Sydney via a weekly Hazelton Airlines flight. This would be a huge amount of money today, but even more so back then.

The money stolen wasn't only from Orange but from banks throughout the entire western region of NSW. Everything was being taken out in the one go. The amount of money passing through a place like that wouldn't be nearly as high today, but back in 1993, everyone dealt in cash.

Forty-two-year-old George Imants Wattle was the mastermind behind the hold-up. Wattle wasn't his birth name; his family were Latvian and they had all changed their surname from Nikolaides via deed poll. Wattle was a partner in a security business in Sydney's Western Suburbs with no criminal record. He had an almost identical twin brother who had not been involved in the robbery.

Wattle had recruited a couple of 20-somethings to help him carry out this robbery, not revealing the target to them until they all arrived in Orange. He obviously had inside information, because he knew that a significant amount of cash went through Orange airport at a particular time each week.

Wattle and his gang of two hit the airport at about dawn. Wattle actually sat in the car while the two young guys went in. Disguised in masks and carrying firearms, they confronted and threatened the two van guards, catching them completely by surprise as they headed towards the plane with the money. Armoured van guards are advised not to get into a firefight with anyone, so they didn't put up a struggle. It was amateur hour, really, because the robbers grabbed three bags, each containing about $500,000 – and left behind a bag containing even more than that because they were rushing. They returned to where Wattle was waiting, loaded the bags into the stolen car and sped away.

Wattle gave the two lads tens of thousands of dollars each, telling them that he had to pay off someone in the armoured van company, so he couldn't give them more. They did not know how much had been stolen; Wattle kept the total figure to himself.

Being young and green, these two knockabouts actually thought all their Christmases had come at once, and therein lay their downfall.

One of them, a lad from Mount Druitt, went to the Hilton Hotel in the city, checked into the most expensive room and invited all his mates over to party with him. Covered in tattoos and sporting mullets, they were seen in the spa and the restaurants, living it up. In this high-class establishment, they stood out like the proverbial sore thumb. The security staff could see that something didn't add up, and one of the cleaners noticed a bag under the bed, half open and stuffed with money.

The Hilton security staff contacted the police in the South Region's Major Crime Squad, as the hotel was in their jurisdiction and there was no connection with the Orange airport job at this stage.

Two detectives from the South Region went to the Hilton – and allegedly took the money from under the bed, let the kids go, and didn't tell us or anyone else.

Meanwhile, we were madly trying to use informants and do anything we could to find out who'd done the robbery. Eventually we tracked the offender from the Hilton Hotel to North Queensland, where he'd gone into hiding.

Once he was in custody, he gave up everyone else. But he immediately made a complaint against the detectives who had gone to the Hilton.

The two police were subsequently arrested and charged for taking the cash but beat the charge in court. Their alleged actions set our investigation back about four to five weeks.

We raided Wattle's home – he was divorced and lived with his elderly mum – but he was gone, and there was nothing we could find of any evidentiary value. We worked out some months later that his twin brother had reported his passport stolen. There were sightings of Wattle from Broome to the Philippines. We established that he had probably gone to the Top End, got onto some sort of fishing trawler illegally, gone to Indonesia and flown on to Latvia, which had no extradition treaty with Australia, and still doesn't.

Predictably, Wattle never came back. He's probably still there somewhere, having taken over a million dollars with him. Back in 1993, that would have been a lot of money in Latvia, which had only regained its independence two years earlier from the USSR.

The second young offender had the misfortune of leaving fingerprints behind at the scene that identified him. After the complaint from the offender who'd checked into the Hilton, the second offender saw an opportunity to capitalise on the situation like his mate had done, and he joined in, saying *his* money had also been stolen by the cops.

It hadn't. We were able to prove all the spending he'd done after the robbery. He bought motorcycles for himself and his mates, and took his de facto wife, her child and other friends on a luxury holiday to Disneyland and Hawaii, paying for thousands of dollars' worth of flights in $50 and $100 notes. This spending spree totalled more than $43,000, within one week of the robbery. He couldn't otherwise explain where the money had come from, especially since he was unemployed at the time.

All in all, it was a good result. We arrested the two young blokes and seized most of the money they'd taken, though sadly the majority of the money went overseas with Wattle.

The two young lads weren't smart, but the bottom line is we never got the mastermind behind the job. The arrest warrant for Wattle is still outstanding.

* * *

There's another duty that the Armed Hold-Up Squad carries out, and that's the hunt for fugitives. There's nothing quite like a good manhunt.

One of the most colourful I worked on was the hunt for Melbourne criminal Christopher Dean Binse, who went by the nickname of 'Badness'. He was a 'postcard robber': he would send postcards from different locations to the investigators on his trail, taunting them as if to say, *Up yours – crime does pay, and handsomely so.*

To track him down, we looked at call charge records for a phone number we thought he was using. One of the numbers he was ringing belonged to a hair transplant clinic in Sydney.

Everybody said it was a long shot, but I went there, introduced myself as a police officer and asked if they had a Christopher Dean Binse on their records. They were adamant that there was no record under that name. I came up with a few variations, but there was nothing similar whatsoever.

Then I showed them a photograph. Bingo! They recognised the man depicted as 'Mr Smith', who came in there all the time. Badness was a very vain individual. It turned out that this company had clinics in all the capital cities, so wherever Badness went, he could go into one of their clinics and all his records would be on file.

I asked them about his next appointment and it turned out that it was at their clinic in Melbourne. So when

Badness flew down there, the cops were waiting for him at the other end.

We put him in Parramatta Gaol, but he's one of the few people ever to have escaped from there. Somehow he had a hacksaw delivered to him in prison, which he used to saw through one of his bars, then he abseiled down onto a sloping roof and leaped over razor wire and a four-metre gap between buildings to get away.

To date, Binse has six successful escapes to his name and a whole bunch of other attempts that didn't work out. He was eventually recaptured after the Parramatta break and ended up serving 13 years in Goulburn's supermax prison.

He also faced charges in Victoria, and there was a personal animosity between him and the Armed Robbery Squad in Melbourne, in particular the legendary Detective Ken Ashworth. After leaving NSW, Badness was arrested at Melbourne airport. He could see the cops coming towards him and he started screaming: 'They're gonna kill me, they're gonna kill me!! The police are gonna kill me!!'

He was an interesting character. He is currently in solitary confinement in Barwon Prison in Victoria.

* * *

The Armed Hold Up Squad lived up to all the expectations I'd had since I was a young constable. The skills I'd proven on the job were vital for the next position I would take on: negotiations.

CHAPTER 9

132 People

1992–2001

It was a dark night and we'd been called to a siege.

I was the primary negotiator. You vividly remember the ones when you were 'it', doing all the talking.

A former South Vietnamese Army veteran, who was estranged from his wife and was clearly psychologically unstable, had taken his five-year-old son hostage in his wife's home. He'd gone in, armed with an M1 carbine – a semi-automatic firearm – to confront his wife, but when he hadn't found her, he'd shot and killed his mother-in-law and tied up his sister-in-law.

The sister-in-law had managed to escape and raise the alarm. She told us her mother had been murdered, but that he was still in there with his young son.

We got the call late in the evening. By the time we arrived on the scene, there was a whole lot of media there. I had to ask myself: *How do I negotiate with someone who's already committed murder?*

The street was cordoned off. There was a brick fence

along the front of the house, about waist high, and we were on the other side, beyond shooting range. The house was surrounded by the Tactical Operations Unit (TOU).

We waited for a long time, calling out to the man through a loudhailer, but he would not engage with us so I turned my attention to the boy. My son, Luke, was about the same age as he was, and thoughts of Luke kept running through my head.

Luke is the baby of the family, the last of the three. At his birth we had a bit of a fright: the umbilical cord was tied around his neck. Alarms went off, lights were flashing, and even though the general rule is that nurses don't run, staff came speeding down the corridor with specialised equipment, pushing me out of the way. Allison and I were really worried, but all was well in the end.

Now I was talking through a loudhailer to this other little boy, trying to get him to stay at the front of the house, talking to us through the front window. I had to keep him away from the front door, so he wouldn't get hurt if the TOU had to go in.

The siege continued for several hours into the night. The father was acting more and more erratically. Finally we came to the conclusion that he was going to harm the child, which meant that we had to act, and act quickly.

The TOU crashed in with a lot of noise, as there usually is in a siege entry situation. The door was kicked down, flash-bang grenades were released to disorient the hostage-taker, and there was a lot of yelling for people to get on the ground.

Then there was the sound of gunfire, as the father fired his M1 carbine at the first man through the door. Even though that officer had a bulletproof vest on, he was hit by a lot of ricocheting shrapnel.

The squad opened up on the father and subdued him. He was wounded but okay.

Understandably, while all this was happening, the little boy was having an absolute meltdown. I was frantically talking to him through the loudhailer, realising it was a matter of life or death for him if he walked into the firefight. He remained at the window, but you could see he wanted to go to his dad. And I could see and hear that he was utterly distressed and scared. I was urging him not to move, yelling at this stage so he could hear me above the fray, but I couldn't go onto the premises to grab him.

I found it quite hard not being able to intervene.

Once the man was under arrest, it became clear just how volatile the situation had been – much more so than we'd realised. Not only had he been armed with the M1, but he also had bullets on the stove with a low flame going underneath them, and aerosol cans in different parts of the house with bullets strapped to them and fires underneath.

At Burwood Police Station afterwards, the TOU guy who got hit took off all his tactical gear and there were bits of buckshot falling off him everywhere. Those guys are dead-set heroes.

The siege had gone on almost all night. At the end of it all the negotiation team regrouped.

'You look like shit, Nick,' said our team leader, John O'Reilly. 'You all right?'

'Do I?' I said. 'Yeah, I'm okay.'

This was a lie. The siege had indeed taken a toll on me, but I was struggling to articulate what had shaken me up. It was the only time that ever happened to me on a hostage negotiation job. The boy had just reminded me so much of Luke, and I'd wanted to protect him, but I couldn't.

My son got an extra-long hug from me when I got home.

* * *

In the 1970s, it was the NYPD who put forward the idea that negotiating is actually a bit of an art, and some effort ought to be dedicated to it. So they brought in a couple of people to start their hostage negotiation team, the first of its kind in the world. It was prompted by the real-life events of the 1972 Munich Olympics siege, as well as the attempted Brooklyn bank robbery in the same year that was the inspiration for the 1975 movie *Dog Day Afternoon*. Later, the developers at the NYPD took the idea to the FBI. Everyone recognised that there was a science at work here, and that it made sense to have police officers study it.

In 1992, I was selected for the crisis and hostage negotiators' course. I was attracted to the idea of dealing with high-risk situations. And so began a years-long career and involvement in the Negotiations Unit that would run parallel to my other policing roles.

Once again, the application process for the course was rigorous, with psych tests, interviews and the submission of references, but I got in. The course was two weeks full-time at the academy, then we were sent out into the field.

At the beginning of the course they said they weren't going to teach us how to negotiate per se, because as police we were already doing it. We already knew about human nature, and we were used to dealing with people in crisis. So they were simply going to give us a more structured format for what to say and do, and what not to do, with a lot of research behind it.

There are a few key principles, including the fact that you never lie to a subject, because that can lead to all credibility being destroyed. You also do anything that you promise to do while negotiating; for instance, if you promise to sit down and have a coffee with the subject once the crisis is over, you must do that. Some subjects might find themselves in negotiations with police on multiple occasions, so it is essential that they knew that negotiators don't lie and that they keep their word.

To be effective as a negotiator you need a broad yet particular set of skills. You have to go in there with a rough plan yet be able to change your approach second by second, knowing that situations will arise that will challenge everything you've planned for. You have to be quick on your feet but also exercise caution so that you don't make any rash decisions. You don't want something to go wrong because you're jumping at shadows. You've got your brain operating at high speed, and you need to think about what has just happened and what the subject has just said. Every word they say has to be interrogated in case it means they're about to kill themselves or someone else.

In the event that anything goes wrong, a very systematic post-operational assessment is undertaken. It's about going back to see what went wrong, what went right and what lessons can be learned. I was lucky, though: I never lost anyone, and the hostage negotiations I was involved in never ended badly either.

You may be a key player in life-and-death situations, so it's only fair that the police regularly ensure you are of sound mind. They go over you with a fine-toothed comb. They look at whether you're coping, whether you're making good decisions.

I knew what the psychs would look for, and I learned sometimes to cover up what I was really feeling – just like I did that night with John O'Reilly. I'm not proud of that, but I didn't want to get kicked off the team.

It can be very hard to show weakness in the operating environment. I was to learn a lot more about these issues years later in my work at the Royal Commission into Defence and Veteran Suicide. There's a stigma, and once you're tainted, you never shake it off. I've seen this repeatedly in my career, and it's convinced me that society has to find a way to remove the stigma and allow men in particular to raise their hand and ask for help when they need to.

* * *

Negotiating was something I enjoyed. You get to use your brain, and it's incredibly rewarding: I've talked people down and saved a lot of lives.

There are four individuals who make up any negotiations team.

First, there are the primary and secondary negotiators. The primary negotiator is the mouthpiece. They talk to the person at the centre of the event, whether that be the hostage-taker, or the guy on the ledge who's about to jump.

The secondary negotiator sticks close by and writes down every detail. They back the primary up and help with ideas. They're also a conduit between the primary negotiator and the rest of the team.

The third position is that of the gopher. They do what it says on the label: they're the one who goes for the coffees and takes care of any other basic tasks that need attending to.

The fourth member is the team leader. They're removed from negotiating, but they're in charge, making sure that the team is functioning, liaising with the tactical team and the commanders, and looking after everyone's welfare.

In any negotiations team, you start off as a gopher, then eventually move up to secondary, then you become the primary negotiator. After that, depending on performance, you may become team leader. I was lucky I got to team leader, but the role of primary was always the most satisfying.

You and your team would go on call about one week in five. Some weeks you might get two or three jobs. On a week when you were on call you could be contacted at any time of the day or night. We used pagers back then. As soon as you got the page, you'd ring up and be briefed on the location and nature of the situation. No matter what you were doing at that moment, you'd drop it and get into your car – you always had access to a car if you were on call – put the blue light on and off you'd go. Obviously, you had to be sober, so the week you were on call, if you had a wedding or a party to attend, you couldn't drink, even if it was your birthday.

The four Negotiations Unit members would head to the location along with a tactical team from the TOU, the two teams working hand in glove. There are always psychiatrists available to assist the negotiators; they understand the terrain and they know the legal framework within which we work.

The idea back then was to quietly surround the place, make sure the person we were negotiating with couldn't get out, and begin to talk. This approach was pioneered by

Norm Hazzard, the leader of the group that consisted of the negotiators and the tactical teams. Statistically back then, there was very clear evidence that the longer the negotiation went on, the more chance it would end peacefully.

Today, this 'contain and negotiate' tactic is no longer automatically implemented because of the 'active shooter or active armed-offender scenario'. These are the bad guys in the USA that we read about with all-too-tragic frequency, the ones who go to a public place like a school or shopping centre with a firearm or other weapon and start randomly killing people. It happens here too: the April 2024 Bondi Junction shopping centre stabbing in Sydney was a recent example. If you were just to contain the shooter or offender, leaving them in there with innocent people, chances are they would kill everyone in there.

The 2008 attacks on the Taj Mahal Palace Hotel and other spots in Mumbai were the turning point, where the use of the 'contain and negotiate' tactic ended up causing a lot more casualties. Today, if police are faced with a political or religious extremist, or any active mobile armed offender, they must go in immediately and engage with the armed offender. This was a major shift in strategy that took a while to implement nationally.

* * *

We'd often be called out in the middle of the night to The Gap, the infamous suicide spot in the harbourside Sydney suburb of Watsons Bay.

One evening around 7 pm, we were called out to The Gap for a guy who was a gym owner. He had a big mortgage, luxury cars, kids in very expensive private schools, but his business was going down. He was too proud to tell his wife or his family that they were going to have to downsize and cut back, so he'd decided to end his life. I was the primary negotiator.

The psychiatrist in this case said to us: 'He's vain. One of the things you might try to do is talk about what will happen to his body if he jumps.' This personality insight was based on the fact that he was very fit, good-looking and an imposing character.

I was the primary negotiator so I began to talk to him about the gruesome details of such a fall, and it worked. You could see it had an impact on him immediately: he actually stepped back from the edge.

Talking someone off a ledge is often a long haul, and you're working quite hard mentally. You've got to stay awake, though, so you need breaks. You'd say, 'Look, I'm going to go and talk to the others now, and I'm going to come back in 15 or 20 minutes. I want you to think about what we've just discussed.' You'd be quite strategic when it came to that thing you'd just discussed; you wanted to leave them with something important to think about.

The other thing we did with this guy was something you wouldn't normally do: third-party intervention. The subject will often say, 'I want to talk to my wife, I want to talk to my mother.' You very rarely allow it, because you have no idea how the subject is going to react, or what history there may be. There are people who want to kill themselves in front of their wife or partner as if to say, *See what you made me do?*

In this case, though, after much questioning we got his wife involved, because we needed her to reassure him. She was absolutely shattered; she had no idea his problems had got to this point. She told him that she didn't care about the money, that they could put the kids in other schools. 'I love you!' she told him. 'Our family is what matters.' There was a lot of crying. By this point, we'd been going for something like nine hours.

One of the things we'd tell the person was that if they came down off the ledge or let the hostages go – whatever the circumstances were – we'd sit down and have a coffee and talk to them. And we always did. As I said: You always do what you've promised, otherwise it destroys your credibility.

I said that to him, and it helped. He came off the ledge, and we had a coffee and a very emotional talk. I assured him that I meant what I said, that things would not seem as bleak when he woke up the next day, and that he had a wife and kids who loved him and needed him. Things would work out.

On this day, I walked away thinking, *We've saved a life and a family here.*

If you got the desired outcome, there was always a great sense of relief and a real feeling of satisfaction. You don't get that instant feedback every day in the police, but in negotiations you do. You either fail or succeed.

* * *

The husband of a family member of mine suicided some time ago. It came completely out of the blue. Like the gym owner, he was an incredibly proud man who'd had a business go bad. He did it one night at home in the garage. His wife and three kids woke up in the morning to find him in the car. I saw the traumatic effect that had on everyone for many, many years after that.

I had been a negotiator for quite a while at that point. I was acutely aware that if we'd saved someone's life, we'd probably also saved a whole generation of people from suffering. Now I could see for myself how true that was. Later in my career I would learn that every suicide cascades down and on average has a serious impact on 132 people.

* * *

I would stay with the Negotiations Unit for years, but that wasn't my full-time role. Towards the end of 1993, after almost three years in the Armed Hold Up Squad, I knew it was time to move on. I'd enjoyed myself, but I wanted more.

I've stayed in each of my policing roles for three or four years on average. Anything longer than five years and you start getting a bit stale – and those you work with start getting sick of your stories.

When a vacancy came up in the Homicide Squad within the North West Crime Squad, I decided to apply. I was successful and a whole new chapter began in my career. Along with my time in Hold-Ups, those years in Homicide would be among the happiest I would have in the police.

CHAPTER 10

No Crime More Serious

1993–2004

Doesn't matter if you're from the penthouse or the outhouse, murder doesn't play favourites.

Homicide affects all sections of the community. The motivations can vary greatly: jealousy, revenge, organised-crime figures knocking out the opposition or someone they've had a dispute with. It doesn't matter whether you're super-wealthy or dirt-poor, there is sometimes a temptation to do the unspeakable, whether you do it yourself or get someone else to do it for you.

Not only does murder affect all levels of society, it can also happen anywhere, at any time – even in circumstances that seem completely safe.

On 20 November 1993, there was a dance party for under-18s at Castle Hill in northwest Sydney. Nothing unusual about that. Three or four hundred kids packed into The Hills Centre. Those sorts of dances went on every weekend, often organised by community and youth groups. They were events that parents felt comfortable sending their kids to. Because the kids were underage, there was no alcohol being served.

That Saturday night, two youths appeared to have some sort of disagreement. They walked away from each other, then one of them spun around, pulled out a knife and came fast and hard at the other, 17-year-old Geoffrey Berrett. Geoffrey was stabbed in his heart and died almost immediately.

That Saturday night, I was at Allison's sister's engagement party, and I was on call. I dropped everything and headed straight over. It was one of the first murders I was involved with after transferring to the Homicide Squad.

It was a difficult investigation given the circumstances. Just trying to work out what had occurred was a challenge. There was a lot of talk among the youngsters. Amid the flashing disco lights and crowded dance floor, everybody had seen fragments of what took place, but no one had the complete picture. A friend of the murderer said something to someone, who said something to someone else, then that person was brought forward to the police. We were left to trace the chain of people back two, three, four steps to get to the murderer.

The youth who stabbed Geoffrey came from a knockabout family; his brother was doing a life sentence in jail, also for stabbing someone to death. Perhaps this youngster carried a knife because he'd been looking for an opportunity to emulate his brother. But we'll never really know.

Interviewing him was quite an involved process. Because he was a juvenile, his parents had to be present. They were separated, and both of them had new partners, so all four of them attended the interview, along with the young man's independent support person – required by law to be there due to the suspect's age – plus his lawyer, another detective and me.

At the beginning of any interview, you have to say who's in the room. I remember we asked the young man on tape: 'Do you agree that apart from myself, Detective So-and-So, yourself, your legal representative, your support person, your mother and her partner, and your father and his partner, there's nobody else in the room?' It must have sounded slightly farcical on the recording.

The trial was held at the Supreme Court in the inner Sydney suburb of Darlinghurst. The accused pleaded not guilty. His barrister was Stephen Norrish QC, who later became a District Court judge. He was a really decent guy who did his job to the best of his ability.

I was outside the court during a lunch break talking to Geoffrey Berrett's mother and father. They were gentle, suburban people, whose son went to a dance party and never came home. The mother was understandably very upset over things that had been said in court, and her husband and I were trying to console her.

Norrish walked past, and she gave him an absolute spray. It was very surprising to see this normally gentle person let fly in this way. Norrish took her recriminations as courteously as he could; he didn't ignore her or disrespect her in any way. I think he understood this distraught mother's need to vent.

It was one of those indelible moments that ambush you and cut right through the professional persona to the awfulness of a crime like this.

The assailant was found guilty and was jailed for a minimum of nine years. Two families were left distraught and severely traumatised.

* * *

I was pretty sure that going to Homicide would be a good step for my career.

The North West Crime Squad was competitive. It included units for sex crimes, child abuse, motor crime (people who deal in vehicle rebirthing), fraud and arson, serious break-and enter offences as well as armed hold-ups. Homicide, rightly or wrongly, saw themselves as the apex. No crime is more serious than the killing of a human being.

There were lots of new skills to get to grips with – forensics, post-mortems, dealing with the Coroner and the victims' groups. And importantly, every case you handle in Homicide is subject to a judicial review. When you investigate drug deals or armed robberies, if you don't resolve them, the cases get boxed up and archived. In Homicide, whether you fail or succeed in solving the crime, whether someone gets arrested or not, there will be a judicial review. You're either going to the Coroner's Court to explain why you weren't able to solve it for the family's benefit, or if you arrest someone, you're going straight to court for a trial.

Anything that carries a life sentence – usually 25 years in NSW, unless a judge determines an offender is never to be released – goes straight to the Supreme Court. So, when you go to trial, you're up against some of the top barristers in the country, because everyone at the Bar wants to represent someone in the Supreme Court.

Homicide work is *satisfying*, but it's also hard work. And most of us had at least five or six cases on the go at the same time; some would carry too many.

Solving homicides requires use of *both* sides of the brain. The factual, logical, scientific side needs to be married with the other hemisphere, which is about intuition, the hunch, the imaginative leap. When the two come together, it provides the vital 'Aha!' moment.

In my view, there are typically two types of detectives. There are those who are very good at the *reactive* stuff. They're the units that can't do much until the call comes in. These offences can be a murder, an armed robbery or a rape. Then they're off to the crime scene, gathering the forensic evidence, witness statements and other tangible evidence; they're reacting to what has already happened. It's very structured and you've already got something to work with.

Then there are those that are good at the *proactive* side of things. They don't have a crime scene. By and large, they've got to make their own luck, such as investigations into drugs and gangs. They have to use initiative, they have to be innovative, they have to think about all the possibilities.

I would contend that a perfect detective is someone who relishes and excels at *both* facets of the work – the reactive and the proactive. They're also able to make a conscious switch from one side of the brain to the other when needed.

If you don't possess the intuition, the proactive side, it's difficult to foster. Most of the detectives I've worked with have that intuition, and some of them have it in spades. You don't need to give them a kick up the arse; they just go. Dare I say, they were born with it.

On arrival at Homicide, I was blessed because there were some seasoned detectives already there who had that kind of intuition. They didn't mentor me, but we were there working with each other all day, every day, and we discussed everything. I soaked up their experience.

In my view, you can only get to the higher reaches by stepping on the shoulders of giants, and I think I've done that in many ways.

It was already paying off. Not long after joining Homicide, I got promoted to Detective Sergeant. Climbing through the ranks would bring more decision-making responsibility, and the weight of accountability that came with it.

* * *

Less than a year later, I was working on what was to become one of the most scrutinised and tortuous investigations in NSW policing history.

No one imagined it at the time, but the assassination of John Newman MP would lead to a coronial inquest, a committal hearing, three Supreme Court trials, and a special judicial inquiry with Royal Commission powers – mainly attacking me and my team – over 15 years.

I became involved the day after the murder hit the headlines across the world, from the front pages of Sydney's morning papers to *Time* magazine.

On 5 September 1994, Newman, the State Member for Cabramatta in Sydney's southwest, had just returned from a Labor Party meeting, and was in the driveway putting a cover on his car. His fiancée, Lucy Wang, had come out of the house to help him. She witnessed a car pull up, then a man armed with a pistol got out and walked towards the MP, shooting him several times. The man then got back into the car before it sped away.

It was billed as Australia's first political assassination. The murder provoked a flood of outrage, and the public and political pressure on police to solve the crime started that first day.

Task Force Gap – a name randomly selected from a pre-prepared list – would initially draw in more than 50 officers from a string of squads, including Asian Crime and Special Branch (responsible for intelligence and national security) to help Homicide in our investigation.

I was appointed to be what police call the 'reader', and it was such a large investigation that I shared the role with my Homicide partner, Greig Newbery. He would remain my partner for about five years, and he was one of the most placid but competent individuals I've ever met. I don't have a huge temper, but I could go off sometimes if things were going wrong or someone repeatedly did the wrong thing and didn't listen. Greig never lost his temper, no matter what. So we complemented each other.

The 'reader' is a crucial role that is used mainly for homicide cases and drives the direction of the investigation. The reader must be across every single piece of information about the case, sifting through everything that comes in and allocating the next lot of inquiries, then getting the results back and doing it again. It's the reader's job to pinpoint information gaps, leads that may not have been followed up, and witnesses who need to be interviewed or re-interviewed.

For the reader and everyone else on the team, one of the key things to consider is victimology – the study of your victim. You try to learn everything about them and the things they were involved in, as well as the people around them – who loved them, who liked them, who hated them. It's about being thorough and methodical, because you cannot afford to charge someone only to then have information come to light that could have provided alternative theories.

You cannot overlook any angle. You discount all the theories that don't stack up, then whatever you're left with, you focus on – and that will hopefully be the right one.

After building up a complete picture of the victim's character and activities, often you will know more about that person than even their closest friends and relatives. You become very involved on a personal level.

The murderer is likely to be someone who has a connection with the victim. A 'stranger murder' is very rare.

If your victim was unpopular, it makes your task harder. People are less likely to want to help you. What do *they* care if you solve the murder or not? So you have to factor that into your inquiries. *Is the person I am interviewing friend or foe?*

Newman had plenty of both.

He was an Austrian immigrant who had been politically active since the 1970s. He had been a deputy mayor of the local Fairfield Council, and by the time he was gunned down in his driveway he had been the Member for Cabramatta for eight years. Newman's life had already been dogged by tragedy: in December 1979, his pregnant wife, Mary, and five-year-old son, David, had been killed in a car accident.

In the 1990s, the notoriety of the suburb of Cabramatta – dubbed 'Little Saigon' – as a centre of Asian drug crime was such that the train that travelled there from the CBD was known as the 'Smack Express'. Around the time of his death, Newman had taken on 5T, a Vietnamese gang involved in drug dealing, serious extortion, home invasions and murder. He made many enemies in his crusade to purge the streets of criminals. The MP didn't hold back with his words: 'The Asian gangs involved don't fear our laws, but there's one thing they do fear – that's possible deportation back to the jungles of Vietnam, because that's where, frankly, they belong.'

Newman was threatening to get the laws changed so convicted gang members could be deported 'back to the jungles' – even if they were Australian citizens. You can imagine how that went down with the Vietnamese community, who made up over 35 per cent of Cabramatta's population.

Even when he wasn't dealing with criminals, Newman could be an abrasive personality. If he didn't like you, you knew it.

There had been a series of criminal incidents in the months before he was killed, including the paint-bombing of his car, death threats and a break-in at his office. CCTV cameras had been installed at his home on the advice of police. However, more recently things had gone quiet, and just days before the attack, the cameras were removed at Newman's request: a move that sparked conspiracy theories after his death.

Homicide investigators have to eliminate all possible lines of inquiry, so there is nothing left unresolved by the time you go to trial, nothing the defence can use to convince the jury that police have pinned the murder on the wrong person.

In Newman's case, ruling out possible suspects was a monumental task. Newman had had conflicts with dozens of people, from members of his karate club to former employees. Not only had he been threatened, but he had also made threats himself.

His relationship with the family of his late wife Mary was fractious. Not long before his assassination, Newman had had a rough exchange with Mary's brother, who had left voice messages calling Newman a prick and saying he was going to get him. But it turned out the brother had been living in Brisbane at the time of the murder and was essentially homeless. When the former brother-in-law heard on the news that Newman had been killed, he immediately went to the nearest automatic teller machine with a camera attached and carried out transactions, to prove he was 1000 kilometres away in Brisbane.

Newman had a black belt in karate and had been president of the Martial Arts Industry Association for a short time; there had been conflict between him and a couple of members. A number of secretaries in his office had left after a short time because he was too tough a boss. He'd argued with the husband of one, who had complained about the way his wife had been treated. Leaving no stone unturned, we investigated all of these leads and eventually eliminated all of these people as suspects.

Even his fiancée, Lucy, had the finger very unfairly pointed at her. Maybe racism was involved – she was a Chinese national – or maybe people thought, wrongly, that she was going to inherit a lot of money as a result of her fiancé's death. Nevertheless, we were required to rule her out as a suspect, and we did.

All in all, there were 97 lines of inquiry. But one suspect soon stood head and shoulders above the rest: Phuong Canh Ngo. A single, 36-year-old Vietnamese refugee with no visible means of support, he was alleged to have been involved with the 5T gang.

Like Newman, Ngo had served on Fairfield City Council and been deputy mayor for a while. He also had political ambitions and had run unsuccessfully against Newman as an independent candidate in 1991. They had clashed frequently in public. Ngo had even joined the ALP and set up a new branch in direct competition with Newman's.

Newman had told Ngo he would never get anywhere in politics as long as he – Newman – was around. They were dark and prophetic words. And indeed, Ngo was forced to give an undertaking to the Labor Party that he would not run against Newman, so long as he was the sitting member of Parliament for that seat.

The year before he was murdered, Newman had pushed for an inquiry into Ngo and his activities with the 5T gang and the Mekong Club, a huge licensed community premises that Ngo, the club's 'honorary president', treated like his own private castle. During the day, Ngo carried out his civic duties, but at night he would be at his Mekong Club headquarters, where he regularly met with members of the 5T Gang. When the inquiry found irregularities in the running of the club, following action against him and the club by licensing authorities, Ngo was banned by the licensing court from holding any position in any club for ten years.

As an example of his activity, Phuong Ngo had had his picture taken with the local police commander in Cabramatta, then had the photo put on the business cards he doled out to members of the Vietnamese community. He was apparently implying that he owned the police, and that anyone who wanted anything from the cops had to come to him first – for a price.

His influence was essentially a mirage – but it soon became obvious that it was causing problems for our investigators. Many people didn't want to talk to us, and even Newman's family were unsettled by the rumours of Ngo's close links to the police.

In fact, the family were initially antagonistic, believing we weren't doing enough to solve his murder. What they didn't know, and we couldn't tell them, was that a covert operation was underway.

The Newman case was the first murder investigation referred to the NSW Crime Commission, often described as the state's most secretive body. More powerful than any other law enforcement body in NSW, it could compel the production of information and documents, issue search warrants and conduct secret coercive interviews.

I had previously worked in the State Drug Crime Commission, that had evolved into the Crime Commission. It was our idea to harness these powers to force uncooperative witnesses and informants to talk. It was innovative. And it worked.

It took months to carry out all the cross-examinations. Some of those compelled to appear and give evidence finally confessed to knowing details about the murder plot but not being involved in the actual murder.

We discovered that three different groups had been approached to carry out the hit on Newman, and before the night of his murder there had been three botched attempts.

One young man, whom I can't name for legal reasons, had information about the lead-up to the murder, and led us in turn to another man who, after a series of covert police operations, revealed he had been approached to commit the murder but had refused.

He knew who had carried out the murder. At last, we had names – including the name of the man who had ordered the execution: Phuong Ngo.

The man claimed that Ngo, after three attempts to recruit a hit man, had decided to organise the murder himself, with the help of three accomplices: David Duy Dinh, Tu Quang Dao and a third man who would soon turn Crown witness.

The Crown's case was that, at Ngo's instigation, an XD Ford Falcon driven by Tu Quang Dao, containing David Duy Dinh and another man (who'd been lured to the car by subterfuge) travelled to John Newman's house at about 9.30 pm, followed by Phuong Ngo in his Toyota Camry. When Newman returned from the ALP meeting, the Crown alleged that Dinh, armed with a pistol and wearing a green army-style jacket and gloves, left the Falcon, shot Newman and returned to the car, which sped away with the Camry close behind.

Within a minute or two, the Falcon stopped at a nearby service station. Dinh allegedly walked to where Phuong Ngo had parked his car close by and gave him a bag containing the gun used in the shooting.

We thought we had enough to charge the suspects, but in the eyes of the Director of Public Prosecutions (DPP), we didn't.

As I mentioned earlier, in any murder case the matter must be reported to the Coroner if no one is charged. In the Newman case, the Coroner eventually decided to hold an inquest – and it would become a turning point in the investigation.

But meanwhile, an opportunity had come up to work on the two side jobs I'd been doing for several years now, and this work would bring benefits to police all over Australia.

CHAPTER 11

Lifting the Lid on Undercover Work

1996–1998

In 1996, I was the recipient of the prestigious Michael O'Brien Memorial Scholarship. It was set up to encourage people within the NSW Police to travel overseas to study different police procedures, in order to implement that knowledge back here. It was named in honour of a great police officer and detective who had passed away from cancer way too early in life.

We'd primarily been using undercover operatives to investigate drug crimes, but I wanted to study a program in Canada where, uniquely, they used undercover operatives in a broader range of investigations. So, following arrangements with the famous Royal Canadian Mounted Police (RCMP), I went over to Vancouver to examine all aspects of their undercover work. I was hosted by three legendary RCMP officers in this space: Pete Marsh, Al Haslet and Rob Blundell. I have remained good friends with them all in our post-police lives, although Pete has sadly passed away.

In Canada, I saw the enormous benefits that could be gained by broadening the horizons of covert operations. I also gathered a lot of information about other aspects of undercover work, from selection and training to deployment practices and, most importantly, welfare and reassimilation back into the mainstream. These were areas in which Australia was somewhat behind. I knew from my own past experience that we had to do much more than what we were doing for welfare and support.

But something else struck a chord with me too. It was the way undercover operatives were treated by their organisations. I had never forgotten my own experiences undercover, when my fellow detectives thought I was on holidays when I was in fact in high-risk situations – not to mention being threatened by a drug dealer and having to deal with it more or less on my own.

Something else I saw was that when an operative in Canada did an undercover job, then ultimately had to go to court and give evidence, they did so in full uniform under their real name. It was about making sure that not just the crooks, but also the cops, saw the operatives for who they really were. For the crook, it becomes a more daunting proposition seeing a police officer in the Mounties' iconic red tunic up on the stand. It crystallises things very quickly for the accused, spelling out that you can't do anything to this guy, he's a cop. We don't do this in NSW.

* * *

On the way home from Canada, arrangements were made for me to attend the two-week, live-in hostage negotiators' course at the FBI Academy in Quantico, Virginia. I wasn't the first person from NSW to go over to do the course, but I was certainly grateful for the opportunity. It probably wouldn't have happened had I not won the Michael O'Brien Memorial Scholarship. The chair of the selection committee said, 'Well, you're going to be in North America anyway, you might as well go and see the FBI.'

The FBI Academy is an interesting place, steeped in history and often portrayed in movies and TV shows. The FBI are renowned as crime fighters, and the course lived up to expectations. We do many things very well here in Australia; in fact, we do some things better than they do. But one thing the FBI are very good at is working on a large scale; they might have something like 500 investigators on a specific case. Whenever something happens, they can get to where they need to and get the job done really quickly, absolutely saturating the situation with resources.

The networking and exchange of ideas were what made the experience valuable. I relished the chance to swap information with the FBI and many other agencies from around the world who were on the course with me, and learn from them. All had interesting perspectives.

Whenever I travelled as a police officer, my aim was to build bridges for ongoing contact, facilitating the exchange of people and ideas. I had to deliver my own presentations and case studies as well; basically, you have to sing for your supper. So I think the Mounties and the FBI got a bit out of me too, but I established long-term contacts that were then available for my colleagues in Sydney. I was later to attend other more senior courses at the FBI and the contact continued.

There is a definite bond between police all over the world, and I've always enjoyed being a part of that – benefiting from it but also giving something back. We share information freely and we don't normally hold back about our successes and our failures. The Mounties say that it's good to learn from mistakes – preferably other people's.

There are a lot of incredible investigators in Quantico, as there are in Vancouver, as there are in Sydney. None of us are perfect, or that far above the rest. I remember the first time I went to Scotland Yard – watching the Brits work brought home to me the fact that they were not necessarily any better than us Aussies. In some ways, they think about things in a more structured way, but we're just as capable, we have just as many clever people per capita, and we can do our jobs just as well.

* * *

Coming back from Canada and the USA, I rewrote the NSW Police undercover training program, with the aim of making it world-class. I also wrote a lengthy paper that made ten major recommendations about undercover work, all of which have now been accepted nationally.

Back when I was with the State Drug Crime Commission, I had made a promise to myself that if I ever had the opportunity to improve and, frankly, fix the experience of undercover operatives when they complete their tour of duty and are reassimilating back into mainstream policing, then I would do that to the best of my ability.

One program we ended up implementing came from the Michigan State Police. When a police officer who had been undercover for a while went back to their normal post, they were fêted with a 'coming-out day'. These days, in the NSW

Police, if an officer takes on undercover work for three years – and we really try to avoid extending it any longer than that – we have our own coming-out day. We usually invite the NSW Police Commissioner, as well as the person's family and the people who will be their new bosses.

Over a couple of hours, there is a presentation on their career in covert operations. By the time it's finished, no one is in any doubt as to how much this operative has done but has never been able to talk about. It's incredibly important for their family to see – not to mention essential for their new bosses to know. You're giving the operative much-needed recognition, and making sure that wherever they land after that, they're going to have some acknowledgement of how much they've achieved.

* * *

I was expected to 'pay the trip off', as they put it, which meant working with the Undercover Branch. I was temporarily promoted to Detective Inspector so I could serve as Operations Controller, effectively running the branch and its operations. The idea was to implement the findings from my trip.

I'd recommended that undercover operatives be used more broadly than just in drug investigations – and I was happy to walk the walk myself.

* * *

'I don't give a shit whether you fucking kill him or what you fuckin' do. You can maim him completely so it ruins his life. I don't care.'

The wire I was wearing had captured everything said by Robert Ernest Neville, who thought he was hiring me as a hitman. He wanted me to kill a young male love-interest who had spurned his advances and taken out a restraining order against him, followed by defamation proceedings. Neville's main motive for wanting to kill the younger man was financial: he feared losing a lot of money from the defamation case.

In February 1998, I'd received a call from Scott James, an old workmate from the Hold-Ups. He knew I was working in the Undercover Branch and he said to me: 'We have a bloke up here in Coffs Harbour who is asking around for someone to kill a young bloke. Can you look at sending someone up to accept the contract – or can *you* do it for us?'

It sounded like an interesting job, so I decided to do it myself. I was confident I could pull it off. Having an ethnic background helped; looking at the background of the suspect, I thought it might be more credible if the assassin he was going to hire was not an Anglo-Saxon.

I drove to Coffs Harbour by myself, listening to KC and the Sunshine Band during the five-hour drive. I had a support officer who drove up separately and we arranged to meet up in Coffs.

Dressed casually in jeans and a shirt, I knew I had to look and act like someone from the criminal milieu of Sydney who was capable of carrying out a murder. I already had a script in my head of how I would play things: there would be no joking or smiling but a fair bit of swearing.

I met Neville as arranged, and he gave me full details of the intended victim and $500 as a down payment, with the rest of the $5000 to be paid after I finished the job.

He suggested one way to get rid of the young man would be to run him off Eastern Dorrigo Way, inland from Coffs. The young man travelled to and from work along this road on his motorbike, and parts of it were mountainous and extremely dangerous. Neville thought this would be cleaner than shooting, and it would look like an accident.

But in the end it would be up to me. 'I don't really care,' he told me. 'That isn't my fuckin' worry any more. I'm going to get him. If you don't get him I'll fuckin' get him myself one night. I've got a small memory.'

We shook hands on the deal and I told him I would be in touch once the deed was done. Then I walked away with the $500 in my pocket and the whole conversation on tape.

Neville was arrested shortly afterwards.

At first he indicated he was going to plead not guilty, claiming he had been entrapped, which was ludicrous. *He* had made the approach and he had been very clear about his intentions.

Eventually he pleaded guilty to the charge of soliciting a person to inflict grievous bodily harm on another person. He was sentenced to seven years and two months in jail. He unsuccessfully appealed the severity of the sentence.

For me this was a rare undercover job that *didn't* involve posing as a high-level drug dealer. But it highlighted what the Mounties had long known: that undercover work could be used in many fields.

* * *

I could have stayed with covert operations, but my heart belonged in the mainstream. I wanted to go back to Homicide.

By that stage, they'd created one centralised unit, the Homicide and Serial Violent Crime Agency, covering serial violent crime and homicide in the whole state, under Detective Superintendent Ron Smith, a legendary Homicide detective. Serial violent crime referred mainly to sexual abuse, a function that later, rightly, was allocated to a specific squad. When that split happened, around 2003, the Homicide Squad relinquished the role of investigating sexual abuse cases.

I'd never worked with Ron before, but they advertised for his second-in-charge, with the title of Chief of Staff. I applied for it and was successful. So in early 1998 I moved back into Homicide, and around the same time was formally promoted to Detective Inspector.

My timing was good, as investigations into the John Newman murder had reached a critical point. On my return to Homicide, I was formally appointed head of Task Force Gap.

CHAPTER 12

A Battle of Wills

1998–2000

The coronial inquest into the death of John Newman started on 2 February 1998 and continued for a number of weeks. Task Force Gap had some compelling findings to present.

We revealed how our team had pioneered a reasonably new investigation technique: using mobile phone towers to track and pinpoint the movements of the people we suspected of being involved in the murder. At the time there were no smartphones, or location apps. I believe we were the first ones in NSW, and probably Australia, to use phone records as a primary source of evidence about the locations of suspects.

We proved that there had been a flurry of activity on the mobile phones of the suspects in the vicinity of the shooting – before and after it took place. We didn't have the content of their conversations, but we were able to show that they had been in the crime scene area at the same time as the murder. We'd also established where and when Ngo had made mobile phone calls as he drove around that night.

This was largely possibly thanks to an expert from Telstra. Ngo's supporters and legal team would later try to blow this evidence out of the water, saying this method was relatively new, that it was unreliable, that Ngo hadn't really been there. The Telstra expert was able to refute all these claims and show the technology was sound.

After hearing all the evidence, the Deputy State Coroner found that a person of interest had been identified as a suspect (Phuong Canh Ngo) and referred the case to the DPP to be considered for prosecution. She also wrote a letter to the Police Commissioner, commending our work on the investigation.

However, the Office of the DPP said: 'No, we don't think you've got enough for charges yet.' So we focused and sharpened our view.

Our team met with the Counsel Assisting the Coroner, Paul Roberts SC, who had some good ideas.

Four cartridge cases and two spent .32 calibre bullets had been found at the scene of the murder. From them, Forensic Ballistics had been able to tell us that we were looking for a 1935 Beretta pistol. In the hours and days following the murder, we had scoured the crime scene and the location immediately around it. We had searched creeks and drains in the area but found nothing.

One significant suggestion Roberts made was to look at Ngo's phone records and see if they could provide clues about where Ngo went immediately after the murder and therefore where the gun had been dumped.

The records revealed that Ngo had travelled to the vicinity of Voyager Point, a 20-minute drive from Cabramatta, where there is a footbridge over the Georges River. He had stopped there to make calls and could easily have dropped the murder weapon into the river. So Roberts suggested we try to dredge the river on either side of the bridge.

I asked myself: *Why didn't we think of that earlier?*

When police divers were told of the plan they were sceptical. But we insisted, and on the second day of the search they found the gun: a 1935 .32-calibre Beretta, just as Forensics had predicted.

I remember the moment Detective Sergeant Ian McNab, who was guiding the search, rang to tell me about the discovery.

He said: 'You're not going to believe this, but I think we've found it.'

I was elated and hugely relieved. Not only had we found the murder weapon, but we had also definitively placed Ngo at the location where it was discovered.

But our work wasn't over. We had to get a ballistic match between the cartridges and the gun.

NSW Police Ballistics could not conclusively say that this was the murder weapon, because after nearly four years on the riverbed it was heavily corroded. A retired firearms dealer told us it was a mass-produced weapon issued to Italian army officers in World War II, while a ballistics expert from the Tasmanian Police Force concluded that it was 'more than likely the murder weapon'.

Not enough. We needed a more definitive answer.

We discovered that the Federal Police in Germany are considered the world experts in ballistics. Officer Leopold Pfoser, a specialist in Beretta guns produced between 1900 and 1940, was assigned to the job.

My workmate Greig Newbery was tasked with taking the gun to Germany to get it tested using the equipment and expertise Australia just didn't have at the time. The chain of possession of the weapon as an exhibit was crucial, so Greig had to be in possession of it at all times and be able to prove where it was at any given moment. The tests conclusively proved that the bullets at the crime scene had come from that gun.

Then something else happened in our favour – although this came not in the form of technology but in the form of a person: Mark Tedeschi QC, the Crown Prosecutor.

There is no doubt in my mind he is one of the best prosecutors in Australia. He has successfully prosecuted many high-profile criminals, including backpacker murderer Ivan Milat and the killers of Sydney heart surgeon Victor Chang. Tedeschi had been nicknamed 'the patron saint of lost causes' by detectives, because of his willingness to take on the cases other prosecutors may put in the too-hard basket.

Mark Tedeschi was in it with us for the long haul. While the DPP was telling us we didn't have enough, he was the first legal mind to say, 'I think we can run with this.'

We met with him many times before he prepared a brief, which went to the Director of Public Prosecutions (DPP), Nicholas Cowdery, for a decision on whether charges could be laid. I think everyone involved – NSW Police and the DPP – recognised we were only going to get one shot at this amid the intense glare of media and public attention.

Finally we were told a decision was imminent, and the team gathered at Parramatta Police Station to hear the news. When the call came through, it was from the DPP himself.

I picked up the phone and Cowdery said: 'Nick, we feel we now have enough evidence to charge Phuong Ngo and the other three with the murder of John Newman.' He told me he would shortly send through a fax to confirm his formal advice.

We were very happy, but we knew it was only the beginning.

* * *

On 13 March 1998, nearly four years after the killing, Phuong Ngo, Tu Quang Dao, David Duy Dinh and a fourth man who could not be named were charged with the murder of John Newman.

The arrests were 'by appointment', as it is known. At our request, the four men and their lawyers attended Parramatta Police Station, where they declined to be interviewed and were charged and refused bail.

After the inquest, Ngo must have known this was coming. He said nothing, but I could tell he was angry.

The task force went out for beers afterwards, but this was not the time for extended celebrations. The Mount Everest of a Supreme Court trial lay before us. We knew this was going to be a battle of wills.

* * *

Once the murder charges were laid there was a shift in community attitudes. Witnesses began to come forward, realising that Ngo's claimed closeness to the police was false.

On the other hand, over the coming years many vexatious complaints against us, and against me personally, would be lodged by those supporting Ngo, particularly during the trial period. None of them would result in any adverse findings, but they were certainly distracting.

The moment Ngo was arrested, he launched the first of many applications for bail. We successfully fought every one. It was crucial to keep him behind bars to show how solid the police case was, and potentially to stop him from interfering with witnesses, tampering with evidence or fleeing the country.

At one point much later, I had a dark encounter with him.

He had been brought from Long Bay Jail to Parramatta Police Station to be interviewed about an alleged extortion and assault charge that had nothing to do with the Newman murder. (He was later charged with these offences but found not guilty at trial.)

Following the interview, my partner went outside to get an independent officer to speak with Ngo, as was required. I was left alone with him briefly. He said a number of things that made it very clear to me that he had been following my career, that he had been watching me and that he knew everything I was doing, at least professionally. I sensed it was an attempt to intimidate me. It took an incredible amount of self-restraint not to lean across the table and grab him by the neck.

* * *

The first murder trial of the four accused was set for 19 July 1999. Ngo had engaged Corrs Chambers Westgarth, one of Australia's most expensive and renowned law firms, and Bret Walker SC, one of the country's best barristers. The instructing solicitor for the defence team was Michael Lee, who later went on to be an eminent Federal Court Judge. Ngo certainly had a crack team.

To this day we have no idea how he was funding his stellar defence team. We had forensic accountants go through his finances and could not find out how he was supporting himself. We suspected he was living off money out of the till of the Mekong Club (and we had some evidence of that from staff) and possibly benefiting financially from the 5T gang operations.

As the trial before Justice James Wood got underway, Crown Prosecutor Tedeschi had the job of deciding which witnesses would appear and what evidence would be tendered. Some of the witnesses did not want to appear in court in person. They were worried about what was going to happen to them: some had received death threats.

After a behind-closed-doors legal argument, we won the right for some witnesses to give evidence by video link. So as not to prejudice the trial, the jury was told the witnesses were not available on the day to give evidence in the courtroom and that was why they were giving evidence remotely. They were actually in the same building, just in another room.

But there was a slip-up when Tedeschi wanted to show one of the witnesses a document. The document was given to the sheriff's officer in the courtroom and just a few minutes later it was seen onscreen by the jurors.

Bret Walker argued that because the document had appeared on the screen so quickly, the jurors could deduce that the witness was in the same building. They might then work out that the witness didn't want to appear in front of Ngo, and that would be prejudicial.

So on 3 August, just two weeks in, Justice Wood ruled that the trial be aborted. And we had to start again.

We were angry, disappointed, deflated. We would have to go up Mount Everest again.

* * *

At the end of the first trial, I approached the team representing one of Ngo's co-accused and pointed out that there was an awful lot of evidence against their client, but that he was probably the least culpable of all of them. He might have been in the car, he might have known about the murder and not told anyone, but he wasn't the author of the crime. He had nothing to gain from the murder of John Newman. I suggested they advise him to reconsider his position.

They did. In the period between the first and second trials, the suspect went to the Crime Commission and gave an 'induced statement', which meant that it could never be used against him. Ultimately, he gave evidence against everybody else and didn't stand trial again because of this. His identity is protected for obvious reasons.

* * *

The second trial began in February 2000 and took three months. The charges against the fourth man had been dropped after the first trial, so there were only three defendants: Phuong Ngo, Tu Quang Dao and David Duy Dinh.

This time the jury couldn't agree on a verdict. They deliberated for seven days and still couldn't reach a unanimous decision.

At the time, all 12 jurors in murder cases needed to agree. Later, in 2005, the law was changed so a majority verdict could be accepted. But the change hadn't come soon enough for us. So the jury was dismissed.

We were to learn later that 11 jurors had been in favour of conviction, with just one against.

I remember Task Force Gap were all sitting together in the police and media box in the old Darlinghurst Supreme Court. I was close enough to see what I thought were tears in the eyes of the trial judge Justice Wood. It was a very emotional and tough time for all concerned, and the result from the jury did not come back until very late in the night after a tension-filled few days.

* * *

It wasn't long after the second trial when something unusual happened.

The phone rang one day and I answered.

A male voice asked: 'Are you Nick Kaldas?'

'Yes,' I said.

There was a moment of silence. Then the voice said, 'I was the foreman of the jury at the John Newman murder trial and I need to talk to you.'

I stopped him in his tracks before he could say more. 'I can't discuss anything with you right now,' I said, 'but ring me back in an hour once I've got some legal advice.'

I didn't ask for his name or number.

Our police internal legal advisers said that if he rang back I could take the call, but under no circumstances could I say anything to him. If *he* chose to talk to *me*, well and good. There was no legal problem with listening.

I wasn't sure if he would ring back, but he did. He told me 'they' – the jury – wanted to meet with me.

Greig Newbery and I met them at a bowling club in Sydney's west. Most of the jurors came and others who couldn't sent their apologies.

From day one of the trial, they told us, there was one juror who had said: 'I am never going to convict this guy. The cops framed him and I'm not interested.' He would not deliberate with all the others.

We later discovered that in the middle of the trial, that juror had commented online that Phuong Ngo was innocent. The other jurors said they had tried unsuccessfully to raise concerns about this juror.

Most of the jurors we met that day broke down and cried, saying: 'We can't believe this is the way the system works! This is incredibly unfair. These people have done it and they should be convicted.'

Greig and I simply listened to what they had to say but said nothing. But by the time we walked away I think they knew we shared their grief, we sympathised and we knew where they were coming from. I hope it gave them some closure.

Of course, it was frustrating to find this out *after* the event.

We carried out an investigation into the online posting and gave our findings to the Attorney General and the DPP, because they are the only ones who can lay charges over a jury matter. But nothing ever came of it. The record of the second trial simply said: 'Jury discharged after failing to reach a verdict. New trial ordered.'

I've had doubts for some time about our jury system's capacity to deal with criminal trials. There are three reasons for this.

First, a complex trial can run for up to 12 months and most people can't afford not to go to work for all that time. I think it rules out a class of society you want to be represented on a jury.

Second, some criminal trials involve cyber technology, complex activities, convoluted timelines and a lot of specialist jargon. It's difficult for the average person with no prior involvement in the criminal system to absorb all that information and make the right call.

Third, a lot depends on how eloquent and charismatic your lawyer is. Juries react to that.

For all those reasons, I am attracted to the European inquisitorial system, as opposed to our British-style adversarial system. In places like France, Spain, Italy and Germany it's not about adversaries arguing against each other, it's about finding out what happened *collectively*. The bench is made up of a number of judges, who all ask questions with the aim of getting to the truth. Most UN and international criminal tribunals as well as most European courts are also inquisitorial, or have a hybrid system. It works very well.

In NSW, judge-alone trials have been permitted since 1990, with the consent of the prosecution and the offender. In judge-alone trials you don't have to instruct the judge not to google the victim or the offender, or worry they'll be influenced by newspapers or social media, as you do with juries. Among other benefits, trials would take a fraction of the time that they take at the moment and there would be zero possibility of juries being interfered with, threatened or influenced.

That system is still not perfect, but it would be a start. Unfortunately, I see no prospect of change and doubt that the legal profession, with some notable exceptions, would ever endorse such change.

* * *

Throughout my married life, I'd worked hard in the various squads I'd been in: I'd done a lot of long shifts, travelled, was away for extended periods – and sometimes we'd played hard as well.

It had taken a toll at home. In 2000, my marriage to Allison broke down and I moved out of the family home.

* * *

In late 1999, Sydney was preparing for the Olympics. The Assistant Commissioner of NSW Police, Paul McKinnon, had been appointed as the head of the Olympic Security Command Centre, which consisted of intelligence, security apparatus and, logically, investigations. His unique leadership skills turned out to be crucial to the success of the operation. He could be abrupt and impatient, but he was ultimately brilliant and without him many doubt we would have got the job done. Accordingly, I was tasked by the Assistant Commissioner for Crime, Clive Small, to establish and lead the Olympic Investigations Strike Force. This meant establishing a crime management framework so we could respond to, and investigate, all levels of crime from petty offences to an international terrorist incident. The job involved implementing operational plans, training staff, allocating resources, researching and establishing necessary strategic alliances such as with the Australian Security Intelligence

Organisation, Australian Federal Police, Australian Defence
Force, and international partners such as FBI, Scotland Yard,
RCMP, Hong Kong Police, and major international Olympic
corporate sponsors.

The 2000 Olympics went off without a hitch, and
while there were some lessons to learn, it again highlighted
for me how important networking and collaboration were
for success. It was an interesting assignment, and halfway
through my time in that role, I was promoted to Detective
Superintendent. I knew I was only going to be away from
Homicide for a limited period, and as things turned out,
having attained the rank of Superintendent, I later returned
to Homicide as Commander.

CHAPTER 13

A Fork in the Road

2001–2004

It's not lost on me that there have been several professional forks in the road of my life when I've been given the choice between two paths.

It's always been obvious to me which of the two paths would be the easier choice. It's the path that would probably lead to promotion and praise. But then there's the other path, the trickier one, which is usually the choice I know to be the right one, and which I can never shy away from.

I'd like to think that my faith and my upbringing, my father's ethos and the way he did things, have always helped me choose. I made a decision very early on that I wasn't going to be a different person just because there might be some benefit in it for me. I hope I've stuck to that.

I don't wear my faith on my sleeve; I don't talk about it publicly, I've always stayed right away from that. Most of the people who've worked with me don't even know about my beliefs.

But my faith is important to me. It's helped me greatly along the way. Certainly, through the difficult times, it's been a strong support and sustenance in my life. My favourite psalm is Psalm 23: 'Yea, though I walk through the valley of the shadow of death, I will fear no evil ...' And there've been several challenging times in my career when I've had those words going through my head.

They were never louder than when I was caught up in a scandal orchestrated by the very police bodies that were set up to stop such things from occurring. A scandal that would force me to fight for – and eventually sacrifice – my career.

* * *

For nearly two decades too long, the NSW Police 'bugging scandal' or, as it was sometimes called, the 'bugging *saga*' – because it *was* a saga – cast a shadow over my policing career and became at times too much of a preoccupation in my life and the lives of those closest to me. The sad and sorry affair has taken up far too much of my headspace, too much of my psyche.

In 2001, a warrant – Listening Device Warrant 266 – appeared in a court matter unrelated to me. Warrant 266 gave permission for 114 people to be bugged. The list of names included serious crooks; lawyers; one journalist, Steve Barrett; and a large number of senior cops – including me.

The warrant had been requested a year earlier by the Police Integrity Commission (PIC), the NSW Crime Commission (NSWCC) and Special Crime and Internal Affairs (SCIA), in connection with an investigation codenamed 'Operation

Mascot'. Sometimes spoken of as NSW's Watergate moment, Mascot was tasked with looking for corrupt officers within the NSW Police Force.

'M5' – whose real name was, and still is, suppressed by the courts – was one of those corrupt officers. He did a deal with the PIC, the NSWCC and SCIA, and became their chief informant, wearing a wire to collect evidence against his former workmates.

The only reason Warrant 266 had come to light was because one of the conversations recorded by M5 needed to be used in a court matter relating to one of the crooks on the list. Now the rabbit was out of the hat.

The production of Warrant 266 set things off. None of the names could be redacted, so everyone who was on the list found out that they *were being* bugged, or *had been* bugged, or *might be* bugged.

Obtaining a warrant to bug anyone is far from easy. You must provide a written statement affirmed on oath – an affidavit – to say that whoever it is you're wanting to bug is suspected of having committed a very serious offence, that you've exhausted all traditional means of investigation and the only way to get the evidence you need against them is by bugging them, by invading their privacy. Bugging should always be a last resort. Finally, you need to affirm that you would only invade their privacy to the extent required to obtain the evidence. The warrant then needs to be examined by a senior judge who approves the bugging by signing the warrant. Warrants only last three weeks, after which the investigators must return to a senior judge, show some progress and gain a further three-week approval.

But in the case of Warrant 266, we couldn't get hold of the affidavits that had been given to the judges, so we couldn't prove what was in them.

Meanwhile, M5 turned up a number of times at my office, engaging me in conversation, wanting to confess all his past sins, fishing for anything, looking to entrap me. His excuses for coming to see me were ridiculous, and as a trained undercover operative, I smelled a rat; it was one of the worst amateur efforts I had ever seen. I told him I didn't want anything to do with him.

I believe there were a number of reasons I was targeted. Firstly, I had made formal complaints against a number of senior people within Internal Affairs. They basically had a conflict of interest in investigating me, yet that was ignored. Secondly, my involvement in the Police Association of NSW – the police union – as Branch official and later as a member of the executive of the union only made things worse. At various times, I'd spoken out loudly, and often, about injustice within the force. I'd had a lot to say about how there was no procedural fairness for cops who were accused of the wrong thing.

Back in the mid-1990s, the Wood Royal Commission had exposed the kind of corruption that had allowed bent cops like Roger Rogerson to flourish. But Justice Wood's findings had ushered in a new era in which oversight bodies could operate in a way that no one else could. They had extraordinary powers, along with legislated secrecy provisions that allowed wrongdoing to be covered up. And in my view there was no real oversight for decades. Successive governments were not inclined to intervene, even though the problems were very clear, and the union was ineffective in achieving any reform. With those extraordinary powers, there should have been extraordinary checks and balances. But that had not been the case.

Wearing my union representative hat, I had stood up against these bodies over the years, and some of my criticisms had hit the mark – hard. These criticisms were well justified, and should have been addressed, instead of leading to retaliation.

The three parties involved in Operation Mascot were our oversight bodies. And if there had been proper oversight of *them*, the saga that would plague my career for 20 years would never have been allowed to happen.

* * *

On 7 March 2001, six and a half years after Newman's assassination, the *third* trial of Phuong Ngo, Tu Quang Dao and David Duy Dinh began. Justice John Dunford was now presiding and the defence counsel for Ngo was John Nicholson QC.

Many of the witnesses in the Newman case had given evidence several times – at the Crime Commission, the Coroner's inquest, the committal hearing, the first trial and then the second trial. That was five times thus far that they'd had to tell their stories.

Now they were back again. They were not only weary, some were simply fed up. And when you've said the same thing so many times, it's understandable that faults creep in, faults that can be homed in on by smart defence lawyers eager to exploit any inconsistency.

My guess is that the jury made up their minds straight away about Phuong Ngo, but the other two defendants caused debate.

David Duy Dinh and Tu Quang Dao were both young men. Dinh had been out on bail and he'd had two children since the murder. His family came to court nearly every day. During breaks he would always make a point of hugging and kissing them in front of the jury. As did Dao. Phuong Ngo didn't have a family.

When the jury retired to consider their verdict, they were out for more than a week. While they were deliberating, we all went back to work.

It's a stressful time waiting for a verdict to be handed down. Juries are impossible to second-guess. When you think a jury are going right, they go left. When you think they are going straight ahead, they stand still.

I often wonder what is going through the jury's minds. Sometimes when you look at jurors they avoid your eyes. That's never a good sign. Other times, jurors shed tears. Being a juror in a murder trial is a huge responsibility, and often it weighs heavily on them.

At 4 pm on Friday, 29 June we got a message that they were coming back, so we rushed to the Supreme Court in Darlinghurst.

* * *

Right in the middle of this, my issues with M5 came to a head. As I sat there waiting, I received an abusive call from him, right out of the blue, asking me to meet him immediately.

I didn't want to talk to him by myself ever again. So I took Greig Newbery with me. He stood next to me while I spoke to M5 in a side street near the court. M5 accused me of maligning him by insinuating he was working with SCIA and the PIC.

I told him: 'I don't know where you're coming from, but I'm not talking to you any more.'

All of this, however, was but a prelude to the PIC hearings that were about to come my way.

* * *

Shortly afterwards, the message came that the jury were finally returning. We all gathered in the court room.

As the court officer asked, 'Ladies and gentlemen of the jury, have you reached a verdict?', I held my breath. I looked over at John Newman's mother and brother. I thought, *After all this time, it will kill them if the accused are acquitted.*

The jury foreman rose from his seat.

'On the charge of Phuong Ngo for murder, have you reached a verdict?'

'Yes. Guilty.'

'On the charge of David Duy Dinh for murder, have you reached a verdict?'

'Yes. Not guilty.'

'On the charge of Tu Quang Dao for murder, have you reached a verdict?'

'Yes. Not guilty.'

I saw Mark Tedeschi at probably his lowest point then. He is an incredibly strong and resilient man, but he was shattered by the result. I think he felt it was one of the biggest losses he'd had in a court battle.

We all felt the same. The evidence against all three was similar. Logically I couldn't see how you could say two of them were innocent and one was guilty. But that was the result.

After the verdict I had to conduct a press conference outside the Supreme Court, before just about the biggest media scrum I had ever encountered – and the hardest. I simply said we must abide by the umpire's decision, that is the jury. I was asked if there would be further investigation as to who the shooter was, as two people were acquitted. I said there were no plans for further inquiries, because we had placed all our findings before the court. The reality was we had exhausted all avenues and reached a conclusion.

* * *

Ngo was later sentenced to life, never to be released.

In sentencing Ngo, the trial judge, Justice Dunford, called it one of Australia's worst murders:

> I am satisfied to the criminal standard that Phuong Ngo's motive for the killing of John Newman was naked ambition and impatience … He could not wait until the next general election due in 1999; and so he needed to remove John Newman … The method he chose was to have John Newman killed … Not only is the deliberate premeditated killing of another human being a most serious offence at any time, the criminality in the present case is greatly aggravated because it involved the killing of a member of Parliament for political ends. It therefore constituted an offence not only against the individual victim, but it was also a direct attack on our system of democratic

representative government and struck at the very fabric of our public institutions.

Listening to those words, I was glad we never gave up on the case when others wanted to drop it because of budget constraints. The reason you go into Homicide is to right wrongs, to hold people to account. You can't just say, 'It's all too hard, let's not worry about it.'

I'd known that a conviction was within reach, and that this case was important for justice in NSW. So I'd done my best as the head of Homicide to ensure it kept going. It was the right thing to do.

Little did I know this was by no means the end of the matter.

* * *

Less than two weeks after Ngo was found guilty, the Homicide team was caught up in another sensational murder.

Most people in Sydney can recall the Sef Gonzales case without too much prompting. Anyone who had a television or radio woke on 10 July 2001 to the shocking news that a mother, father and daughter had been slain in their home at North Ryde in Sydney's northwest.

The murders were truly gruesome. I wasn't one of the investigators, but as the head of Homicide I was across the details. I didn't go to the crime scene, but I certainly saw the photos and was briefed throughout. At certain crime scenes, we put down stainless-steel grids raised off the ground for people to walk on, so they don't walk on the blood and other evidence that is on the floor. Normally you'd have just one or two of these grids. At the Gonzales murder scene, the floor was covered in them because there was so much blood.

The officer who ran the investigation was Mick Sheehy, a very thorough, methodical detective, absolutely tenacious, and just a terrific guy. The 22-year-old son, Sef, was a suspect from the start. There really wasn't any other plausible explanation. For a long time he convincingly hoodwinked everyone into believing that he should be pitied. He made an appeal on television, offering a reward to anyone with information about the killer, and notoriously sang the Mariah Carey song 'One Sweet Day' and gave the eulogy at his family's funeral service.

Yet this was a young man who had decided to massacre his father, Teddy, his mother, Mary Loiva, and his sister, Clodine, so that he could inherit his parents' wealth, and lead – in his mind – a fabulous, rich life without ever having to work for it.

At the house, the words 'Fuck off Asians KKK' (signifying the Ku Klux Klan) had been painted on one of the walls, in an attempt to convince police this was a racially motivated crime. While keeping an open mind, we were sceptical regarding the racial motive for a number of reasons. First, we had never come across a break-and-enter and murder committed in the cause of anti-Asian racism. Second, the KKK had no presence or reach in Australia that we were aware of. Third, nothing was stolen, and fourth, traces of the paint from the graffiti were found on Sef's clothes.

His defence team later claimed there could have been Colombian drug lords after him, but that was garbage. At one stage he produced an email that he said was from a Filipino businessman warning him that people wanted to harm his father. It proved to have been faked. There was no international conspiracy to kill him, no evidence for it whatsoever.

More significantly, Sef's statement about his movements and actions had so many holes in it that it unravelled more with each telling; it just didn't add up. Due to the many lies he told police in a series of interviews – all of which were investigated and disproved – he had to fundamentally change his story repeatedly.

He had made inquiries regarding the size of his inheritance from his parents, as well as having put an order in for a new flash car that he could not have afforded normally. Additionally, witnesses came forward to say that his car had been seen in the driveway at the time of the murders, when he said he wasn't there. It was a strong brief of evidence.

The reality of it was that Sef Gonzales resented his parents telling him what to do and restricting his money flow. The family were devout Catholics, and the two children had had a very conservative upbringing. Sef was a failing student who was never going to meet his parents' expectations and anticipated being cut off financially.

Yet having an obvious suspect rarely translates into an instant charge. Much needs to be done to prove every aspect of the Crown case, and to ensure that no defence team can negate the evidence. Because Sef was wily and kept changing his story, detectives needed to deal with every issue he raised.

For a while it looked like the case was going to be a hard one.

* * *

Towards the end of 2001, I was dragged in for hearings at the PIC in connection with M5 and Operation Mascot. I faced the same accusation levelled at me by M5 himself: that someone had leaked his identity to me as an informant for Internal Affairs and the PIC. As I have explained, this was just ridiculous. I had never worked with M5, never been in the same squad as him, never conducted an investigation with him. Detectives don't just turn up at the office of someone they barely know and confess all their sins. I was well aware there was no love for me at Internal Affairs or the PIC. So they sent in an amateur who was missing a back story or an excuse for coming to see me. None of it made sense.

There was a second lot of PIC hearings in late 2001 and early 2002, in relation to allegations about two of my informants who were due to get a reward. In a bugged conversation, one was overheard to say to the other that I'd been very fair to them and that he was going to give me a bit of the reward money. The second informant immediately said, 'I don't think that will happen, mate. He's not the type, he won't take it.' That was the end of the matter. The offer was never made, and I would never have accepted it. I later learned that the PIC decided to sit on this matter for a considerable number of years, using it as an excuse to say I was under investigation and in the process blackening my name without giving any details. The matter could have been clarified in a simple interview. They chose to leave it hanging there.

Ultimately the PIC couldn't prove either of these accusations. And like everybody else on Warrant 266, without those affidavits, I couldn't prove anything either. Meanwhile, I had no choice but to get on with life. But there would be a shadow hanging over me and my career for the next decade. I had been named in a bugging warrant as a suspect.

In 2003, after a crescendo of complaints from over 100 people, Strike Force Emblems was set up to investigate the matter, but they too could not get access to the affidavits behind the warrant. Emblems reported back, but the findings would be kept secret for over a decade. In 2012, Sydney newspaper the *Sun-Herald* would finally run articles revealing information that journalist Neil Mercer had received about Emblem's findings.

And it would be many more years and another, even more damaging inquiry, before any of us saw any justice – justice in which I would play a central role.

* * *

With perseverance, Mick Sheehy and his team finally cracked the Gonzales case, and a year in, they had enough to charge Sef with the murders of his father, mother and sister.

The case took its toll. From the actual murders in July 2001 through to the conviction in May 2004, everyone in the Homicide Squad office was supportive of the team doing the investigation. We knew that our colleagues were going through a tough time.

We might be cops, used to dealing with the worst life throws up, but we're still people. You might harden up and not show it, not buckle, not break down. But when you see human beings who have been chopped up, their blood coating the walls and floor, then you realise the crimes were committed by the victims' loved one, it's normal to be affected on some level. You begin to realise you're not ten feet tall, nor are you bulletproof. I decided to bring in mandatory regular counselling sessions for the Homicide Squad staff. Some disagreed with me, but the reality was, people who I cared about were hurting and I had a responsibility to help them. It's possibly the only issue I had ever had any disagreement with the troops about in Homicide. The plan was implemented and even those who opposed it ultimately said it was the right decision.

As a commander in charge of a squad, I had to be conscious of all that. I had to make sure that we had enough support for the guys investigating the murder, and fortunately everyone was fine.

It was a hard-fought trial – with Mark Tedeschi again acting as Crown Prosecutor – and to this day Sef is still arguing his innocence.

But by the time the baby-faced Sef was safely behind bars, I was in the middle of a war zone.

1. My great-grandfather Kaldas Morcos, outside our family home in Assyut (Assiut) in the 1930s. In the Arabic world, you adopt your father's name, then your grandfather's name and possibly your great-grandfather's name – so in Egypt I would have been Naguib Samy Naguib Kaldas Morcos.

2. My grandfather Naguib Kaldas.

3. My sartorial idol, my uncle Alfonse Naguib Kaldas in the mid-1920s.

4. My parents, my sister, Dallal, and me on our annual summer holiday by the beach in Alexandria, Egypt.

1. As a kid, I loved playing cops and robbers, c.1962–63.

2. My proud mum took this photo on the day of my graduation as a cop, 1982.

3. The NSW Police Academy graduating class of 1982. I'm in the back row, second from the right.

1. Great friends and fellow cops, c.1986–87. Back row: Greg Rosman and me; front row: Alex Ramsey (aka Roger Ramjet), Darren Spooner and Doc Holliday.

2. In 2004, I went to Iraq to oversee the rebuilding of the Iraqi police and security forces. I enjoyed a big fat Cuban cigar and a Corona beer with other cops after a hard day!

3. Here I am in Iraq with two members of my protection team (faces pixelated to protect their identities).

4. Deputy Interior Minister Hussein Ali Kamal was a heroic figure in the face of the insurgency in Iraq. He was in charge of the national crime squads, national criminal intelligence and the Iraqi Interpol office, which we established together.

In the course of my career, I met many well-known and important people.

1. Louis J Freeh, then Director of the FBI, was to become an important figure for me, as a mentor, friend and adviser in the business world. This photo was taken in early 2000, when he visited Australia to be briefed on the Sydney Olympics security preparations. *(Tim Flynn)*

2. In 2008, I met the then Director of the FBI, Robert Mueller, later the author of the *Report on the Investigation into Russian Interference in the 2016 Presidential Election.*

3. With His Holiness Pope Benedict XVI, 2008.

4. After the 2012 Hyde Park riot in Sydney, I met with Sheikh Mousselmani, head of the Supreme Islamic Shia Council of Australia.

5. With His Excellency the Honourable David Hurley AC CVO DSC (Retd), the then Governor of NSW and later Governor-General of Australia, 2013.

6. In 2015, I was honoured to meet Ban Ki-moon, eighth secretary-general of the United Nations, during his visit to Government House, Sydney.

1. At the NSW Police Academy, following a graduation ceremony in 2008. *(Glen McCurtayne/SMH)*

2. Standing in front of the NSW Mounted Police. *(NSW Police)*

1. Giving evidence during Operation Prospect, the Office of Ombudsman's inquiry into the 'bugging saga', 2015. *(Cameron Richardson/Newspix)*

2. In March 2016, I announced my retirement from the NSW Police Force. My decision made the headlines. *(The Age)*

3. My last day as Deputy Commissioner, ending a 35-year career with NSW Police.

1. Natalie and me at our wedding in Italy, 2009. With us are my best man, Bob Reid (who was the former chief of investigations at the Yugoslav Tribunal), and his wife, Ann Sutherland.

2. Natalie and I spent some time travelling in Egypt in 2018. Here we are in Luxor with my kids.

3. In 2019, I received an Honorary Doctorate for Services to the Community from Western Sydney University. I'm pictured here with Peter Shergold, then chancellor of WSU.

1. It was an honour to serve my country as chair of the Royal Commission into Defence and Veteran Suicide from 2021 to 2024, alongside co-commissioners Dr Peggy Brown and James Douglas KC. *(Leanne Kelly)*

2. My 2023 address at the National Press Club was a significant step in highlighting the issues we were discovering in the royal commission. The response was overwhelmingly positive from veterans and the public. *(Troy Deighton)*

3. After 12 hearing blocks and nearly 6000 submissions, my co-commissioners and I delivered the final report to the Governor-General, Her Excellency the Honourable Ms Sam Mostyn AC. *(Leanne Kelly)*

CHAPTER 14

A Bag of Human Fingers

2004

Around midnight in early January 2004, I landed at Baghdad International Airport in an Australian military C-130 Hercules. All military flights into Iraq had to do a 'tactical landing' – straight down, no gradual descent – to avoid being shot.

I was with one other Australian adviser. On landing, we were told there were insurgents on the road into Baghdad, and we'd have to spend the night in a tent on the tarmac. About 45 minutes later, we were woken up and told we needed to move immediately. Things had changed, and an opportunity to move had come up. I would soon get used to this constantly and rapidly moving threat environment. So we donned bulletproof vests and set off, our protection team armed to the teeth, in two armoured SUVs, with the Aussie flag flying from the bonnet. We careened our way into the capital at the fastest possible speed, barely slowing down for checkpoints.

That first drive into Baghdad set the tone for what I would be immersed in over the following nine months.

* * *

In March the previous year, a coalition of US, British, Australian and other troops had invaded Iraq and toppled the Saddam Hussein regime.

Then in December, Saddam Hussein had been captured. The coalition was helping to rebuild the government of Iraq, which included rebuilding the law enforcement bodies along modern, democratic lines. I had been approached by some Australians connected with the FBI and the US Drug Enforcement Administration (DEA), who were looking for senior police advisers for Iraq. They wanted people with high-level Western law enforcement experience, from countries that were part of the coalition, and as an Arabic speaker, I had an extra skill to offer.

I had a number of lengthy phone conversations with Steve Casteel, a legendary former DEA special agent, who had been appointed by President George W Bush to oversee the entire rebuilding of everything to do with security in Iraq. He went through my background and asked me many questions; I asked him many questions in turn. A lot of them he couldn't answer.

I accepted that it was going to be a 'flying by the seat of the pants' effort, which was not unattractive to me. I'd been the commander of Homicide for some years and spent more than a decade on and off in that squad. I was not getting on with the hierarchy, nor my immediate superiors, and felt it would be good to do something completely different for a while.

So I asked Steve: 'How do I apply?'

He didn't hesitate. 'Nick, you've just got the job. When can you start?'

* * *

Things moved quickly. I applied for 12 months' unpaid leave from the NSW Police. I was assured they would keep my job as the head of Homicide open for me.

I was to be deployed by the Department of Foreign Affairs and Trade (DFAT) as part of Australia's contribution to the coalition effort, which was being managed by the Australian Agency for International Development (AusAID), the government organisation that ran Australian overseas aid programs. I would travel to Iraq with another Australian, a fireman who would be helping to rebuild the country's fire brigade and emergency services.

I was required to nominate beneficiaries for insurance policies. Kidnapping of high-worth individuals was a very real danger in Iraq, so I also had to complete forms that included personal details only *I* would know; these are known as 'proof of life' questions. This was so that if I was kidnapped and held hostage, during the negotiation process they could ask the kidnappers questions, and if the answers were correct they would know I was still alive.

These things certainly brought home to me the fact that there was significant risk involved.

The insurgency that had flared up since the toppling of the regime would take years to abate. Huge numbers of people were being killed; I had read about a number of Western advisers from coalition countries being targeted specifically. I was later to be in no doubt my position of senior police adviser would make me a somewhat attractive target.

Despite this great personal risk, I also felt a sense of duty. I was in a unique position to be able to help the Iraqi people, understanding more than most about the culture and history of the region and being able to speak Arabic fluently. I knew I was part of something historic.

I had some difficult conversations with my family. My mother had a bit of a meltdown. I talked to my kids about it and told them that I thought what I was doing was important. My son, Luke, who was eight or nine, didn't want me to go because he thought I would die. My daughters who were 11 and 13 years old were more supportive, but they weren't happy either. My youngest daughter, Laura, was always close to me, and she was particularly anxious. I felt bad about worrying them, as they had been through a bit during the breakdown of my marriage to their mother, but I did my best to reassure them.

Finally, on a Sunday at the start of 2004, I flew out of Sydney. As I tried to focus on what was ahead, the whole world I knew disappeared below me, beyond the cabin window.

* * *

That first night, we arrived at the Hamra Hotel, in the Red Zone of Baghdad. There was a very large, protected compound known as the Green Zone, and the rest of the city was the Red Zone.

I would stay in the Hamra Hotel for the first week or so, commuting each day to the Republican Palace in the Green Zone. All marble floors and sweeping staircases, the Republican Palace was where Saddam Hussein had once met dignitaries and visiting heads of State, but it now served as HQ for the coalition occupiers of Iraq.

I immediately asked to be housed in the Green Zone instead: as well as making me somewhat safer, it would alleviate daily travel. After some time, I was able to be moved from the Red Zone into an American trailer. There was a whole colony of them on the edge of the Green Zone, which unfortunately put them within easy reach of insurgents' mortars. Eventually the Americans would sand-bag the trailers, but they couldn't do anything about the flimsy tinfoil roofs. So if a mortar landed in your little square of trailer park, there were no ifs, buts or maybes – you were gone. If it landed next door, *they* were gone, but *you* might be okay because there were two layers of sandbags between you and them.

The trailers were cosy spaces, about as big as my dinner table at home. Every four men shared one bathroom. I used to get up at 5.30 am to beat the rush for the showers, then go back to bed for another hour or two.

Eventually the Australian Government rented a nice, double-brick, two-storey house in the Green Zone. At any given time, there were probably six or seven of us living there, and it became a little bit of an Australian compound. Our protection personnel, the Control Risk Group – made up of former SAS personnel from Australia and New Zealand and a couple of former police tactical operators – lived in a house next door.

Everyone in the Control Risk Group was armed and I wasn't. It soon became patently clear to me that I needed a gun; I'd used one in the police for 25 years at that stage. However, my request was rejected by Canberra. Essentially they were saying: 'You're an AusAID adviser. We can't have you carrying weapons.' It was ludicrous.

Finally, a deputy secretary from DFAT, Zena Armstrong, came to Baghdad. I took her to the palace ballroom, which had been converted into the main dining room, catering for thousands. They used to liken it to the cantina in *Star Wars* that was populated with Jedi knights, Wookies and all manner of aliens. We had Gurkhas, Māori, Fijians, all the European nationalities. And I was the only person in the room – other than Zena – who didn't have a weapon.

She looked around and saw my argument, then sorted out the approval. I was finally issued with a Glock 17, the same weapon I'd had in Sydney. It just showed me how out of touch people in air-conditioned offices in Canberra can be.

There were a couple of times when we were going through an area in the Red Zone when you could tell from the crowds that something was kicking off. On those occasions I was glad to be armed, but in all my time there, I never pointed my gun at anyone.

The standard operating procedure was that you did not stop driving and have a look. Didn't matter if it was a shoot-out or a dead animal lying in the road, you just kept going.

The insurgents would use any distraction to try to get us to stop. It was common to hear about dead donkeys lying in the road that had been cut open and filled with explosives. If you ran over one, it would go off; if you stopped and tried to pull the animal off the road, it would go off. You just had to try to swerve around it.

The possibility of injury or death was never far away.

* * *

I was working in the office of the Interior Ministry under Steve Casteel and Chief Police Adviser Doug Brand, a deputy chief constable from South Yorkshire who'd spent most of his career with the London Metropolitan Police. There were about a dozen senior police advisers that made up the leadership team under Doug, and a couple of hundred police advisers across the country.

After a few months, I became Doug's number two. I grew very close to both him and Steve.

The magnitude of our mission in Iraq quickly became clear. I was sometimes asked whether I supported George W Bush's 2003 invasion; my answer was 'No'. But it was clear that the Iraqi people had suffered greatly under Saddam Hussein's rule, and they would need our help if they were ever going to stand on their own two feet again.

To make sense of the present, it's important to understand the past. Aside from the Israel–Palestine conflict, it is my view that most of the hostilities going on in the Middle East are primarily about the Sunni–Shi'ite split within the Islamic faith. It can be likened to the Catholic–Protestant conflict in Ireland.

The Shi'ites are a minority in most Islamic countries and are widely oppressed. The extremists, Al-Qaeda, Islamic State, the Taliban – they are all Sunnis, and they hate Shi'ites. They don't even see the Shi'ites as real Muslims; they see them as infidels.

Iraq is largely made up of three disparate groups: the Kurds (who have dreams of their own nation), the Sunnis, and the Shi'ites, who are actually the majority within Iraq, making up 60 to 65 per cent of the population.

Saddam Hussein was a Sunni, and he oppressed the Shi'ites quite savagely, as he did the Kurds. Just about every

Iraqi I got to know had a story about someone they knew of or cared about who had had something terrible done to them by Saddam's regime.

The coalition had a number of priorities. Primarily they were about 'standing up', or establishing, the Iraqi national police and other law enforcement and border protection bodies. Another was to demobilise the militias; every ethnic and religious group had their own. I'm not going to tell you we succeeded, but we did our best to incorporate them into the Iraqi military and police, so that they could become a legitimate part of the new republic.

Saddam's Ba'ath party had ruled Iraq since 1968. After the US invasion, Defense Secretary Donald Rumsfeld had insisted the coalition sack anyone in the public sector who was a member of the Ba'ath party.

The entire military was also disbanded. That affected something like a couple of hundred thousand people who had been militarised, armed and battle-hardened. All of a sudden, their country had been invaded, and overnight everyone from the lowest-ranking private to the highest-ranking general was out of a job, with no prospects of employment. What did we – the coalition – think was going to happen? We made it a very attractive proposition for them to go over to the other side.

Rebuilding a police force in a peacetime environment would have been tricky enough, but doing so in a war zone, with an active insurgency afoot, and with Saddam Hussein sitting in a US military facility just up the road, was a whole other story. His presence cast a very ominous shadow over everything.

Added to this was the complication that the Americans often had a limited understanding of local culture and religion. When we wanted to do a press conference saying something unsupportive of the Shi'ites, you couldn't get a Shi'ite Iraqi official or policeman to do it. It took me five minutes to work that out, but explaining the same concept to some of the Americans took longer and was met with blank looks and cries of: 'But this is his job! This happened on his patch, he *must* get up and say this, this and this!' I would have to tell them it wasn't going to happen.

The American political sphere back home also had very unrealistic expectations about how quickly we could re-establish security. They thought that democracy would be lauded and welcomed, and that they, the liberators, would be greeted with flowers. Needless to say, that wasn't what happened.

* * *

To me, the police in Iraq were heroes. Simply turning up for work every day was a risk to life and limb. They were targeted *on the way to* work, targeted *while they were at* work, and targeted on the way home. The chief of the Major Crimes Squad moved into his office and did not go home often because he didn't want to draw attention to where his family lived.

To get the Iraqi Police back up on their feet, we needed to bolster numbers as quickly as possible, so we were running four academies. There was one in Baghdad; another in Erbil, in the Kurdish area up north; a third down south in Basra, in the Shi'ite area; and a fourth in Jordan: our main academy, which was pumping out 800 to 1000 trainees at a time.

We established an eight-week training regime. Those already in the Iraqi Police who wanted to stay and had been vetted only had to go through a cut-down, four-week program.

The same training in peacetime circumstances would take months, so this was a steep learning curve for them and us. We had to make up a curriculum in a very short space of time. We had the discussion about quality versus quantity, but it was a matter of life and death.

A part of my task was to identify and 'hothouse' talented Iraqi police, so they could eventually take charge. We picked Jamal Allamedine as an incredible individual with huge leadership potential. We wanted him to be the police chief, heading up the greater Baghdad police force, which was 14,000 strong.

Jamal was a very tall, broad-shouldered man, incredibly dignified, with great charisma and presence, and his English wasn't bad, although some Americans didn't think so. I'd tell them that English language skills had little to do with it. He could use an interpreter while we were there; we would be gone in a couple of years. It was about putting the right people in the right places.

Yet Jamal's appointment kept getting held up. Finally, Doug and I went into bat. He was ideal, we said, and we worked with him very well. It was then that we found out Jamal had been 'removed from circulation' for a couple of days and 'interviewed', because he had been a senior member of the Ba'ath party, Saddam's former regime.

Addressing me as 'Najib' – the non-Egyptian Arabic pronunciation of my name, Naguib – he told me at one point in Arabic in a meeting: 'Najib, even the dogs were in the Ba'ath party. You couldn't survive in Iraq if you weren't.'

I liken it to not being in the Communist Party in Soviet Russia. You weren't going to get anywhere unless you were in the party.

He did get the role, but he only held it for a while. There were a few assassination attempts on him by insurgents, and he received reliable information that the insurgents were not about to give up on killing him. It finally got to him and he wanted out. He ended up leaving the country. Many years later, we had a reunion in Jordan and it was great to see him, a real leader.

We also appointed General Ra'ad as the chief of the Major Crime Squads. Similar to Jamal, there had been so many attempts on his life by insurgents that he used to set off the metal detectors at airports because his body was riddled with gunshot.

* * *

But the Iraqi insurgents weren't going to wait while the coalition forces trained the locals to keep them in check. And one of the worst was cleric and political leader Muqtada al-Sadr. The Sadr family were notables in the Shi'ite world, and Sadr became a thorn in our side. He was destabilising the country for his own ends, undermining the population's confidence in the Iraqi Government and the coalition forces while deliberately fomenting tension between Sunnis and Shi'ites.

Sadr was holed up in the Imam Ali Shrine in the city of Najaf, 160 kilometres south of Baghdad, considered holy ground for Shi'ites. He was operating it as a State within a State, breaking every law. A number of women complained about being grabbed off the street by his thugs and placed in his prison, where terrible things happened to them. He also ran his own court and his own militia, the Jaysh al-Mahdi (Mahdi Army), one of the worst insurgency groups. He was standing over the local police and the military, and they were too scared to do anything.

Things came to a head when he was accused of the murder of his biggest rival cleric, Grand Ayatollah Abdul-Majid al-Khoei, and 13 others at a Najaf mosque. Warrants were issued for the arrest of Sadr, along with a number of his associates. There were many meetings among coalition forces and Iraqi police and authorities about how we were going to take him down.

Eventually, one of Sadr's henchmen, Mustafa al-Yaqoubi, was detained by coalition soldiers and all hell broke loose. Sadr effectively declared an insurrection. All our facilities in Najaf and the surrounding area came under intense attack. First it was mortar shelling, then vast numbers of insurgents arrived on foot, firing at our camp.

The commander of the coalition forces at that time, General Ricardo Sanchez, ordered action. I was directed to mount an operation to arrest Sadr and his cronies, codenamed 'Operation Law and Order'.

After a number of trips down south, I'd managed to muster around 700 police, mostly from the southern city of Basra: all Shi'ites, by necessity. We were going into one of the most holy places for Shi'ites and it would have been sacrilege to take Sunni (let alone US) boots on that ground. We had to use Shi'ites – or at least try to.

I went down there with my protection team and a very reliable police major-general from Baghdad. We organised accommodation in the military camp in Najaf and briefed the troops on the mission at hand: raid Sadr's compound, get Sadr and arrest him.

The look on the faces of the mostly Shi'ite troops said it all. Once they were told it was one of the most prominent Shi'ites in the country we were after, they sent a delegation of senior police to meet me, who politely said they simply could not do what we were asking.

After a day of bargaining and negotiating, the religious factionalism proved an insurmountable hurdle.

I received strident calls from Doug Brand, who was in the company of a number of senior US military. The generals were demanding the operation go ahead, no matter what. But the Shi'ite police simply would not act against one of their own, let alone one from such a revered family. We had no choice but to abandon Operation Law and Order.

It was a hell of a day, one that ended with me going to sleep with a sense of profound disappointment.

Sadr was never arrested, and he remains a member of parliament in Iraq, with a sizeable following.

* * *

Along with Muqtada al-Sadr's Shi'ite insurgency, we also faced the al-Qaeda insurgency, led by Abu Musab al-Zarqawi, a former Jordanian criminal radicalised in jail. Zarqawi's methods went beyond even what al-Qaeda was comfortable with. Deadly, effective and ruthless, his hatred of Shi'ites was as strong as his hatred of the coalition forces.

On a May spring morning in eastern Baghdad, one of our Iraqi colleagues, the Deputy Interior Minister, Abdul-Jabbar

Youssef al-Sheikhli, had a convoy waiting outside his house to pick him up. He came out but realised he had forgotten his keys, so he went back inside to get them.

Witnesses would later recall seeing a white Caprice motor car rolling down the hill just before he walked out again, then zig-zagging outside his home and exploding.

The suicide bomb hit the convoy, killing five and injuring twenty. Charred car wreckage was scattered everywhere. The deputy minister was injured but survived because he was still walking out of his house.

Doug Brand and I felt we had to go straight out there to show our solidarity and see if we could help. By the time we arrived with our protection team, the local community had gathered on the street. A couple of people began to scream at us, saying that this was all our fault, that we were not protecting them.

Doug and I spoke to them – me in Arabic, Doug in English – in an effort to de-escalate the situation. Our bodyguards tensed as we became hemmed in by the very large crowd.

One guy kept tugging at my sleeve. I brushed him off a couple of times, then finally turned around to see what he wanted. He was crying and holding a plastic shopping bag. It was full of human fingers and a hand.

I shall never forget the look of despair in his eyes. It brought home to me the evil we were up against. I stayed with him for a while and tried to console him. I have no idea who he was, most probably a neighbour of the deputy minister.

The attack was later claimed to be the work of a group linked to al-Qaeda and Zarqawi. In a website posting, a statement said that the driver of the Caprice was a 'martyr', who 'drove a car bomb to take al-Sheikhli to hell'.

After about an hour, we drove back in silence. We knew that could have been any one of us. As I looked through the tinted window of the SUV, I wondered: *How do we stop this? Are we ever going to win this thing?*

There were times when I felt what we were doing was futile, times when I knew we were losing. I couldn't focus on those thoughts. I had to keep looking ahead and thinking about the good I was doing while I was here. And we did many good things. We helped the Iraqis establish properly structured major crime squads, an Interpol Office, National Criminal Intelligence Office, and enhancements to their forensic capabilities and internal oversight.

I'd usually call home every two or three days, but I made a point of ringing my kids that night after attending the bombing scene. I didn't tell them what had happened that day. I could never tell them about events like that. I just wanted to hear their voices.

* * *

There was one time when the violence came even closer to home.

A young American college graduate, Scott, was working as an assistant in our office. He was a very noble-cause sort of guy, who really wanted to help the Iraqi people. Against all our rules, and without telling anyone, he used to go to Baghdad University every Wednesday in a softskin – a non-armoured vehicle – with two young Iraqi police officers. He'd deliver lectures championing democracy and deriding the evils of dictatorship under Saddam.

One Wednesday Scott was going across to the university at the same time he always did, via the route he always travelled: all things that we were warned against. He and the officers were ambushed by insurgents. The others were shot dead, and Scott's injuries were so horrendous he had to be medevacked to Germany and then to the Walter Reed Army Medical Center in Washington, DC.

A month or two later, Steve Casteel and I went to the US capital for some meetings. We tried to visit Scott a couple of times, but the extent of his injuries was such that we weren't allowed to see him.

He pulled through in the end, but you can imagine how it left everyone feeling. We had a small office of about 25 senior police, but at any given time, there were only about a dozen of us there. It had a massive impact on everyone.

* * *

Prior to my deployment, I'd had a session with the Commonwealth psychologists, who told me that people could often develop bad habits in a war zone because of the stress.

I remember thinking, *That's garbage. I've been in the cops 25 years. Nothing's going to happen to me. I'm good to go.*

At the end of most days, the senior cops would get together and wind down. A favourite spot was a terrace within the palace that looked out over an incredible pool. We'd take it in turns to bring a carton of beer and someone would always have Cuban cigars.

For the first few weeks they'd ask if I wanted a cigar and I'd always turn the offer down. Then we had some really tough days – such as the shooting of our colleague or the attempt on the deputy minister's life – and next thing you know, I'm having two cigars a night. I would later discover that living in a war zone had even bigger effects on me.

Being away from home was tough for everyone. There were some guys in our office whose wives or partners left them while they were in Iraq. It happened often and felt heartless.

The main concern I had was my kids and my loved ones. I just wanted to get home safely so I could see them again. This thought helped to keep me going during the long weeks.

We worked seven very full days; there were no weekends off. On Friday afternoons all the Aussies would try to have a bit of a get-together in the Green Zone. We'd have a beer and a laugh; it was a release at the end of a shit week, knowing you were about to go into another shit week.

For us advisers it was six weeks on, one week off. On the week off they'd get us out on a C-130, either to Kuwait or Jordan. I preferred Jordan, because it was much easier to travel from there to Lebanon, or to Egypt, where I got to see my many family members. Ultimately, one week wasn't really long enough to wind down, kick back and uncork the pressure valve of being in Iraq before it was time to return. It wasn't easy to suddenly switch from being in Baghdad, armed and on guard all the time, to the relative freedom and comfort of another location. It took a little while to adjust. But it was better than nothing.

I vividly recall my first week off. I went to Amman, Jordan's capital, with two other guys. We stayed at the Marriott, an old-fashioned hotel in the centre of the city, which was nothing short of an oasis. None of us had had a decent coffee for six weeks, and we went straight to the little coffee shop on the ground floor and had about four or five cappuccinos in a row. We smoked Cuban cigars, we did some sightseeing, we went to restaurants, we caught up with friends, and we treated ourselves to nice things. We slept on nice beds, and each had our own private shower. But most importantly, we were not on guard; we simply relaxed, with no one trying to kill us. I also visited Beirut and caught up with some Australian friends.

I have since been accused of being addicted to the Marriotts and their nice beds.

* * *

The looming, immovable deadline for all of us was the formal handing back of authority to the Iraqis on 30 June 2004. Everyone anticipated that all hell would break loose at that time. We expected the insurgents to launch attacks that day to make their point.

A secret decision was made to formally hand over control on 28 June, two days earlier than planned. Head US diplomat Paul Bremer and his number two slipped out of the country that night, and John Negroponte came in as the new US ambassador not as the head of the Coalition Provisional Authority running the country. It was a surprise move, and it worked, deflating any attack plans the insurgents might have had.

* * *

Finally it got to September. AusAID wanted me to stay in Iraq for as long as I could, but I was beginning to think of my future back in the NSW Police. I was now around the nine-month mark; my term in Iraq was supposed to be 12 months max.

While I was in Iraq, a position came up back in Sydney: chief superintendent, second in charge of Counter Terrorism and Special Tactics. It required extensive investigative experience and knowledge of the 'operating environment': the field of terrorism. I was in Iraq, terror centre of the world, and had more investigative experience than most. I had spent most of my career in major crime and had commanded the Homicide Squad and many other investigations. Additionally, I had lost my position as commander of Homicide; NSW Police had reneged on their promise to keep it open for me. I did not have a specific role to go back to.

So I applied for the job and did the interview by phone from Baghdad.

Very soon afterwards, I got a call from the head of Counter Terrorism, Norm Hazzard, who was the Chair of the selection committee, and a second member of the selection committee, who both congratulated me on having won the job. Norm said the difference between candidates could often be very slight; you could win by just one or two points, even half a point sometimes. I was apparently ten points ahead of the nearest person.

Then, a couple of days later, I was notified by Human Resources that I *hadn't* got the job. Nothing had been amiss in my application; I was told the Commissioner had overruled the committee's decision and appointed someone else. He had the power to do this and was not obliged to explain. This was a misguided and unfair process introduced after the Wood Royal Commission.

Naturally, I was upset. I had the qualifications, and I had been told by the selection panel that I was way in front of the other candidates. It didn't make any sense at all.

My attempts to call the Commissioner and the Deputy Commissioner went unanswered. This wasn't good. After two and a half decades in the force, I wondered whether I had a future in the NSW Police. Had I become persona non grata?

Everything felt unstable and uncertain. I decided to head home and try to sort things out.

For what I thought would be the last time, I got into a Black Hawk helicopter to go from the Green Zone to the airport. They're great fun; they travel in pairs and fly very low and very, very, very fast. I looked down on the beautiful ancient city of Baghdad and the Tigris River with mixed emotions. I was worried about whether my enemies outweighed my friends back home. I was also feeling very melancholy, thinking about all the new police mates I'd made, whose company I'd loved.

Would I ever see them or this city again? I very much doubted it.

Little did I know how wrong I was.

CHAPTER 15

Like Coming Down From Drugs

2004

Arriving back home, I couldn't wait to see the kids. That was the first thing I did, and they were really glad to see me. If I tried to have a cigar in their presence, they were quick to tell me that I stank and they were not going anywhere near me, so I had to pull back a bit.

My elder daughter, Simone, was about 13 and was demanding a mobile phone: 'All my friends have one, Daaaaaad!' So the deal was she could pick one – a nice Nokia, she chose the colour, size etc. – but I needed to hang on to it for a week or so, because I didn't want to pick up my police phone just yet.

I was expected to go to Canberra and debrief with the various government agencies of what I had learned from my experience on the ground. So I used Simone's phone to line up the various meetings I had to go to.

I attended one formal debriefing with most of the government agencies – DFAT, the Australian Federal Police

(AFP), the Australian Trade and Investment Commission, the Australian Security Intelligence Organisation, the Australian Defence Force and others. I was pontificating about my meetings with the Iraqi Interior Minister and various other senior officials when my mobile phone rang. And the ring tone (which my daughter had picked) was a loud rendition of 'Barbie Girl' by Aqua!

Everybody looked at me. I felt I lost some credibility.

* * *

On my return, I still had my NSW Police rank – detective superintendent – but I didn't have a position. There were two spots open at State Crime Command, the home of the major crime squads where I was attached – not promotions, but at my rank. The two vacancies were Commander of the Fraud Squad (later renamed Financial Crime Squad) or the Gangs Squad.

I had first choice. I chose Gangs, responsible for investigating and dealing with outlaw motorcycle gangs and some ethnically based organised crime groups.

As it turned out, though, it would be a few weeks before I was able to take up the position.

* * *

Just a couple of weeks after my return, I was still attempting to settle back into Sydney when the AFP rang. There was a claim on a jihadi website that three Australian security contractors had been kidnapped, along with two others described as 'East Asians', after their convoy was ambushed in the Sunni town of Samarra, in the north of Iraq. A militant group had released a statement claiming responsibility and giving the Australian Government 24 hours to withdraw its troops: 'We tell the infidels of Australia that they have 24 hours to leave Iraq or the two Australians will be executed, without a second chance.' The Australian Prime Minister, John Howard, announced the withdrawal.

The AFP asked me for contacts in Baghdad. I got my black book out and gave them details for all the key players I could think of.

None of these guys in Iraq spoke much if any English and the AFP had no presence on the ground. There were difficulties in all directions. After a couple of hours of to-ing and fro-ing, they realised they couldn't do this on their own. They needed me back in Baghdad.

They were ready to deploy two AFP officers and a large number of military assets, but I knew the language, I knew the ground rules in Baghdad, I was accredited as a hostage negotiator up to the highest national level, and I had all the key connections and the trust of the Iraqi senior police and government. I could navigate them through an investigation fairly quickly.

I knew it would be a challenge, but my conscience kicked in and overrode any doubts. The statement might be a hoax, but it was just as likely to be genuine. I had to do what I could to save Aussies whose lives could be in danger.

While the safety of those who had been kidnapped was obviously our primary concern, there were other things in play. Spain had just pulled out of the coalition, and other coalition partners were jittery. There was also an Australian federal election looming. The Howard Government were worried about the perception that Australians were fair game in war zones, and everyone realised we needed to either put this thing to bed by proving it to be fake, or rescue the kidnapped Aussies ASAP.

I was sworn in as an AFP officer and flew out that night with the other two AFP officers and a senior bureaucrat on a commercial flight to Iraq via Dubai. One of my deputies, Detective Inspector Maria Rustja, was left in charge of the Gangs Squad in my absence.

While on the tarmac at a military base in Dubai, my Aussie phone rang. It was a female journalist called Natalie O'Brien from *The Australian*. I didn't know her – at least I didn't think I did – but she was trying to confirm a rumour she'd heard that I had been called back to Iraq. I didn't give anything away. Little did I realise that she would come back into my life much later.

We flew out of Dubai with a large number of Australian military personnel. On arrival in Baghdad, the first thing I wanted to do was establish the identity of the Australians we were looking for. Lives were at stake, so it was essential that we got this right.

Time to do a headcount of Aussies in Iraq, thought to number about 900. There was a large group working in various private capacities, yet what became clear to me was that there was no centralised registration. So we conducted a systematic audit of all Australians registered with our embassy, of which there were very few, but more significantly we had to meet with and interview companies known to employ Australians.

That was great in theory, but in practice a lot of Aussies didn't *want* to be registered. They were running away from disgruntled wives, overdue alimony, lawsuits and who knew what else. It was often the case in Iraq that employers didn't ask why you were there or where you'd come from; they just wanted to know that you were capable of doing the job you were being paid for.

You can't force people to appear on a list, though a lot of people did come forward and register.

* * *

After a few weeks of investigation on the ground, with the full support of the Iraqi Police and particularly their major crime units, as far as we could tell, there were no Aussies missing. The kidnapping was a furphy, which was obviously a relief. It was good to put the whole thing to rest.

All up, I was back in Iraq for a few weeks. It allowed me to catch up with many Iraqi colleagues, and I learned that around a fifth of the Major Crime Squad police who we had appointed had either been targeted or assassinated. I asked about a couple of people in particular, and my inquiries were met with a rueful shake of the head, which of course meant they were dead. A lot of the guys in senior positions had been Sunni because Saddam had been Sunni. Now there had been a Shi'ite takeover, which had led to a lot of vengeful acts.

After the good we had tried to do and the things we had achieved, it was doubly distressing to learn of these deaths. I felt incredibly sad to have lost colleagues, and frustrated by the futility of Iraq's never-ending cycle of violence and tragedy.

* * *

When I look back on my time in Iraq, I can see I learned a great deal about myself. I found out that I'm more resilient than I thought I was.

I've often reflected on danger and the effect it has on people. I accept it's not for everyone. Some people in Iraq simply could not cope. Someone I was working with, and became good friends with, just could not function in Baghdad. Others were blasé.

I didn't know how I was going to react to the extreme daily danger, to the carnage, to the massive human tragedy. But I had lived through the Six-Day War in Egypt as a ten-year-old, and seen my dad face all sorts of threats as he tried to make a living in an increasingly hostile environment in our country.

I look back now on all the life-threatening environments I have lived and worked in, and I can honestly say that the danger never daunted me. I took all necessary precautions, remained focused and just got on with the job at hand.

In Iraq, I found that I could cope fairly easily. I could function, and I could actually perform at a high level. I also found that I could use all those negotiation skills that I'd picked up over the years to deal with people from different cultures and diverse levels of bureaucracy. I could hold my own with ministers, a huge range of multinational ambassadors, and legal, military and law enforcement figures. And I think I performed well and contributed significantly.

* * *

But then there was the downside.

After my first tour as senior police adviser, the experience really hit me when I got home. That adrenaline, that hourly rush, wasn't there any more. I'm guessing it's what coming down from drugs feels like.

I was in a supermarket with my kids one day and went to use my credit card, but I couldn't remember my PIN. It had been months since I'd used it. There was no EFTPOS, no ATMs, no banks in Baghdad that we could access. You had to do everything in cash.

This simple act of forgetfulness floored me. I had tears in my eyes; I actually had a bit of a meltdown in the supermarket.

I was never jittery while I was in Iraq; I couldn't afford to be. I was armed, alert and ready to roll, all day, every day. I worked hard during the day, and drank and mingled at night.

But coming back was a huge adjustment, and I couldn't explain it to people. There's no doubt in my mind now that I had severe post-traumatic stress disorder for quite some months. I had all the symptoms. I was hypervigilant and would jump out of my skin at sudden noises. If someone banged a table I'd tense up, because to me it was like a mortar going off. I found it hard to concentrate and my mind would race back to things I didn't really want to revisit.

I was not able to clear up what happened with my withdrawn promotion, and the Commissioner and responsible Deputy refused to speak to me. The Police Association declined to assist, even though I am aware that the Secretary, under his own initiative, did bring it up a number of times with the hierarchy, to no avail.

Coupled with this, a kind of sadness and a sense of not quite belonging in this environment slowly set in and made me withdraw for a while. I had seen a lot of blood spilled, felt a lot of frustration about the unfairness of what had happened, and it took a while for all of that to hit me. It wasn't a delayed reaction to the fear and danger, it was more depression than anything else.

I never talked about it to anyone at work or at home – not even the policewoman I was going out with at the time. I thought it would be unfair to expect her to understand. Besides, in the police, it's not the done thing to take your work troubles home. Like most cops, I had bottled things up for decades.

On one occasion I was at a meeting of crime squad commanders. At the end of the meeting, a friend of mine pulled me aside and said: 'Nick, we lost you about ten minutes into that. Are you okay? I don't know where you were, but you weren't with us.'

I should have put my hand up and got help. But I suffered in silence. I wasn't well – but I never admitted it to anyone. I didn't feel that I could.

At that time, I simply could not show that kind of weakness and continue as a detective superintendent with promotional prospects. I had failed to get an explanation from the hierarchy as to why my promotion was stopped, so the last thing I was going to do was tell them I was not well.

So when it came to the Commonwealth Government's psych debriefing process on my return, I lied and faked my way through it. I'd been through a lot of these psych debriefs in my undercover and negotiating work. I knew what to say in order to pass them. After that, I just ploughed on, and within a few months the symptoms faded into the background.

I'm not proud of the fact that I couldn't admit I needed help, but it has to be seen in context.

I felt there were people intent on destroying my career. I'd been bugged, I'd appeared twice before the PIC, I'd been refused promotion, and the top of the organisation would not have any contact with me, which still irks me. If I had made a decision that was so vital to someone, I would have looked them in the eye and explained why. To this day they never have.

In short, I felt I could not show any weakness or it would certainly have been used against me. It would have given these people the ability to justify the decisions they'd made about me, allowing them to say: *See? We didn't promote him because he is broken.*

I'm not proud of the fact I bottled things up, and during my tenure as the Chair of the Royal Commission into Defence and Veteran Suicide I saw first-hand the damage this does, but I could not see an alternative and that was how I coped at the time. I came to the conclusion that the broader society has a problem with the stigma attached to sufferers of mental ill-health. I hope our efforts at the Royal Commission have helped in some small way in this regard.

CHAPTER 16

Hunting the Maltese Falcon

2004–2005

If I'd missed out on promotion to the role in Counter Terrorism, I at least had a position to come back to after my second tour of Iraq. In late 2004, I took up my job as Commander of the Gangs Squad.

The Gangs Squad is proactive; you have to create your own work. We set about investigating gangs, primarily bikie gangs, and their criminal activities, then arrested the bad guys and tried to seize their assets.

We got some good results. The biggest bikie group in the State was the Rebels Motorcycle Club, headed by national president Alex Vella, known as 'the Maltese Falcon'. He had survived for many years without being convicted; he had let others get caught instead. He was a bully: he stood over people internally and externally.

He was from Malta and we found out he had never bothered to get his Australian citizenship. Had he applied, he would probably have failed based on his character. I oversaw the effort to formally alert the Federal Government to that fact and to recommend, strongly, that if he ever left the country he should be refused access back into Australia. It was a much quicker, simpler process than trying to have him expelled if he was here. We lodged all the paperwork, and I went to Canberra for various meetings to stress the importance of this effort. Decapitating such an organised group was a very positive move.

We patiently waited for him to leave the country, but this didn't happen until 2007, when he went to Japan to watch his son compete in a boxing match. I'd moved on from Gangs by that point, so I oversaw the response but was not hands-on. The squad lodged every available piece of information with the Federal Government so that he would be declared not a fit and proper person to be allowed back into the country. We're talking about a person who had got away with stabbings, had links to a methamphetamine factory and had been involved in all manner of other crimes.

We had trouble getting the federal authorities to agree with us: a number of senior bureaucrats were obviously worried about being threatened by the bikies in reprisal. That time we were unsuccessful and he was allowed back in.

It took a few more years, but it was Immigration Minister Scott Morrison who finally signed the paperwork and jammed him overseas when he was on a trip to Malta in 2014. He's still stuck over there, even though he's gone to the media and has friends lobbying on his behalf.

Vella's absence created a vacuum at the top. The Rebels were in a mess without him.

It was a roundabout way of doing things, but the Gangs Squad had to be innovative. It was like getting Al Capone for tax evasion rather than for the hundreds of mob crimes he oversaw. Some of the crooks don't touch anything themselves. They direct others to do things and those people will never dob them in. They won't talk on the phone and they won't talk in premises. It's very difficult to gather direct evidence of their culpability.

* * *

In early 2005, in my spare time, I got elected to the executive of the Police Union, representing all commissioned officers – nearly 1000 in NSW. I probably became more strident in my criticism of the police oversight bodies that had targeted me and so many others. I fought back against all the injustices I perceived were going on – not just my own, but other people's too.

I've no doubt that taking on this role boosted my popularity in the police force. The rank and file saw me as someone who was going to say what needed to be said on behalf of those who couldn't do it for themselves. But it also left me open to more reprisals from the people I accused of doing the wrong thing.

* * *

In mid 2005, I was once again asked for by the Federal Government. Australia had been called on to assist the Iraqi Government in setting up the Iraqi Special Tribunal, to carry out the trial of Saddam Hussein and all the leaders of the former regime responsible for countless crimes against humanity between 1968 and 2003.

I later learned there had been a lot of discussion and different schools of thought about what should happen to him. The Americans wanted to take him to the International Criminal Court (ICC) in The Hague, which would have ensured he received a fair trial and absolved America of responsibility for his eventual fate. The biggest irony in all this was that the US were not even signatories to the ICC, though that didn't mean they couldn't refer people to it.

The Iraqis, of course, didn't want to go to the ICC at all. They thought that they would lose control of Saddam and they were never going to let that happen. There was also the fact that the ICC didn't have the death penalty; the Iraqis wanted their pound of flesh.

The US had legal custody of Saddam, but he had to be handed over to the Iraqis, particularly after sovereignty was restored. It was decided that he would be tried at the Iraqi Special Tribunal, to be established by the Iraqi Government with support from the coalition nations, of which Australia was one. They were very keen for the tribunal to be run properly and to show fairness.

The Australian Government wanted a needs analysis done on the ground, and they had a policy of not deploying anyone to conflict zones like Iraq and Afghanistan unless they had a proven track record in that kind of environment.

I fitted the bill. However, my application for unpaid leave was rejected by the NSW Police Commissioner. Apparently I was too valuable and could not be spared, even though I could not be promoted.

He was overruled. A letter was dispatched from the Commonwealth to the Premier of NSW and the Commissioner, stating that I had to go as a matter of national interest.

So back I went to Baghdad, along with an analyst from the Crime Commission who had spent time in Iraq working on war crimes issues. We worked out of the Australian Embassy, now within the Green Zone, with Control Risks Group protection. We realised fairly quickly that the security situation had become much worse. The Green Zone had been breached many times, with suicide attacks in the Hajji marketplace where coalition forces could buy all sorts of things.

We were there for a couple of months. In essence, we were preparing the Iraqis to be able to conduct the Special Tribunal themselves. It was about learning, finding out where the gaps were in Iraq's abilities, and trying to help them plug those holes.

After many interviews and meetings, we established that the Iraqis did not need what most Western governments thought: training for judges and investigators. They were very good at those things. What they needed was training in dealing with the media – particularly the international media – as well as training in archiving, record keeping and other administrative processes. Saddam had effectively frozen these activities back in the 1970s, and Iraq had missed out on a great deal of progress. Ultimately, we recommended that about a dozen Iraqis visit Australia and take part in a planned program that I and others would facilitate, and take back material to help them with the trials.

It is a matter of history now that although Saddam faced 12 major charges, he was tried on the first one and convicted, appealed, lost the appeal and was executed. The remaining cases were never heard.

In Baghdad, the hunger for vengeance was always going to triumph.

* * *

Each time I've left Baghdad International Airport, I've looked out the window and thought, *This is probably the last time I will see Iraq. I'll never be back.* Being on that plane came with an experience of mixed emotions: sadness at having to say goodbye to my Iraqi colleagues, relief at saying goodbye to the demons I'd left behind on the ground, a sense of pride in thinking of what we'd achieved while we were there, and hope as I looked to the future and the prospect of getting back to normal life.

But leaving Iraq for the third time, I also felt an overwhelming sense of regret. I had seen much conflict between various arms of US government, particularly the Defense and State Departments. I had seen many great leaders, but also witnessed first-hand how poor leadership and dysfunctionality at the highest levels of the US command had sown the seeds of future suffering and allowed bad decisions to unleash terrible forces on Iraq.

CHAPTER 17

A Lightbulb Moment

2005–2007

I loved being Commander of the Gangs Squad. It was much more of a kinetic, knock-'em-down, drag-'em-out kind of environment than Homicide, more at the sharp end operationally. I was really enjoying getting out with the troops again and getting good results.

But I still had not been able to resolve why my promotion to Counter Terrorism had been scuttled. The Commissioner and Deputy Commissioner continued to refuse to meet with me or discuss the issue.

While working in Gangs, I applied for two more jobs on promotion, both of which I knew I had the right qualifications for. But again, I heard from those involved in selection that I'd missed out. I was more hurt than disappointed. It seemed clear to me that I was under a cloud because of my inclusion on that warrant and unfounded corridor talk by certain people in Internal Affairs. The more I said I hadn't done anything wrong, the worse it got. I couldn't fight back. There was nothing I could do.

And there was another issue in play that I suspected had been going on for years. Sadly, some of what I heard being said about me by very senior police was simple racism.

In so many of my years in the police, my Egyptian heritage had been nothing but an asset, opening doors into sectors of the community that had been closed to Anglo-Saxon cops. But now it seemed being 'different' was holding me back.

I became aware that a very senior officer habitually referred to me in meetings in my absence as 'Ahab the bloody A-rab', which was greeted with much laughter by others.

But you can either jump up and down, yell and scream and walk off in a huff, or smile, keep going and right the wrongs when you can.

I did the latter.

* * *

In late 2005, the winds finally changed. Terry Collins was appointed the new deputy commissioner in charge of Specialist Operations, which included the crime squads, where I was.

I had no history with Terry and we barely knew each other. But he is a man who has a very real sense of fairness, and in my view he is incapable of lying. He came across my application for one of the jobs I'd missed out on and asked: 'How is this bloke not working in Counter Terrorism? He's led murder investigations, he's worked in Iraq ...'

Norm Hazzard was due to retire from his post as the inaugural assistant commissioner of Counter Terrorism and Special Tactics, and there was no clear or acceptable successor. Terry, against the wishes of others, asked me to stand in for Norm while he was on leave, and when Norm retired in March 2006, I applied for the job.

I was successful, with Terry's support. He later told me others had objected to my promotion, but when he pressed them for the reason, there was none.

Leaving the Gangs Squad meant that I was out of State Crime Command, where my heart had lain for a good couple of decades. But it was time to move on, and my experience in Iraq had prepared me to deal with the terrorism threat that we faced after 9/11, which had already resulted in similar attacks all over the world, including the 2002 Bali bombings that claimed 88 Australian lives.

Norm Hazzard had done a great job in setting up a one-stop shop that enabled NSW Police and the NSW Government to deal with all forms of terrorism. He brought together the investigative and intelligence arms of countering terrorism with the operational arms. I had the nucleus of a good team, and began to recruit more people who would help me refine and shape our counter-terrorism response.

We identified some key areas for change and, over the next year or so, translated them into a number of new initiatives.

First, we recognised the need for more engagement with communities that were vulnerable to radicalisation, and those affected by terrorism. I set up the Community Contact Unit, tasked with building bridges to at-risk communities across the State, understanding their needs and problems and communicating our intentions, at a time when there was no crisis. This community engagement effort has borne fruit over many years and become a model for others to follow.

A second key need was to maintain vision on what was happening around the world and to understand what it meant for Australia. We established the Strategy Unit, a team of clever young men and women who monitored what was happening globally, engaged with academia and think tanks and kept us well informed about international developments in the world of counter terrorism.

And finally, we needed to ensure that the mistakes of 9/11 did not recur here.

When I'm asked to lecture, I often talk about a report from the 9/11 Commission, which investigated that most fateful day in modern US history, and the failures that allowed it to happen. The 567-page report, which was 20 months in the making, said that there had been a lot of miscommunication and 'a failure of imagination' on the part of the CIA, the FBI, law enforcement and Congress. It really resonated with me, and I think a lot of cops could learn much from that stinging rebuke. Proactive crime-solving means thinking about what's possible, what your adversary is conjuring up, and what *you* can do to ensure they're not successful, and, most importantly, sharing information as required with other units or agencies.

I had a good relationship with AFP Commissioner Mick Keelty, and told him and my own team that if we were to avoid the mistakes of 9/11, we had to work together closely, maintaining a free flow of information, so nothing would slip through the cracks. There needed to be no bars between the two agencies.

When I arrived in Counter Terrorism, there was already a joint AFP and NSW Police team working on these issues, but its numbers and charter were very limited. I proposed we merge *all* our investigative staff with those of the AFP, so they would literally be working together on every investigation, using the same databases. Intelligence agencies could join them if required. We committed to not carrying out any counter terrorism investigations separate from that team, and the AFP also did so at that time.

It took a while to implement this change, and there was some scepticism within my own organisation, but in the end we made it happen, and it has been a success, with most other States following the model.

We also streamlined the operational areas that made up Special Tactics: the Bomb and Rescue Unit, Dog Unit, Tactical Operations Unit, Protection Operations Unit (dignitary and VIP protection) and the Intelligence Cell. These formed the State Protection Group. We brought together all arms of the organisation that were responsible for responding to all acts of violence, whether politically or religiously motivated or otherwise. We held regular retreats for the senior people from all units and we thought through ways of coordinating our efforts to achieve better results.

I was blessed with the senior team I had; we were humming. I represented NSW on the National Counter Terrorism Committee, Australia's peak policy body, and felt I was contributing on a national level, as well as mixing with counterparts on the international stage.

I felt that the State government of the day noticed and were pleased with what we'd achieved.

* * *

Late in 2006, I was having drinks at the Marble Bar at the Hilton Sydney with an old colleague Dan Ruming (affectionately known as 'Camel', he unfortunately died an untimely death two years ago), our journalist friend Steve

Barrett and others. Steve told us he had invited a colleague from *The Australian* called Natalie O'Brien, who had just moved back over from Perth. She was lovely, he said.

She joined us, and as she walked down the stairs, I remember thinking, *I know her!*

I realised I'd met her many years earlier. I'd been at the Shark Hotel in Sydney's Liverpool Street, where a group of journalists and police had been having drinks. Natalie and I didn't really talk but I certainly noticed her; she stood out to me, really gorgeous. She was with her husband, who very sadly later passed away from cancer.

Then I recalled a phone call on the tarmac in Dubai, on the way to my second stint in Iraq. It suddenly occurred to me that the call had been from the same Natalie O'Brien!

Seeing her again, I felt the same way as I had all those years ago in the Shark Hotel. She was tall and elegant, and had a presence that affects me to this day. We talked about the Middle East and I found out she had spent time there and knew a great deal more than the average Aussie. I felt I didn't need to explain things, she just seemed to get it; all the issues I was interested in, she was there already.

We met up a few times after that and got to know each other. The thing that struck me about her was that she really knew how to work a room. I now know I could leave her alone in a pub full of drunken cops and she'd be fine. We could go to a function with ambassadors and ministers, and she would hold her own. Natalie can have a conversation with anyone. I always say that she's much smarter than I am.

Yet commencing or maintaining a relationship was difficult. We had a sort of conflict of interests: Natalie was a senior journalist (Investigations Editor at *The Australian*), and as a high-ranking cop, I was in charge of things she was professionally concerned with.

I knew that there were those within NSW Police who had the ear of State Government ministers. I imagined them saying: *Kaldas is going out with a journalist. He's going to leak everything, he's a liability.*

For this reason, Natalie and I had to be secretive about the fact we had begun dating. This took a toll, and we ended up in a cycle of on-again, off-again.

* * *

Meanwhile, I was happy in my role at Counter Terrorism. I felt we were making great headway.

Towards the end of 2007, Terry Collins announced his retirement as the Deputy Commissioner. I decided not to apply for the position.

I was summoned to Terry's office and found him irate.

'What's this I hear about you not applying for my job?' he asked.

I said, 'I'm not going to, I'm happy doing what I'm doing and we're really kicking goals.'

As was his habit with people he genuinely cared about, he unleashed a tirade of abuse. Finally, he said: 'If *you* don't apply, how will you fare if so-and-so or so-and-so gets the job, and you have to work for *them*?'

It was a lightbulb moment. There were some people in the senior ranks I knew I would struggle to work for. I applied the day before the position closed and won the job.

This time there was no opposition, and I knew I had the support of the NSW police minister and the government.

I felt a sense of relief. After all those years, the whispers in corridors that could never be substantiated seemed to have come to an end. Put bluntly, the promotion of Terry Collins restored a process of fairness and transparency that had simply not existed before in relation to me. Moreover, the Egyptian and Arabic community and the migrant community more broadly organised a large function with hundreds of attendees to celebrate my promotion. They saw it as a breakthrough that a first-generation migrant, and an Arab at that, could rise to be a deputy commissioner in the biggest police force in Australia and New Zealand. I was humbled, happy and very proud indeed. I saw it as one for the good guys.

* * *

In November 2007 I commenced my role as Deputy Commissioner, Specialist Operations, which gave me command of just about everything in NSW police that wasn't administration or a police station. They included Counter Terrorism and Special Tactics; my former home, State Crime Command; the Special Services Group – water police, helicopters, covert operations and ancillary areas; the Forensic Services Group; the Police Prosecutions Branch; the Police Communications Branch (radio and IT); as well as Special Crime and Internal Affairs.

It was a huge span of control, but I made time to walk the floor of every one of the commands I had; the troops really appreciated it. I also relished the opportunity to be innovative.

I felt that Special Crime and Internal Affairs (SCIA) was one area in need of reform. But not long after I was promoted, the Federal Police made an appointment with me for a classified briefing. It was about Mark Standen, who was number two at the NSW Crime Commission and a co-leader within the SCIA framework. I learnt that the AFP had been investigating Standen for some time in relation to a major drug conspiracy, and it was clear he was involved in the importation of massive amounts of drugs through the Netherlands to Australia. He had a lot in his head: he knew about every drug crime that was being investigated in NSW through his role in the Crime Commission and he knew or could have access to information about every informant who had given up drug suppliers to the Crime Commission. It had been easy for him to manipulate the system. There were serious corruption allegations against him going right back to the 1970s, but that had not stopped his rise.

Obviously I was to keep the matter confidential, apart from briefing the Commissioner, Andrew Scipione. Their operation came to a head shortly thereafter. I was informed in advance that they were about to arrest Standen and a number of others.

I emphasised to the Commissioner how outdated, irrelevant and dysfunctional SCIA's structure had become, and how Standen's arrest demonstrated its disastrous lack of accountability. There were people who had been there for 10 to 15 years and hardly knew what basic police work was any more. Because they were working in Internal Affairs, many there felt the rules did not apply to them. They had not requalified for pistol shooting, first aid or any other mandatory training for years and they had climbed the ranks without doing any normal police work for decades. That closed-mindedness is what caused the problems, and it is often what happens with oversight bodies. People stay far too long and are exempt from normal accountability. That had to change and I was now in a position to change it.

There was some irony in all this. Thanks to the ongoing bugging saga, I'd been on SCIA's target list for a long while; now I was the deputy commissioner in charge. It was a surreal feeling to arrive in the SCIA office with my staff officer, and tell them I was the new boss and things were about to change.

I appointed a new commander and changed the name. We dropped the 'Special Crime' part of SCIA, which had simply been a way to compete with the crime squads without any of the accountability that went with major State Crime Command investigations, and changed 'Internal Affairs' to 'Professional Standards'.

The new commander advised me later that, having gone through all the SCIA standard operating procedures, he could not find the word 'fairness' anywhere. Modern, standard accountability mechanisms did not exist or were not enforced: firm terms of reference at the beginning of an investigation, declarations of conflicts of interest, regular reporting, post-operational assessments – none of that existed or was not checked or enforced. These had all been introduced into major crime investigations at State Crime Command by Clive Small. But there were almost no rules at SCIA. It was astounding.

We had to give every SCIA operative a tough choice: come back into the mainstream and follow the same rules as everyone else, or leave NSW Police.

Many people transferred to other departments but most could not cope in the real police world: after being in Internal Affairs for so long, they had little credibility among other police. Sadly, many left the force not long after leaving Internal Affairs.

It gave me no pleasure, because there were some good people at SCIA who didn't deserve to be discredited in that way. They'd been let down by the command and its leadership, and the leadership of the Police generally.

My own issues with Internal Affairs weren't over, but as Deputy Commissioner, I felt I was making great strides.

Then, out of the blue, one of the biggest cases from my past resurfaced – forcing me to step aside from my role and fight for my reputation and my very career.

CHAPTER 18

A Character Is Assassinated

2008

In early 2008, I was contacted by a producer from the ABC's current affairs program *Four Corners*. Almost seven years after Phuong Ngo had been locked up for the murder of John Newman, Ngo's supporters were mounting a campaign to challenge his conviction, and *Four Corners* were putting together a program that would investigate their claims.

Following on from Phuong Ngo's conviction and sentence, and his failure to be granted leave to appeal to the High Court in 2004, an activist group called 'Free Phuong' had been started. The group had some political clout: Meredith Burgmann, former president of the NSW Upper House, was a strong supporter of Ngo. Two academics from the Australian National University College of Law, Emeritus Professor Don Greig and Tasmanian academic Hugh Selby, also championed his case.

I actually thought the campaign was a bit of a joke. In my view, Ngo's supporters had no evidence and not a leg to stand on. There was an insinuation that the conviction had been some kind of Anglo-Saxon racist plot against a refugee. The irony was that I, the lead investigator, was an Egyptian refugee, and the prosecutor, Mark Tedeschi, was of Jewish-Italian stock. It worried me that *Four Corners* had apparently been gullible enough to buy the story being peddled.

The producers wanted to meet with the detectives of Task Force Gap. None of the other cops on the case wanted to talk to them, but I pointed out that we couldn't complain later on if we didn't give our side of the story.

We had one three-hour meeting with *Four Corners* and told them everything we knew.

* * *

On the night of Monday, 7 April 2008, *Four Corners* went to air with an episode called 'The Newman Case'. Central to the program's allegations was the story of our discovery of the murder weapon.

Four Corners had found a 'leading corrosions expert' who thought it 'surprising' how quickly the gun had been found in the river. He asserted that the gun was too rusted to have been in the river for four years (though following further research, he altered his opinion on this). He went on to make the serious allegation that the gun had been planted.

Let's just pause and think about that for a minute. Our investigation, Task Force Gap, had been able to prove that immediately after the murder, Ngo had been in the vicinity of the location where the gun had been found. We had matched the bullet casings found at the murder scene to that exact gun. The only way we could have been in possession of the murder weapon and framed Phuong Ngo with it would be if *we* had committed the murder ourselves.

It just didn't add up.

And what about the large number of people who had given evidence that Ngo had approached them to kill John Newman? All these people – most of whom didn't know each other – would have somehow had to conspire to all tell the same lie.

Then there were the sightings of vehicles near the crime scene by neighbours. There were several people who had given evidence of seeing cars matching the descriptions of Ngo's and his accomplices' cars in the lead-up to and at the time of the murder. Had all of *them* lied too?

Four Corners went on to question the mobile phone tracking evidence presented at the trials, and gave airtime to an alternative killer theory, with the help of one of Ngo's most passionate supporters, Marion Le.

Le was a migration agent. She had taken over as President of the Mekong Club after Ngo's arrest, and had held frequent press conferences saying Ngo was innocent.

On the program Le asserted that nearly four years after the murder, a man by the name of Albert Ranse had confessed to her that he was the murderer of John Newman, and that he had acted alone. *Four Corners* aired selective recordings of Albert Ranse's ramblings, secretly taped by Le while Ranse was drunk.

These and other matters had already been traversed thoroughly at Ngo's trial and completely debunked. The trial judge, Justice Wood, had even demanded that Le be investigated and charged for breaches of listening device legislation. We had put together a brief of evidence in relation to her actions and she was charged but acquitted on appeal.

The government had not granted Ngo an inquiry in 2004 after the failure of his appeal, despite the pressure and the associated media interest. However, on 29 May 2008, seven weeks after 'The Newman Case' went to air, James Spigelman, the Chief Justice of the NSW Supreme Court, received an application from Hugh Selby asking for a review of the case.

It was a mere 20 pages of speculation, but later, more comprehensive submissions were made. On the strength of them, Chief Justice Spigelman ordered an inquiry into the conviction. My legal representatives advised me that this was the only time in Australian history that a judge, not the government, had ordered such an inquiry. At that stage, they informed me, NSW was possibly the only State in Australia where a judge can order up a Royal Commission–style inquiry without any of the accountability that elected representatives had to face when making such an important decision.

I remember thinking: *When will this ever end?*

On 5 June, Chief Justice Spigelman appointed his inquirer: Justice David Patten, a retired and distinguished District Court judge. He would be given wide-ranging powers, similar to those of a royal commission.

I strongly felt that the inquiry was unnecessary, and had been granted under questionable circumstances. We were heading into the unknown.

* * *

Naturally, the Patten inquiry occupied the front pages of the newspapers. The attacks against the work of Task Force Gap became quite personal.

I've always taken the approach that criminal investigations and trials are a contact sport. There's more than a good chance that you're going to get attacked in court – a lot. People are going to call you names. People are going to question your motives and methods.

My view remains that I chose this life, nobody forced me to become a detective. So I took it on the chin. All of us in Task Force Gap did. We agreed that we were going to stick together – and hopefully the truth would come out.

We weren't the only ones who were incensed. While the Free Phuong campaigners celebrated, John Newman's loved ones were devastated, and angry. Newman's elderly mother, Helen Naumenko, was quoted in the press as saying: 'They could not let him go. No, no, no, no … They got the right man. Phuong Ngo had my son killed. They got the right man, they got the right man.'

* * *

There's a saying around the courts that the witness box is the loneliest place in the world.

During the Patten inquiry hearings, I was in the witness box for quite some time, as were my Task Force Gap colleagues. My former colleague Ian McNab, the detective who led the search of the river where the gun was found, probably had the worst time of it. There were six or seven QCs at the Bar table, only one of whom I could count on being friendly and that was my own barrister, Peter Bodor

KC. There were lawyers representing Crown Prosecutor Mark Tedeschi KC; lawyers representing the DPP; lawyers representing the NSW Police, the NSW Crime Commission and the NSW Government, and a whole team of lawyers representing Phuong Ngo.

One of the unexpected moments of the inquiry was when Bret Walker SC, the prominent and highly distinguished barrister who had represented Ngo at his first trial, was criticised by Ngo for inadequately defending him. I think it's the only time I've ever seen Walker give evidence himself. I don't think he enjoyed it.

* * *

In our line of work, our families put up with a lot. We're often late for important family events like birthdays, weddings and anniversaries – or we miss them altogether. We frequently put ourselves in physical danger.

Sure, there are times when our loved ones get cranky with us, but for the most part they are forgiving and they understand these things are part of the job. But during the Patten inquiry, the media coverage was brutal. The very public tarnishing of the force's name and reputation – I don't think any cop sees this sort of thing coming. It lands on you, and your family, like a grand piano.

Those in Phuong Ngo's corner made it personal; they made it about me and the team, and the media bought it. That was what made it worse for my family. Ngo's supporters often weren't calling out the rest of the investigating team; it was all about Nick Kaldas.

I was accused of many things: at best, I was incompetent; at worst, I was corrupt. The *Sydney Morning Herald* ran an article about the *Four Corners* story, in which journalist Paul Sheehan wrote that the 'program questioned whether the conviction of Phuong Ngo had been a miscarriage of justice, based in part on sloppy conduct by Kaldas'.

It took a toll on everyone around me. My kids were teenagers by this point – Simone 16, Laura 13 and Luke 12. I didn't shield them from it, but neither did I go out of my way to tell them I was going through a tough time.

I could talk to my brother and sister and their spouses about it, and they could understand what was going on, but my mum struggled with it all.

All my mother's friends rang her and said, 'Nick's in trouble, your son's in trouble. He's going to jail! What are you going to do?'

She would ring me up asking: 'What's happened? Are you going to be okay?'

* * *

In the end, the inquiry went on for about nine months. I can only imagine how much it all cost.

On 17 April 2009, Chief Justice Spigelman released Justice Patten's 211-page report. After sitting through 39 days of hearings, hearing the evidence of countless witnesses and reading a significant number of statements and reports, Justice Patten was convinced that what he'd heard and seen 'actually increased rather than diminished' the case against Phuong Ngo.

Of those who supported Ngo, Patten had this to say:

Regrettably the strength of the evidence available against Mr Ngo was virtually ignored by his supporters in their submissions to the Inquiry. Unsupported allegations of gross impropriety were substituted for analysis of the facts. While Mr Selby's submission to the Chief Justice, on its face, raised matters calling for investigation, they lost all significance, in my opinion, when scrutinized at an open hearing and in the light of cross-examination and submissions by senior and experienced counsel.

Justice Patten also felt the need to address the *Four Corners* program's unfounded accusations about me and the rest of Task Force Gap:

Mr Bodor [my barrister] ... contended that there was 'not one scintilla of evidence [which] points to any wrongdoing or improper activity by Mr Kaldas'. I agree ... there is no evidence that the investigation of Mr Newman's murder was conducted otherwise than professionally and competently.

In November 2008, before the inquiry had completed its findings, *Four Corners* had won a Walkley Award for 'excellence in journalism' for 'The Newman Case'. I thought it was ludicrous, and I wasn't alone in this thinking. After Justice Patten's report was published, John Hatzistergos, the NSW (State) Attorney General, commented: 'You give people Walkley Awards for this sort of garbage? What that program did ... was seriously tarnish confidence in the judicial process, [and] attack the credibility of some very fine prosecutors and police officers with what I believe were baseless means of pursuing such allegations.'

I'm all for investigative journalists who bring to light miscarriages of justice, but the work of *Four Corners* in this case was not, in my view, subject to the checks and balances that Task Force Gap's was. They hadn't gone through the rigorous processes that our team had gone through.

Even the ABC's own *Media Watch* program couldn't support its colleagues. In an analysis of 'The Newman Case' in May 2009, host Jonathan Holmes observed that 'at the heart of investigative programs like this one are the innumerable decisions about what to leave in, and what to leave out – decisions that have to strive for fairness. I don't pretend they're easy. But I have to say, in the instances we've singled out, that in my opinion *Four Corners*' judgments don't stack up.'

Four Corners have not apologised – nor did they give the Walkley back.

* * *

I'll never forget how delighted I felt when the team called to tell me the news about Justice Patten's report immediately after it was released. But by then, I was working on the other side of the world, on *another* politician's murder.

CHAPTER 19

'They've Killed a Lot of People, Nick'

2008–2009

In late 2008, in the middle of the Patten Inquiry, I'd received a call. 'Nick, you were born for this job, you've got to go for it,' said Nick Cowdery, the NSW Director of Public Prosecutions, over the phone. 'You've got exactly what they need, and I've told them all about you.'

It turned out to be a phone call that would change my life and take me nearly halfway around the world, then a little bit further.

* * *

On 14 February 2005, a parked open-top Mitsubishi Canter truck packed with explosives had been detonated outside a Beirut landmark, the 1930s St Georges Hotel. The car bomb had ripped through the motorcade of former Lebanese prime minister Rafic Hariri on Beirut's famous Corniche, killing him and 22 others and wounding more than 220.

All hell broke loose. On 8 March, between 150,000 and 200,000 anti-Hariri protesters marched through the streets of Beirut, in support of the main suspects, Hezbollah. They became known as the March 8 Alliance.

On 14 March, those who were upset about Hariri's assassination marched in response, demonstrating against Hezbollah and the Syrian and Iranian influence. It is estimated that more than a million people marched, and they continued to do so for many days. They became known as the March 14 Alliance.

The country was polarised.

The Lebanese Government needed help. The UN International Independent Investigation Commission (UNIIIC) was established on 7 April 2005 to assist them in investigating the murder of Hariri.

Eventually it became clear that conducting the investigation in Lebanon was not going to work: everyone involved was at grave risk. The Lebanese Government completely handed over jurisdiction to the UN, and, four years later, on 1 March 2009, the Special Tribunal for Lebanon (STL) was born out of a United Nations Security Council Resolution. For a number of reasons I'll get into later, the investigation moved from Lebanon to The Hague in the Netherlands, the international city of justice. But a chief of investigations was needed.

Nick Cowdery was very active in his role as NSW DPP, and regularly took part in international prosecutors' conferences. At one of these, he caught up with his Canadian counterpart, Daniel Bellemare, who had just been appointed the prosecutor of the STL. Bellemare told him he was looking for someone with three things: homicide experience, familiarity with

Arabic language and culture, and a proven ability to serve under difficult circumstances in the Middle East.

As Nick observed, I was born for the job. And I was instantly attracted to the ethos behind it. The UN Security Council had called the STL a 'tribunal of an international character based on the highest international standards of criminal justice'. It was hoped that its work would not just be an attempt to hold Lebanese assassins to account, but also a new beginning for justice in the Middle East.

I applied and won the appointment. I sought a leave of absence from NSW Police, which was granted, and in early January 2009, off I went.

* * *

One of the reasons I'd decided to take the job was Natalie.

Things had still been a bit erratic between us. I felt we needed to get away from the environment that was causing us to falter if we were to make a go of it – and I had decided I really wanted to. I could see that the best way to distance ourselves from all of it was to get out of the country – get away from everything.

Before I left for Beirut, I said to her: 'I've made my mind up. You're it. I want to marry you and spend the rest of my life with you.'

She accepted my proposal!

We agreed that I would go to Lebanon for a couple of months and then relocate to the Netherlands, where Natalie would meet me.

I left Australia feeling a mix of trepidation and excitement. I was about to take on one of the most complex murder investigations of my career, one that would have historic international implications, but at the same time I couldn't wait for Natalie and me to start our new life together.

* * *

Of all the nations in the Middle East, and the world for that matter, Lebanon has to be one of the most complex. I'd thought Iraq was complicated, with its mix of Kurds, Sunnis and Shi'ites, but in Lebanon the religious landscape is even more byzantine, with 17 different sects, and a convoluted history of who has been in bed with whom.

I would argue that it's difficult to be a functioning democracy if you have more than one military and judicial power. And the militant group Hezbollah – formed with assistance from Iran to fight Israel's 1982 invasion of Lebanon – soon grew to resemble a proxy Lebanese government. They had their own militia, ran their own jails and courts in the south of the country, and had significant control over the airport and the ports. They even had a satellite TV station. A lot of the security and police positions were held by Hezbollah sympathisers, and Hezbollah members occupied seats in the Lebanese Parliament and the cabinet. Incrementally, they took over more and more of the apparatus of the State. They called themselves 'The Resistance' and claimed to be standing up against Israel. Maybe they were, but that wasn't their main aim any more. And Hezbollah's stranglehold on Lebanon was impeding the proper running of the country.

Iran and Syria and their proxy in Lebanon, Hezbollah, were united by their religious beliefs, and acted as one. Iran, of course, was the godfather of Shi'ites, in the region and globally. The members of the Assad regime in Syria were all Alawites, a sect which is Shi'ite in origin and compatible with the broader Shi'ite movement. These three entities never betrayed each other's interests. Being part of this triumvirate made Hezbollah an even more powerful force.

In the middle of this, Rafic Hariri decided that something had to be done. As a young man in the late 1960s, he'd gone to Saudi Arabia, got into the building game, become a billionaire and come back with a vision to help his country. Civil war had broken out in Lebanon between 1975 and 1990; thousands died and over a million were displaced. Hariri did a lot of rebuilding and eventually went into politics, serving two terms as prime minister – 1992 to 1998 and 2000 to 2004. He believed that there were a lot of things in Lebanon that needed fixing – and first on the list was Hezbollah.

In 2004, during his second term as prime minister, Hariri – a Sunni Muslim himself – worked to unite the Sunnis, the Christians, the Druze and others against Hezbollah. He looked like he was going to get his way. He was going to have a majority and he was going to take the country in a better direction.

Later that year, Resolution 1559 was passed by the UN Security Council, calling for non-government militaries to stand down and disarm. That was a huge deal for Hezbollah, as it effectively meant they were being asked to disband, which they deeply resented – and they blamed Hariri. Even more significantly, the resolution forced Syria to withdraw all forces from their occupied areas of northern Lebanon. It was a very big hit for the Syrian regime.

Gearing up for his third run at office, Hariri also found himself in strong disagreement with Syrian President Bashar al-

Assad. The Syrians had invaded the northern part of Lebanon during the civil war under the pretext of stopping bloodshed but had remained there illegally for some years, exerting a malign influence on Lebanese politics in favour of the Syrians and their allies. The Syrians wanted the President of Lebanon, Émile Lahoud, to have his term extended because he was seen as friendly to them and to Hezbollah. Hariri wasn't bending.

Hariri was 'summoned' to a meeting with President Assad in the Syrian capital, Damascus. Afterwards, it was a two-and-a-half-hour drive across the desert and mountains from Damascus back to Beirut. Hariri had a medical condition that meant if he became upset he would bleed from the nose. The reports from his staff were that on the way home he was bleeding profusely, such had been the volatile nature of the meeting.

This meeting is believed to have been the occasion when Hariri signed his own death warrant. Some months after that fateful day, he was assassinated.

Hariri certainly had his critics, and many allegations were made against him, but ultimately, from the information we gathered, he was killed by those who simply did not want him to achieve the aim to which the majority of Lebanese aspired: disarming Hezbollah and curtailing their activities, and expelling Syria from Lebanese land.

I'm not sure whether the Shi'ite-aligned powers, and the Syrian regime in particular, had realised how strong and widespread the condemnation of Hariri's murder would be. Within a few months, Syria were forced to withdraw all their forces from Lebanese territory due to the international pressure, and Hezbollah stood accused, in the eyes of the world, of the heinous murder of innocents.

But *proving* Hezbollah had been involved was an entirely different thing.

* * *

Almost 20 other murders or attempted murders had happened over the four or five years preceding Hariri's death, and tellingly, none of the victims had been Shi'ite.

Three years after the assassination, events took another deadly turn. Wissam Eid was a 31-year-old senior intelligence official within the Internal Security Forces of Lebanon. He had a senior role in the investigation into the murder of Hariri. He had done pioneering work in communications analysis to see who had been in the area at the time of Hariri's assassination. He was threatened and told to stop investigating. He did not.

On the sunny winter's morning of 25 January 2008, 50 kilograms of explosive wreaked havoc in a car bomb attack. Eid, a bodyguard and two civilians were killed and dozens of bystanders injured. It sent a clear message to anyone who was helping the investigation.

Eid would have been one of my deputies. When he was murdered, it became obvious that intelligence staff, witnesses and everyone involved in the investigation was in danger. The danger was not only real but pressing. In 2007, the Lebanese Government passed an Act of Parliament ceding jurisdiction over the investigation to the UN. This was accompanied by a UN Security Council Resolution to establish a court to deal with the matter, the STL. Due to the murder of Wissam Eid and other threats, the UN decided it was no longer safe to establish the tribunal in Lebanon. It was decided it would be based in The Hague, in a large, comfortable building donated by the Dutch Government. It's important to note how historic this was. This was the first tribunal to deal with terrorism as a distinct crime, and to seek arrest, trial and conviction for that crime.

* * *

Even though the tribunal wouldn't be fired up properly until 1 March, the UN wanted me to come to Lebanon two months early to meet with the departing UNIIIC staff, debrief them, help select the new staff, and supervise the moving of exhibits, documents and people from Beirut to The Hague.

Not everyone wished me a bon voyage. Before I left, and before Justice Patten had completed his inquiry, someone in Sydney leaked material to Hezbollah about the Patten inquiry, arguing that I was corrupt, that I was under a cloud and that they mustn't let me take up this role in Lebanon. I was front-page news in a pro-Hezbollah Lebanese newspaper called *Al-Akhbar*, 'The News'. Predictably for Hezbollah, I was accused of having worked for the CIA in Iraq and of being a Zionist sympathiser. The UN considered all the evidence, and I submitted a report to them putting my side of the story. The appointment stood.

Sometime later, after we were established as a tribunal, the journalist who wrote the story maligning me, and who had remained a strong critic of the STL, visited The Hague and met with the STL's media people. I asked to meet with him. We had a cordial discussion, and he admitted that he had it wrong and that I had been completely cleared. I would almost say we hit it off.

When I landed in Beirut, a protection team and my predecessor were waiting for me at the airport. This was just the second time I'd been back to Beirut since our family had fled from Egypt; I'd visited once during my time in Iraq. I tried to recall what the city had been like in 1969, and where we'd stayed, but I could not. The 15-year civil war was also a distant memory; Beirut was now full of bustling shops and restaurants, and teeming with life.

We climbed up into the mountains to the Monteverde Hotel, which served as both the office and home for all UNIIIC staff. My first task would be to gather everyone and everything together. There was a lot needing to be shipped to the Netherlands: containers filled with all the mangled bits of cars that had been blown up; evidence from all the crime scenes, including forensic material – even bits of a suicide bomber – all kept in temperature-controlled environments; and a mountain of files.

Fortunately there were a lot of really good people at the UNIIIC who had done a great deal of the work already. Some people had to be moved on for various reasons, and a lot more positions had to be created and advertised and interviews held.

* * *

Within a few weeks of my arrival I was contacted by two successful Lebanese–Australian businessman whom I knew from Sydney. They were in Beirut and they wanted to catch up and take me out to dinner. We arranged to eat in the busy Place de l'Étoile.

During the meal I could tell they were anxious. Finally, one of them said as politely as he could, 'Nick, we're here to give you a message: you need to be really careful. You shouldn't do what we think you're going to do. It'll be terrible for you and those who work for you.'

'Thank you for looking out for me,' I replied, 'but I'm going to do what I need to do.'

'We don't want anything to happen to you,' they repeated.

'It won't.'

'They've killed a lot of people, Nick.' Of course they meant Hezbollah.

I'm sure they felt they were being my friends. They cared about me. But it didn't dissuade me one iota. I was always going to call it as I saw it. This investigation was always going to be based on evidence, not politics.

I was certainly under no illusion as to what Hezbollah were capable of. There was evidence that Hariri had been on very good terms with the head of Hezbollah, Hassan Nasrallah (who was killed by an Israel air raid in 2024). Nasrallah allegedly guaranteed his safety every time Hariri went to see him. If Hezbollah were in some way involved in the assassination – and it was an 'if' for me at that point – then it seemed Nasrallah's guarantee only extended to their meetings. That's Lebanon.

I also had quite a large protection team throughout my stay: six to eight people. When I later returned to Beirut, following the move to the Hague, the protection team expanded: I had Lebanese Army armoured personnel carriers with turret-mounted guns at the front and back of my convoy, as well as a core protection team close to me. But to be honest, I felt this was overkill. It's my view that Hezbollah are methodical, and look at killing through the prism of a cost–benefit analysis. I was a senior UN official; I'm sure they thought the outcry from my assassination would have far outweighed any benefit to them.

I'd long since learned that I could operate at a high level without being obsessed by the possibility of dying. It was my dad who taught me that if you let the fear master you, you're not going to get the job done. And it seemed to me that Hezbollah and their leadership were simply bullies. I was against bullies. And I wasn't going to bend.

* * *

We established a field office in Beirut with a very small number of staff and a lot of security around them, and the rest of us prepared to move. The UNIIIC ceased to exist and the STL was born. We all ended our contracts of employment with UNIIIC and I came back to Australia for a week or so, to sort out personal logistics and close up my home.

And with that, I headed to The Hague.

CHAPTER 20

Cold, Hard Evidence

2009–2010

When I arrived in The Hague at the start of March 2009, it was freezing. I think that was because of the biting winds that blow in off the North Sea. Even so, I couldn't get over how beautiful the city was: the cobblestone streets, the medieval architecture. I loved it, especially the big square in the middle of town called the Plein, with grand buildings on each side and people sitting outside them drinking coffee.

I made a decision to live in the middle of the city and got an apartment just off the Plein, never wanting to be too far away from good coffee.

Natalie didn't join me for a little while. It took her a few months to tidy up her affairs. She couldn't get time off from her job at NewsCorp, so she resigned. Then she followed me to The Hague, where our work was in full swing.

* * *

We were designing the STL Investigation Division as we went along. We'd tried to bed down as many positions as we could while we were in Beirut, but some were not clear, or we simply ran out of time, so we had to finish the recruitment process after we moved to The Hague. All up we had about 150 staff: investigators, analysts, forensic staff, administrators, record keepers and so on.

We had to be careful who we hired. There were next to no Americans in the team, simply because they would have been accused of being biased. As long-time allies of Israel, the US are held in deep suspicion by all the Arab States in the Middle East.

It didn't end there. In any UN organisation you set up, you cannot normally have the number one, two and three positions filled from the same country; the roles have to be geographically dispersed. That meant I could not get an Aussie as my number two or three.

I wanted someone as my second-in-command who operated on the same wavelength. My search took me to London, where I knew a lot of the senior police, including the Metropolitan Police Commissioner, Sir Paul Stephenson. He had around 45,000 staff at his disposal, the biggest English-speaking police force in the world.

I'd been aiming for a particular officer, who had declined my offer but told me his own offsider was about to retire and was looking for something meaningful and exciting to do. I said, '*I've* got something for him that's meaningful and exciting – he won't know what hit him!'

I didn't know Mick Taylor, the offsider in question, but his reputation preceded him: he had worked as one of the senior investigators on the 2005 London bombings, among many other cases. He and I had a couple of lunches together and I felt comfortable with him. We thought the same way about many issues, the Australian and English police being very similar in their structured and strategic ways. I talked Mick into applying for the position. (I'm not sure he'd thank me for that today.)

We still advertised the job, and Mick stood out from the crowd. I was very happy to bring him on board as my investigative deputy. If I was out of town, he would fill in for me, attending meetings with my authority and speaking on my behalf. He was credible, incredibly hard-working and loyal, and he fitted in very well. Just a terrific guy.

* * *

In any UN tribunal or investigation, there are a number of agendas at play. We had to be alert to the fact that there were those who wanted us to succeed and many who wanted us to fail – not necessarily for bad reasons: a lot of them thought we would start another civil war in Lebanon if we accused Hezbollah of carrying out the murders.

So many experts in the history and politics of the region told us we weren't going to get anywhere. Since the start of the civil war, no one had succeeded in indicting anyone for a political assassination in Lebanon. But that kind of thinking just spurred us on.

* * *

Soon after the STL got going, I'd realised we would need to shift the entire approach of UNIIC's investigation.

In any major investigation, and certainly a murder investigation, you start with your basic building blocks – the crime scene, forensic evidence, initial witnesses, statements, a canvass of the area, photographic exhibits. You put all that together and it gives you a rough picture of what actually happened. Later, you move on to victimology, learning as much as you can about the victim – who hates them, who loves them, what their last movements were, and so on. This is really important in any murder investigation, as we'd shown in the Newman case.

What had happened, in my view, was that the UN investigation, while assisting the Lebanese authorities, had raced towards the geopolitical angle: who was politically opposed to Hariri. That direction was simply not going to solve it. They had moved straight to motive without actually doing enough of the groundwork.

I told my team that we'd get to the geopolitical later. We would in time meet people in Washington, London and Paris and have those discussions, but they weren't what was going to solve it for us. We needed cold, hard evidence admissible in a courtroom before we could actually lay charges.

* * *

Typical of the misinformed lines of inquiry pursued by my predecessors at UNIIIC was the arrest of four senior generals not long after Hariri's assassination, who were accused of being complicit in the murder. The generals had now remained in custody for almost four years. The issue had become quite controversial and caused a lot of divisiveness in Lebanon. It was continually making front-page news. Some of those who were pro-Hariri and anti-Hezbollah were convinced that these four generals should be hanged, drawn and quartered – and they wouldn't hear of anything else. So, one of the first things I was asked to do when I got to The Hague was to carry out a comprehensive review of the case against them.

Muhammad Zuhair al-Siddiq, a lowly soldier in the Syrian Army, claimed to have been in a car with the four generals when they carried out a reconnaissance tour of the site of the Hariri assassination as part of their planning and plotting. There was another low-ranking Syrian soldier named Husam Taher Husam, who made the same allegations. He later retracted his statements on Syrian television and disappeared. But there were so many problems with al-Siddiq's version of events that it couldn't possibly have happened.

We could not accept that al-Siddiq had ever met the generals, for a start. Each of those four generals had a protection team that would have been bigger than a US president's. The idea of the four of them in a little car, driving around the suburbs of Beirut with a rank-and-file soldier from Syria: it just did not make any sense. It was also concerning that investigators accepted such a version of events.

Yet the Lebanese authorities arrested these men. I don't doubt that there is a possibility that one or more of the four knew more than they were letting on, because they were very senior and had enormous intelligence resources throughout the country, but the bottom line was that we did not have any evidence that incriminated them beyond doubt.

We tracked down al-Siddiq, who by then was in the United Arab Emirates. I took a team across with me, including a polygraph (lie-detector test) operator from the Belgian Police. Polygraphs would not be considered evidentiary at the tribunal, but I didn't want to leave any stone unturned. I wanted to offer al-Siddiq the opportunity to take the test, even if for no other reason than to see how he reacted to the idea.

He immediately agreed to be interviewed. He came in with a lawyer and, in a moment of bizarre comedy, sported the most ridiculous hairpiece I've ever seen: he had what looked like a raccoon sitting on top of his head.

We audio- and video-recorded everything from the minute we met al-Siddiq, so that there could be no he-said-she-said debate later on. We had strong doubts about him, but we needed to explore every possible avenue of investigation.

Over two days of interviews, we asked a lot of questions and he didn't have any answers. Then we offered him the opportunity to take the lie-detector test.

'I'll take your lie-detector test, I've got nothing to fear!' he proclaimed.

Then his lawyer interrupted. 'I need a word with my client.'

They left then returned a few seconds later, and al-Siddiq said he wasn't going to do it. The conclusion we reached was that everything he'd said was rubbish.

* * *

Next we spoke to the generals themselves. A colleague and I interviewed the most vocal of the four, Major-General Jamil al-Sayyed, the former head of the Lebanese General Directorate of Security, and a Shi'ite.

General al-Sayyed was a short, stocky, very urbane man in his fifties. We interviewed him twice in Roumieh Prison, for about four to five hours each time. Roumieh is 15 kilometres outside Beirut and is often described as overcrowded and holding many notorious offenders, including Al-Qaeda members and other terrorism suspects. Tough school. Al-Sayyed had his own cell, which he insisted on showing me. It was reasonably comfortable, but nothing flash.

When we started talking, he was calm and rational. He'd drawn all sorts of charts for us in an effort to prove that he couldn't possibly have been involved. As he spoke, he got more and more animated. In the end he broke down crying.

'This isn't right,' he exclaimed. 'What's happening to me is not right!'

I told him to take a deep breath and have a break for five minutes. Before we left, he told me that I was his last hope of getting out.

* * *

Eventually we pulled it all together. I finished the review and wrote a report – very thoroughly, I hope – that said the evidence was simply not there, and all four generals should be freed forthwith.

Jamil al-Sayyed and the others were released shortly thereafter. Al-Sayyed sued many people, almost anyone involved in his case, but he has never criticised or attempted to sue *me*.

All those who were pro-West were very upset, seeing the release of the generals as a betrayal. There was a fair bit of bad press for a few weeks afterwards.

The huge and powerful Hariri clan were also unhappy. But Hariri's son Saad, who, like his father, would go on to serve two terms as prime minister, was very supportive of the tribunal and of me personally. He told the media: 'We want the truth, we want justice, and all these victims must be justified.'

* * *

Some in Lebanon had thought the arrest of the four generals was going to lead to bigger and better things, but it had now proven to be a dead end. Our team were heading in a different direction. Our sights were fixed on Hezbollah, because all the evidence pointed in their direction.

The events of that fateful day in February 2005 had played out as follows.

Just before 1 pm on the day in question, Rafic Hariri had left the Lebanese Parliament Building and walked to the Café de l'Étoile on the Place de l'Étoile, where he had coffee with some constituents.

After about 20 minutes, he headed towards his home in his six-car convoy via a secret route decided at the last minute. His convoy had the same security plan and the same level of vehicular armour as that of a US president – the only difference being that he liked to drive his car himself.

Five minutes later, as the convoy approached the St Georges Hotel on the Corniche, it encountered a slow-travelling, white Mitsubishi Canter flatbed truck, packed with explosives covered by a tarpaulin. The explosives were detonated, killing Hariri, eight members of his party and 13 bystanders, and leaving a 9-metre-wide crater in their wake. In all, 23 people were killed. Around 220 people, passing in the street or working nearby, were injured, some sustaining terrible wounds. Several nearby buildings were severely damaged, and others had their windows blown out, such was the force of the explosion. Both the historic St Georges Hotel and the building across the road were shattered, hollowed out, and at the time of writing had still not been rebuilt.

We started on the forensic and ballistic evidence, including all the available details from the crime scene. Astonishingly, it had been swept clean within 48 hours. There had been no thorough, extended combing of the scene and surrounds. I still struggle to understand how they justified that. I don't know whether it was incompetence, or a malicious and malevolent act, but it set the investigation back significantly.

We had received information that a member of parliament had signalled to Hezbollah when Hariri was leaving the Parliament Building and indicated the direction he was heading in. We knew the assassins had used nearly 3000 kilograms of military-grade explosives and that the device had been detonated by a suicide bomber sitting inside the vehicle. Hariri had a jamming device in the back of his car, which would have blocked any remote detonation. We knew it had been functioning.

We also discovered that the Mitsubishi Canter had been stolen in Japan, so it was a right-hand drive. It was smuggled to the United Arab Emirates and sold legitimately to a dealer in Tripoli in the north of Lebanon, a very strongly Sunni area. Whoever was behind the killing bought the car in Tripoli. They also bought mobile phones there, which they used to coordinate the murder. They bought the SIM cards in Tripoli as well, and for a few months they intermittently went back there and reactivated the phones to make it look as though the attack had been carried out by someone from that part of northern Lebanon.

All of this was done to throw us off the scent and try to lay the blame at the feet of the Sunnis.

Soon after the blast, a martyrdom video and letter were delivered to two news outlets, Al Jazeera and Reuters. The video was a suicide note from a 22-year-old man called Ahmad Abu Adass, a Sunni Palestinian youth living with his parents in Beirut. In the video, he said he represented a previously unheard-of group who had sworn to 'inflict just punishment' on Hariri. This didn't make any sense, because Hariri had been a follower and staunch defender of Sunni Islam.

It turned out that the group claiming responsibility didn't exist. Adass's family informed us that he had been attending a nearby mosque, where he had been befriended by a man named Mohammed, whom the family never met. Mohammed picked Adass up on the morning of Sunday 16 January 2005, nearly a month before the bombing, and Adass was never seen again.

It was clear that whoever had orchestrated the martyrdom video had done everything they could to frame the killing of Hariri as a Sunni Muslim plot. Adass was just a youth, without the means, ability or expertise to mount such a sophisticated attack. He had never even driven a car. He was simply a pawn, used then almost certainly killed. It was a brutal plot.

We were able to acquire Adass's DNA from his toothbrush, among other things. We also had DNA evidence retrieved from the suicide vehicle and the crime scene. The two sets of DNA didn't match. Adass was definitely not the suicide bomber. He was a patsy.

There were still bits of the bomber being found two or three years after the murder, on building-site cranes and in other places. We had a good portion of his nose. We also had hair follicles.

One of the leading agencies specialising in hair follicle examination was the AFP laboratory in Canberra. Someone had to take the exhibit to the AFP in Australia, and I was the logical choice. I had the exhibit expertly packed in a small Esky with dry ice, hopped on a plane and took a short trip home to see the family.

We also brought together a group of experts in isotope analysis, which can show where a person spent time in the months before their death, what they were eating, and literally what air they were breathing.

The results of both these sets of analysis led us to believe that the suicide bomber had spent time in a conflict zone, as he had a significant amount of lead in his system. We formed the view that he was from the Horn of Africa – perhaps Somalia or Ethiopia – or possibly just across the Gulf of Aden in Yemen.

This was helpful in a number of ways. First, it was yet more proof that Adass was not the suicide bomber. Second, we hoped it might prompt someone to come forward with the more specific information about the real identity of the bomber. Third, it would allow us to make inquiries in that particular region that could enable us to identify him and answer a host of other questions like how he got to Lebanon and who else was involved in the assassination.

I'm not going to tell you it was a success – it was a very long shot – but we had to try.

* * *

Victimology was another important line of inquiry we took to build our case. But whatever paths our investigation took – and there were many – the persistent allegation from all corners was that Hezbollah were responsible.

In any investigation into an organised crime group – and I would argue that Hezbollah falls into that category – there are a number of things you should do. You study their background, their structure, their aims and objectives, how they operate. It's important to look at what they've done in the past, and whether there are any disgruntled former members who could turn and tell you everything you need to know.

The last question was easy to answer. There are no former members of Hezbollah: they're either still there, or they're dead, because no one ever leaves the organisation alive. In Hezbollah, everyone is married to someone else's sister. If you left, you would lose your whole family. It's one of their control mechanisms, and when it comes to control, they are truly ruthless.

Since we weren't going to be able to learn anything from former members, we had a small team look at similar incidents from the past that we thought Hezbollah might have had a hand in.

There were quite a few.

In 1992, Hezbollah had played a significant role in the murder of four men in the Mykonos Greek restaurant in Berlin – three members of the Kurdistan Democratic Party of Iran, who were agitating for Kurdish rights in Iran, and their translator. The four had been due to meet with a former Swedish prime minister, who had pulled out of the meeting at the last minute due to a crisis at home. It's likely he would have also been killed if he had been there.

Two men were convicted of the murder: a Lebanese national and alleged experienced Hezbollah operative, and an Iranian intelligence operative. Three others were complicit but were safely in Iran. The former president of Iran, Abolhassan Banisadr, gave evidence at trial that the order to kill had come directly from the Iranian Supreme Leader, Ayatollah Ali Khamenei, and the Iranian President, Akbar Rafsanjani. Ultimately, convictions were obtained in three of the four cases, and warrants issued for the outstanding co-conspirators. The interoperability of Iran and Hezbollah in carrying out the murder was clear. It highlighted the fact that we were not just up against a group with terrorist intent, but possibly up against governments as well.

We looked at a second pair of incidents in Buenos Aires, Argentina. In 1992, a bomb targeting the Israeli Embassy resulted in the death of 29 people. Then in 1994, a second bomb targeting a Jewish community centre was responsible for the death of 85 people, injuring over 300. The prosecutors, led by Alberto Nisman, formally accused the government of Iran of directing the bombing and Hezbollah of carrying it out. That was the hypothesis for the prosecution case. Again, there was evidence of Iran and Hezbollah operating in unison.

There were many twists and turns in the ensuing investigation, and at one stage two former presidents of Argentina (Cristina Fernández de Kirchner and Carlos Menem) were accused of attempting to derail the investigation. Nisman was a tenacious investigative prosecutor and fearless in pursuing his case with an unwavering determination. Thirty years after the attacks, in April 2024, the federal court in Argentina ruled that the attacks were ordered by Iran and carried out by Hezbollah.

Hezbollah was also involved in the 1996 Khobar Towers bombing in Saudi Arabia that killed 19 US Air Force personnel.

We organised to meet with the two prosecutors of both the 1992 Berlin attack and the two attacks in Argentina, one of whom was Albert Nisman. Both prosecutors were very helpful in painting the picture of what they were up against: a well-coordinated, highly effective organisation that was ruthless against its enemies and had a very sophisticated modus operandi. Their tradecraft was second to none.

In early 2015, just a few years after our meeting, Nisman died in suspicious circumstances. To summarise a long and complicated matter: after a ten-year investigation, Nisman was due to testify before the Argentine Congress and present his evidence that Iran was behind the bombings. He had actually identified the Iranian leaders who had ordered the bombings, and was likely to testify that the Argentine Government had covered it up. Hours before he was due to give evidence, he was reportedly found dead with one bullet wound to the head and a .22 calibre pistol on the floor next to him in an apparent suicide. The door to his apartment was locked from the inside – however, a number of things just didn't add up. For example, why, after a ten-year investigation, would he take his life now? There was also no suicide note found and no gun powder residue on his hands.

The matter remains unresolved, but having met the man, and having spent a week or so with him, it is very difficult for me to accept that a person as passionate, ethical and motivated as him would choose to be silenced just before his years of work were to be recognised by parliament and the world. Describing the matter as unresolved simply does not do it justice.

All of this research helped us paint a picture of Hezbollah's methodology. What was patently clear was that we were up against not just Hezbollah but the might of all the Shi'ite-affiliated powers in the Middle East.

* * *

Our big break came when we cracked the phone analysis. The investigations started by Wissam Eid became central. There were only two phone companies in Lebanon, and Eid and his team had got hold of every phone record for a period of six months. They had begun to work out how to identify which phones were active in the vicinity at the time of the murder.

After Eid's death, we took this communications analysis to a whole new level. We had millions of call charge records: so much data that we had to invent a whole new system to make sense of it.

Eventually, we identified four different groups of phone numbers – which we respectively called the blue, yellow, green and red networks – that had operated together and spoken exclusively to each other. The red phones became known as the 'murder phones', as they had been used solely by the Hariri assassination team. After Hariri's murder, they had been shredded, but the assassins had left a trail of phone records in their wake that proved the murder phones had been in the vicinity at the time of the murder, and that the killers had done a 'dry run' a few days before the actual event. The five phones had all been involved in coordinating on the day of the murder. They were all linked due to those five phones moving in sync with the five suspects' normal phones for some months. In effect, we aimed to show that the murder phones had in fact moved closely with the suspects' real phones over a period of time.

* * *

But we still had to be able to demonstrate to the court and the judges in graphic detail what had taken place and who had been where on that day.

So in June 2009 I used my connections to set up a meeting with the FBI in Washington, DC. I travelled there with my head of intelligence, a former Canadian military officer, and my head of forensics, a former senior French gendarme, who both remain dear friends. We then visited the laboratories at the FBI Academy in Quantico to discuss the creation of a detailed 3D mock-up of the bomb site. They produced models of the scene before *and* after the explosion that helped us greatly.

If an explosion is conducted in an open space, its impact dissipates and the detritus goes in every direction. Conversely, if there is a hard structure around the site, the explosion will be contained and reverberate, causing worse carnage. Chances were nothing in that zone would survive.

Using the 3D models created for the tribunal by the FBI, we were able to demonstrate that was what had happened in the case of the Hariri bombing. The explosion detonated between two very solid structures, the St Georges Hotel and another big building on the other side of the road. Rafic Hariri had had no chance of surviving, nor had the 22 others who died that day.

Hezbollah would have warned their own people to stay away from the area that day. But it was clear they hadn't cared about the countless innocent people who were killed or badly injured.

* * *

We also tried to do something else, and I can't say we succeeded brilliantly. We reached out to all the victims' families and the media in Lebanon, to try to keep them as informed as we could about what we were doing and to answer their concerns.

We had a team in Lebanon as well as staff from the Hague who met with the surviving victims and the families of those who had perished. The guys in Lebanon were taking the lead, doing some media, holding a few press conferences, trying to show we were actually getting somewhere in the investigation and were serious about holding people to account.

I don't think we succeeded in changing the minds of the surviving victims or the families of those who had lost their lives. They were resigned, saying, 'This is Lebanon, you're never going to get to the bottom of it.'

Meanwhile, Hezbollah were calling us names and trying to taint our investigation, comparing it with previous investigations that had gone nowhere and been discredited, as well as alleging that Israel and the USA had infiltrated and influenced our investigations. Hassan Nasrallah actually gave speeches naming me personally and directly accusing me of corruption. It's funny – as I've mentioned, when I'm in physical danger it doesn't faze me. But I did object to allegations that our investigation and my leadership lacked integrity and was essentially corrupt.

It wasn't a picnic, that's for sure; again, it was more like a contact sport.

* * *

At least there were happier things happening in my personal life. In November 2009, Natalie and I got married in Italy. It was a small ceremony with a few friends and relatives, held in an old castle right on the Mediterranean, in the town of Zoagli, near Genoa. It wasn't possible for my kids to be there, but my sister was. It was a relief for me and Natalie that our relationship could finally be 'official'.

We didn't really have a honeymoon, just a few days staying at the nearby coastal towns of Santa Margherita Ligure and Camogli and exploring the local region. We're both obsessive travellers, and as much as we wanted to spend time travelling around Europe, I had to get back to work. There was much still to do.

* * *

Upon my return, we progressed the examination of the communication records as a priority. A great deal of work also had to be done on the 'provenance' of the records that the tribunal held or inherited from the previous UNIIIC. We had to prove how they'd come into the tribunal's possession, as well as have them authenticated by the source, the phone companies. We also tracked financial transactions back to our suspects, which helped prove the movement of money to purchase the necessary equipment for the assassination, the phones and other items. Other lines of inquiry had to be finalised and either ruled in or out.

There also needed to be more engagement with the Prosecution Division, who would pick up the task of presenting the evidence in the tribunal, once the trials began. It was up to the prosecutors to make the final decision about evidence to be tendered. Some of the expert evidence was ultimately left out.

By April 2010, we had built a cohesive, effective investigation team, and laid the foundations for a solid case. We knew this hadn't been Hezbollah acting alone. The other two in this cosy relationship – Syria and Iran – had obviously wanted Hariri killed as well. We had expert evidence to indicate that the three entities would always act in unison. Even so, it was Hezbollah operatives whom we had in our sights.

I had reached the point where I felt it was time for me to go, knowing the investigation division would be in good hands, with my deputy Mick Taylor more than ready to fill my shoes. I had been gone from Australia for almost 18 months, I still held the position of Deputy Commissioner in Sydney, and I felt the need to go back.

I wasn't required at NSW Police just yet, though, so I took a two-month break to travel with Natalie, first stop Jordan. I wasn't working, but Natalie was. She had a short-term contract in the outreach office of the UN that was managing the upcoming Iraqi elections. She was helping the UN get in contact with Iraqi refugees who had fled to Jordan and were still eligible to vote.

The Jordanians are all really friendly people, hospitable as Arabs typically are. The capital, Amman, is a gorgeous city, modern but chock-a-block with ancient ruins. We rented an apartment there, which had a satellite dish that received 900 channels. I spent most of my time watching old 1950s and '60s Arabic movies in black and white, hundreds of them; they brought back memories of the open-air cinemas of my childhood, under the stars on the banks of the Nile.

We travelled, too, to the valley of Wadi Rum, the desert wilderness made famous in Lawrence of Arabia, and to Petra, the city half-carved into the rock, once almost completely buried in sand.

We then went to Egypt, and Natalie got the full Egyptian experience because we stayed with one of my aunties, who lived in Garden City, an elegant tree-lined residential quarter of Cairo. It's very European and idyllic with its proximity to the Nile Corniche, perfect for evening strolls and watching the Nile feluccas ply their trade. I especially enjoyed the traditional home-cooked meals my auntie made for us.

After that, we flew south and had five or six days cruising the Nile, taking in everything. I'd seen all of the classic tourist landmarks before, but they still took my breath away. The bonus prize for Natalie was that she got to meet my six million cousins along the way.

It was one of those periods between gigs that I really enjoy – a chance to rest, relax and re-energise. It was a time for me to reflect on the past and imagine what lay ahead. I knew I would be going back into the fray in NSW. Still, I didn't think I was done. I had many initiatives I wanted to see implemented and there were always wrongs to right.

Above all, there was the pull of family – my kids were in Sydney and I missed them dreadfully, plus my mum's health

had not been the best. Sydney was where my roots were now –
no longer on the banks of the Nile.

Had I known then what would happen on my return to
Australia, I might have been forgiven for choosing to stay in
the religious and political cauldron that is the Middle East.

CHAPTER 21

Return Home

2011–2016

In early 2010, I returned to NSW Police and resumed command of Specialist Operations. However, it was always planned that the deputy commissioners of Specialist Operations and Field Operations would swap roles after a few years to broaden our horizons and ensure fresh approaches in both commands. I was comfortable with that plan, and so was the other deputy commissioner, Dave Owens. He was a classmate from my time at the academy, and we had remained friends. We made the switch in August 2011.

It was a smooth transition. I assumed command of all police stations in NSW and a number of ancillary units. The number of staff I had was much larger but with far less diversity. My focus then was on driving down rates of crime, supporting commanders to achieve their individual goals, and strengthening the connection between frontline police and the community. I introduced a number of measures, including one where local area commanders had to report on the number and nature of events or meetings they had with communities.

We dip-sampled these reports to ensure they were effective encounters, not just an officer passing someone in the street. Commanders had to take this issue seriously. Crime statistics were already heading in the right direction, but with a strong focus we drove them to historically low levels.

Ironically, a couple of years later, after Dave's retirement, the issue of the Brothers for Life crime wave arose, and at the instigation of the NSW Government and Premier Barry O'Farrell, the State Crime Command was added to my portfolio. This meant I was in command of all the major and organised crime squads and the intelligence arm of NSW Police as well as the frontline police – where the rubber meets the road. This constituted the majority of the organisation and was somewhere in the vicinity of 13 or 14 thousand staff.

I saw it as an opportunity to ensure unity of command and intent across the organisation. The operational outcome was outstanding, decimating one of the worst organised crime groups.

* * *

On 11 August 2011 – the same month I moved into Field Operations – a NSW Supreme Court jury found former NSWCC and SCIA heavyweight Mark Standen guilty of conspiring to import and supply 300 kilograms of pseudoephedrine – a drug key to the manufacture of methamphetamine – with a value of $120 million. The deal had involved the world's biggest synthetic drug cartel.

Standen was given a 22-year jail sentence, with a 16-year non-parole period. The news reports talked of the 'fall from grace' of one of the country's most senior law enforcement officers, now a convicted drug trafficker.

I felt the sentence was more than justified. Standen was part of the team that had investigated me inappropriately for so many years, and this verdict spoke directly to the integrity of their investigations.

This was a dark time for justice in NSW. And the following year, it would become personal.

* * *

In September 2012, I received an unmarked white envelope. There was nothing special about this envelope, but it contained what 114 of us had been desperate to get our hands on for a decade: photocopies of the affidavits that had convinced more than a dozen judges to sign warrants to bug us and secure Listening Device Warrant 266. I later became aware that many others had also received similarly startling material: various affidavits and other documents, which clearly showed that the warrants were not legally obtained.

Astoundingly, there was no information nor allegation whatsoever in those affidavits in relation to me, or to a large number – around 70 or 80 – of the other 113 people named. Our names were on the actual warrant as people to be bugged, but in the affidavit, there was nothing to justify the bugging of any of us. No evidence of any offence. Not one word. The affidavits clearly showed that those requesting the warrants had acted at best inappropriately, and at worst illegally.

Not only that, the warrants had been rolled over – renewed by a judge – every three weeks for two years. A couple of dozen judges had been signing these again and again and again.

As well as Warrant 266, I found there were other warrants relating to my former wife's home phone, located in the home where only she and our kids lived. I subsequently discovered my office and my mobile phone had also been bugged.

Looking over what I'd received, I was incandescent with anger. I'd long suspected the whole wretched thing had been illegal, and now I knew for sure. Even though I felt validated, I was outraged.

All those years of living under a cloud, all that corridor talk, and these affidavits showed me that they had nothing on me. There was not one shred of evidence against me. Maybe now, at last, I'd be able to hold those accountable to justice.

Who would have been able to get their hands on the affidavits to leak copies to us all? Whoever it was, they certainly wanted us to have this information, to be able to see it. They knew what they were doing by giving out this information, because they knew that I and others were not the kinds of people who would sit on it.

* * *

By this time, Dave Owens had retired and his position had been taken over by Catherine Burn, who had spent some years as co-leader of the SCIA team that had targeted me. As the senior Deputy Commissioner, I was well placed to be the next Commissioner, if I wanted it.

I knew that if I spoke up about the affidavits it wasn't going to go well for me. I knew that I would be up against the establishment – the NSW Police hierarchy, and the entire legal fraternity of NSW. I could have done nothing with them and let someone else do the heavy lifting, as my lawyers strongly advised.

I thought about it overnight. But the truth of the matter is there was never really any conflict for me. Yes, this deeply affected me personally, but there were at least 113 others, many of them not in a position to complain on their own behalf. It was about sticking up for those who were not in a position to help themselves.

Weighing up all the advice I'd been given, I came in the next morning, sat down at my keyboard and typed up a formal report to Commissioner Scipione, telling him what I was now in possession of. This wasn't just a report I was lodging, it was also a demand for an investigation into the actions of senior public officials – including the Commissioner himself as the former commander of SCIA. Additionally, I requested my complaint be classified as a 'Public Interest Disclosure', and that I be afforded the protection of the legislation governing whistleblowers. This request was acknowledged and accepted in writing by Internal Affairs, and later the office of the Ombudsman, the body tasked legislatively with the protection of whistleblowers. Ironically that office did the exact opposite.

Doing the right thing rarely turns out right.

Commissioner Scipione initially referred my and others' allegations to Internal Affairs, keeping the matter within the organisation. But asking NSW Police Internal Affairs to investigate themselves just wasn't going to fly.

The matter was all over the media. It became clear that this had been festering for a decade, and the large amount of incriminating evidence confirmed everyone's worst suspicions that the warrants were illegal. It was now too big to sweep under the carpet as successive governments had done. There was a huge amount of pressure on the NSW Government to do something about it.

Because the PIC, the NSW Crime Commission and SCIA – the former Internal Affairs – were all compromised and stood accused, none of them could investigate. The Premier, Barry O'Farrell, spoke to me after we had completed a press conference together. He said, 'We're going to give it to the NSW Ombudsman to investigate.'

The NSW Ombudsman, Bruce Barbour, asked for a significant budget and legislation that gave him royal commission powers and secrecy provisions. His investigation began in October 2012 and took the name of 'Operation Prospect'.

He hired a whole new investigative team, and began holding secret hearings. Of course, I didn't know any of that at the time. But my turn to appear before the Ombudsman would come.

I'd been given whistleblower status, with all the protection that should bring. But I would soon learn that meant nothing.

* * *

On 26 July 2013, nearly 20 years after MP John Newman was murdered, the core team who'd solved the case – Greig Newbery, Ian McNab, Wayne Walpole, Mark Jenkins and I – finally received the New South Wales Commissioner's Commendation for Service, usually awarded for outstanding police work, at the regional police headquarters in Parramatta. In total, 23 of the investigation team involved over the years were recognised, along with Crown Prosecutor Mark Tedeschi.

Justice Patten had said in his 2009 report that not only had we not done anything wrong as alleged, but that we deserved a commendation for our outstanding work. Now, finally, our many years of work were being recognised.

I have a photo from that day of the five of us with John Newman's mum, who was 92 years old at the time. We had kept in contact with her and it meant a great deal to me that she was there. She was just a wonderful lady and couldn't thank us enough. Sadly, she has since passed away, but to this day, the rest of the family are very supportive of us.

I look back on our efforts proudly. We were up against incredible odds and constant criticism, yet we were innovative and we persevered.

What was the lesson for me, in the John Newman murder investigation, trials and subsequent inquiry? It was the importance of tenacity, which was shown by all the detectives involved.

We had John Newman's own family against us early on. The community were not supportive of us in the beginning, nor were our own hierarchy. Then we had the media against us, and we had every allegation under the sun levelled at us.

But when we were the victims of unfair complaint after complaint to Internal Affairs, nobody ever said, 'This is getting too hard, I want out.' There were five of us from Task Force Gap who really stuck with it all the way through. We are all still very tight because we've been through a crucible of fire.

* * *

Other work I'd done in the past was finally coming to fruition.

On 16 January 2014, the trial of five men accused of the murder of Rafic Hariri and 21 others began in the courtroom in the STL building in Voorburg, just outside The Hague. The building had been specially outfitted with all the trappings required for the trial hearings, and the ballroom restyled as a courtroom.

There were five accused: Salim Jamil Ayyash, a senior operative in Hezbollah's assassination squad; Mustafa Badreddine, a Hezbollah military leader; Hussein Hassan Oneissi, a Hezbollah member; Assad Hassan Sabra, a Lebanese national; and Hassan Habib Merhi, another Hezbollah figure. These were the men we had tracked down via the mobile phone records and a number of other means.

The UN prosecutorial process was lengthy and tortuous in its attempt to be incredibly fair to the accused. They were not in court as the charges against them were read out. Hezbollah had announced that they would never give up the five men, and their whereabouts were unknown. Their trial would be held in absentia. The legal phrasing was that they had absconded and did not wish to participate.

The judgement against them would not be handed down until 18 August 2020, a full 15 years after the assassination.

Of the five we charged, one, Mustafa Badreddine, had been reported killed fighting in Damascus in 2016, so the case against him was dropped. Salim Ayyash was found guilty on the basis of conspiracy to commit a terrorist act and sentenced to five life sentences. The other three of the five – Oneissi, Sabra and Merhi – were acquitted due to 'insufficient evidence'. After all those years of work, it was a disappointing result.

Worse still, and even more of a puzzle, the presiding judge effectively said the prosecution had not proved the connection between Hezbollah and the murder. This was despite the fact that at least four of the five were publicly known to be Hezbollah operatives, and one of them was working directly for the head of Hezbollah, Hassan Nassrallah, who had acknowledged they were his men and had refused to hand them in.

Fortunately, the UN system allowed for appeals against acquittals. The STL was beginning to run out of funds, but the prosecutor appealed against the acquittals of Oneissi and Merhi. And on 10 March 2022, they too were convicted in absentia. No conviction has ever been recorded against the fifth man, Assad Hassan Sabra, and I regret that the prosecutor declined to appeal his acquittal – to say nothing of the many other Hezbollah operatives who were doubtless involved. Interpol Red Notices, which are circulated worldwide, have been taken out for the accused, meaning these men can be arrested if they surface anywhere in the world.

Even though this was not a perfect result, at least the truth had come out and the victims' families had received a measure of justice. I felt comfortable that we had done our best and achieved more than most people expected, under the constant glare of media and public attention, particularly in Beirut, where our investigation had been front-page news daily.

We had stood up to the bullies and delivered some degree of justice.

Hezbollah had a black eye.

CHAPTER 22

Speaking Truth to Power

2015

I said the following as I was giving evidence at the NSW Parliament inquiry into Operation Prospect, which would blow the lid off the Ombudsman's expensive five-year-long investigation.

> I have spent most of my career in organised and major crime. I have spent some time in Iraq as a senior police adviser with coalition forces and in 2009 I was headhunted by the UN Special Tribunal for Lebanon. I led the international investigation into the assassination of the Lebanese Prime Minister Hariri. I received many threats from Hezbollah and other proxy groups.
>
> I fear no man and I have operated in trusted circles with a top-secret level of clearance from our national government and our allies, entrusted with much classified and internationally sensitive information.
>
> No one has ever questioned my integrity, nor have I ever been doubted nationally or internationally.

In Sydney, with decades in major investigations, I have been cross-examined by more QCs than I can remember in hotly contested trials, yet I have never been denigrated, humiliated and had my every action and thought so unreasonably maligned as I experienced in Operation Prospect – that took a toll.

* * *

On 5 September 2014, on the twentieth anniversary of the murder of John Newman, I was due to join my colleagues for lunch with Newman's family. But I was summonsed to a secret hearing for Operation Prospect that morning. I had been assured I would only be there for a short time and would be able to make the lunch. I did not get out of the hearing until after 6.30 pm – about ten hours later.

In that time, I faced an onslaught of aggressive questions. I'd quickly realised the investigators had gone through every email, notebook and diary entry I'd written for the past five or six years. I was not asked one question about my complaint or the issue of the illegally obtained warrants. Not one. It was all about the documents: *How did you get the incriminating affidavits? Who did you show them to? Who did you discuss them with?* I've never been humiliated the way I was at that hearing.

It appeared to me that the inquiry had no interest in investigating the wrongdoing committed by SCIA and PIC. I later learned that my experience was the same as all others who had been dragged into secret hearings. No questions about the bugging or the warrants, just about who had revealed the wrongdoing and who knew about the incriminating evidence.

I and others felt the focus of Operation Prospect was on brutally silencing the complainants, no matter the cost to the individuals, and yet again sweeping it all under the carpet.

When Prospect had been set up in 2012, it had solely been meant to look into how the warrants had been issued to bug people who had had no allegation whatsoever made against them – including me. But it seemed to me that somehow it had been entirely refocused onto who had *revealed* the wrongdoing rather than the *actual* wrongdoing. So victims of the bugging, complainants who were supposed to be *protected*, were being treated as *offenders*, suspected of leaking documents that revealed truths many wanted to remain covered up. The whole thing had gone off the rails.

I was aware that at least one former police officer had to be taken in an ambulance from these hearings after collapsing from the torrid examination. I had to do something. I could have said nothing and hoped for the best, but I did not have that in me. I had to stop this travesty of justice from continuing. This was another fork in the road, and I took the right road, to stand up against a dreadful wrong.

With no report from Operation Prospect on the horizon, I made my own inquiries into the Office of the Ombudsman's investigation. I asked: *Who had oversight?* The answer came back: *No one did.* The inquiry answered directly to parliament.

I spoke to all the opposition parties – Labor, the Greens, the Shooters and Fishers Party – and many others who were affected did so too, and they agreed that there should be a parliamentary inquiry. The Shooters and Fishers Party leader, Robert Borsak, led the charge and became the chair of the inquiry. Greens MP David Shoebridge, who would become the inquiry's deputy chair, told parliament that for 'well over a decade a cloud has hung over the NSW Police Force' due to the bugging saga, and 'it is the job of the Parliament to shine light where nobody else is willing to do it'.

The office of the Ombudsman wrote to every member of the Upper House, urging them not to have an inquiry, and this was supported by the Minister for Police. The Upper House felt otherwise. They instituted the NSW Parliament Select Committee Inquiry into the Conduct and Progress of the Ombudsman's Inquiry 'Operation Prospect'.

Speaking after the inquiry was announced, Shoebridge said: 'What we have is a secret police investigation that obtained secret warrants, that was then reviewed by a secret police investigation and is now being considered by a seemingly endless secret Ombudsman's inquiry ... This secrecy must stop.' He summed it up brilliantly.

* * *

One of the very few things that's ever really tested me was the bugging saga. It didn't make me give up, but it whacked me about a bit, because I was up against the whole system.

The Police Union tried to be neutral, which disappoints me bitterly to this day. We were heading into a State election and the government just wanted to shut it down. There was a right and a wrong. The hierarchy of the Police Force should have had an interest in seeing the right thing done, but they just didn't – and had not done so for a decade. And the government had a bottomless pit of money to fight me in court and elsewhere.

Before the parliamentary inquiry began, for the first time in my life I took some sick leave. Doctors insisted. I ended up having a battery of tests with a heart surgeon. Coronary disease takes men in my family young: it took my father, many of my uncles and both my grandfathers before their time.

I knew I was about to face the biggest choice of my career. If I truly spoke my mind, publicly, it would make me radioactive. But I was never going to stay silent. Too many people had been destroyed by the initial bugging operation, then, even more unfairly, by Operation Prospect, which had been intended by parliament to right the many wrongs.

* * *

On Friday, 30 January 2015, the day I gave evidence at the inquiry, I made a decision to walk straight through the front door of the NSW Parliament, to front the inquiry in full uniform and with my head held high.

I was mobbed by the media, but I was not going to sneak in through a back door. I had nothing to hide, I wasn't going to skulk in the shadows. I wanted the world to know what had been going on – and the NSW Parliament was the only body with the power and protections to be able to reveal the hidden machinations of Operation Prospect.

The men and women of the NSW Police Force rightly expected me, as one of their leaders, to speak out when there was an injustice.

Once again, the words of Psalm 23 – 'Yea, though I walk through the valley of the shadow of death, I will fear no evil' – were ringing loudly in my ears.

I was allocated a side room so I could confer with my lawyers. One of them said: 'Nick, it's not too late, why don't you just let someone else do this? You don't have to.'

Many friends who were involved in politics and some who were actually members of Parliament had said to me, 'If you do this, you will never be Commissioner. Just let it go.'

Under no circumstances could I do that. So many good people had been damaged by SCIA and the PIC. I knew I had to do this, come what may.

The Macquarie Room in Parliament House was standing room only, and the atmosphere was daunting. It felt like every political and crime journalist in Sydney was there. I later found out that many of the NSW Police crime squads downed tools and watched proceedings in the meal rooms.

In that wood-panelled room, with its scarlet walls, I had the instruments and agencies of law in my sights, those who had clearly failed the people of NSW. This was my declaration of war.

The parliamentary inquiry finally allowed details to be shared under the protection of parliament. It was held in public, with all the evidence given on oath and remaining on the public record. What I said to the committee was widely reported: that the long-awaited time had come for me to speak truth to power, and to speak the truth *about* those in power, no matter what the consequences.

As I told the inquiry, 'I and other legitimate complainants had no right to silence in Operation Prospect, could not even discuss with doctors or psychologists what was being done to us.' It was hard to believe this had happened in NSW in the 21st century.

I thought I'd been prepared for what I would hear, but I was wrong. The Ombudsman, Bruce Barbour, gave evidence that I had been the target of 80 bugging warrants over a period of three years. *Eighty* warrants – I simply could not fathom rolling over or renewing that many warrants over three years. Don't forget, part of the renewal process was that you had to show progress to a judge. No criminal in NSW history could have been subject to such intense surveillance, let alone with no result. I watched Barbour's evidence in my office with the door closed. Then I went to the bathroom and was physically ill. It suddenly dawned on me just how much venom, lies and injustice had been heaped on me over a decade by the PIC and Internal Affairs.

* * *

In a matter of months, the parliamentary inquiry did what the Office of the Ombudsman couldn't do in five years and with tens of millions of dollars. It determined in February 2015 that the inquiry should not have incorporated both the legality of warrants and the leaking of confidential information into a single inquiry. 'Combining these two issues has resulted in participants being considered both complainants and perpetrators, and has delayed the completion of the inquiry', the select committee found.

It called on the government to establish an open and independent review of how surveillance warrants were granted, to apologise to people inappropriately named in warrants, and to formally amend the onerous secrecy provisions that had dogged witnesses during Operation Prospect.

More significantly, in relation to me, it said: 'That on the evidence before this inquiry there is a compelling case to make a specific apology to Mr Kaldas, which we now do, and we call on the NSW Government to do the same.'

My friend Steve Barrett, a Seven Network journalist and one-time producer of *60 Minutes*, had been the first witness called; he said the bugging had destroyed his career, as informants dared not trust him any more. The select committee also recommended a specific apology to him.

In my view, it wasn't just the police force and the government who needed to apologise. The Supreme Court judges who signed or renewed warrants for about three years to bug people against whom there was no evidence of wrongdoing have never been asked one question, nor been forced to account for their actions. Judges are our safety net, they're our legal guardians. In any warrant application, it is the judges who make the final call on whether people's privacy needs to be invaded. We entrust them with that power.

When it came to the bugging saga, all three of these parties had failed miserably.

* * *

In the NSW Police Force there are many people who do their basic two or three years on the street and then choose to do non-operational roles. After that they literally don't leave the building. There are many areas to work in where you can avoid crooks, you can avoid being on the frontline, and therefore you can skate up through the ranks without anything on your Internal Affairs record. There are no complaints against you because you haven't rubbed up against the reality of operational risk, you haven't made decisions that have been scrutinised by judicial processes in a trial or at a Coroner's inquest or a commission.

I and many operational police officers have experienced intense judicial scrutiny and other processes that have shaped us. For those who have managed to avoid that scrutiny for the majority of their careers, it is hard to see how they will ever have credibility with the rank and file who are out on the road day in and day out.

I think it's a tragedy that a lot of the leadership personnel – not just in NSW but in other police forces as well – have managed to avoid real police work for most of their careers. It hasn't cost them, because they've known how to talk the talk and how to handle the political end of town. But what happens is they simply don't have the credibility with the rank and file of the force. They never will.

Non-operational duties may be fine for a while, perhaps for those who don't aspire to high office, but not for life. There are some who simply don't want to do the work, they don't want to be at any risk of criticism, they don't want to get hurt, they don't want to take any chances. Ironically, they're usually more ambitious than the man or woman out there on the street.

This is not a problem exclusive to the world of policing. My observation is it happens in business all the time, but in business you more or less get judged on your results. If you've been a failure, you're not going to get anywhere. In the police, you can fake it.

In the UK, my sense is that before you'll get anywhere, you have to have been a detective or an operational officer, you have to have been at Scotland Yard, you have to have run major operations and investigations.

I think that needs to happen here. I think senior police should be required to have been at the sharp edge, to have run operations, to have made heat-of-the-moment decisions, to have arrested people, so that their reputation among more junior police is such that those junior police will follow them.

Politicians are the ones who appoint police commissioners, and they don't actually care how the men and women of the force feel. Their main criterion is: *Will this person disagree with me?*

In some parts of Canada, rather than have the politicians of the day select the commissioner, they have a process where they seek feedback from the public and the police rank and file. They talk about these opinions, factor them in and *then* they pick the commissioner. As a consequence, they end up with people who have credibility.

I don't think many politicians in NSW would ever accept that. I think that in the past the main criteria has often been: *Will this person do what they're told?* I clearly did not satisfy that criteria.

I've thought about this a lot over many years and have always tried to make sure that those I promoted were people who had done the work. There were mates whom I *didn't* promote because they didn't have the level of ability that was required. There were some who I promoted even though I did not get on with them because they were the best person for the job.

It has to change. The people of NSW, and the men and women of the NSW Police Force, deserve better.

CHAPTER 23

Guard of Honour

2015–2016

When the parliamentary inquiry had finished I received three boxes full of cards and letters of support, many from people I didn't know, saying it was clear I had been hard done by. I also received a beautiful bunch of flowers with a heartwarming card signed by many leaders of the Egyptian community, who also organised a dinner with my wife and me. The palpable support of the community and the police rank and file gave me great comfort. It meant so much more than the opinion of those above me. It always has. It always will. I had a moral victory, even though nothing had been resolved in relation to the illegal bugging.

On a superficial level, my relationship with the Commissioner, Deputy Commissioner Burn and others was cordial, but beneath the surface it was anything but. Most mornings at work, you could cut the air with a knife. Three days a week we had operational briefings very early in the morning. You'd be in for half an hour and then out. Still, in that short sliver of time the tension was palpable. I had no support. I was on my own in those meetings.

I was hitting my head against a brick wall. Natalie said to me, 'How long are we going to keep doing this?' She was obviously worried about my wellbeing. But I did not simply want to cut and run. I told her: 'I'm not going to walk away after this. I can't walk out and retire with my tail between my legs. I'm going to stay in the police for at least another year and then I'll reassess where I'm at.'

During that time I received numerous other job offers, both in Australia and internationally. I resisted them all.

In June 2015, the parliamentary inquiry was sadly obliged to hold another two days of hearings following a leak of information allegedly from the Ombudsman's office to the media. That matter also remained essentially unresolved.

I'd been on the front pages of the papers for many weeks during the initial hearings, and now the media attention continued. I'm not going to say that it didn't take a toll on me, it did, but what really upset me was the effect it was having on my family, my kids and my marriage.

In the end, Natalie, in her own diplomatic way, said: 'There is a big world out there, Nick.' She was right.

* * *

Some of the job offers I'd received had seemed very rewarding, but none of them had really grabbed me. Then in February 2016 I was approached by the UN to lead a soon-to-be-established international inquiry. The Syrian Assad regime had been accused of using chemical weapons against their own people.

That got my attention.

I decided to resign from the NSW Police – but on my own terms, and at a time of *my* choosing, not someone else's. I didn't want to be one of those guys who sit in coffee shops and whinge and whine about how badly they've been treated. Once I retired, I wanted to be out of town, busy doing something useful – looking forward, not back.

So I accepted the offer from the UN to become the Chief of Investigations of the OPCW–UN Joint Investigative Mechanism, a collaboration between the UN and the Organisation for the Prohibition of Chemical Weapons. My team and I would be based in The Hague; I was very familiar with the city now and knew I could live there comfortably.

It would be a tough gig, but one I knew I would enjoy. I loved the idea of once again doing something that mattered on the international stage.

I advised Commissioner Scipione I was going to lodge my papers and retire. I wanted to go quietly. But someone leaked to the press the fact that I was leaving in a huff. So I declined all media interviews, and decided to simply hold one press conference on Friday 4 March 2016, outside the Sydney Police Centre in Surry Hills.

Unbeknown to me, word about my surprise departure had got around the building. Chief Inspector Rick Steinborn felt something needed to be done.

Somehow he very rapidly organised a 'Guard of Honour'. When someone has served in the police force for decades, the Guard of Honour is a tradition for their last shift.

When I walked out for my press conference, I was astounded to see dozens of police in various uniforms, paying their respects with a salute. I had a tear in my eye, really struggling to hold it together. It all just hit me at once. Thirty-five years of blood, sweat and toil were coming to an end.

'I've decided to go,' I announced. I would take some leave then officially retire in June. 'It's best for my family at the moment, and I'm moving on ...'

I actually couldn't reveal what I was about to do because the UN had instructed me not to announce any details to the media, for security reasons. I just explained it as vaguely as I could.

This was the end of the biggest chapter of my life, and I needed to tell people how I felt about all those years. It was the people I was going to miss, not the politics.

One of the things they do on your last day is have the official police photographer take pictures of you, alone and with your staff, in full uniform, as it will be the last day you wear it.

I still treasure those photos. Looking at them now, I find it hard to picture that young recruit who turned up for his first day at the academy with longish hair.

On that last day, I went out for lunch at a Lebanese restaurant in Ryde, with my family and immediate staff. It was a very long, emotional lunch that lasted into dinner. I was presented with many gifts.

Over the weekend, my staff, loyal to the end, helped me pack up all the memorabilia and personal possessions in my office. Over 800 text messages flooded in, and I had hundreds of missed calls that day, all from well-wishers. I later tried to respond to every single one.

The following day the newspapers all splashed my departure on the front page, two of them describing me, rather flatteringly, as 'the best commissioner we never had'. I had a vision of where the organisation should be heading, but that was simply not going to happen. I was at peace with that.

It was a bittersweet time. I am not usually emotional, but in the days following my departure I often found myself with tears in my eyes.

It slowly dawned on me that I would never again wear that uniform, or be part of that team. But at the same time, I was happy and excited about the challenge that lay ahead.

I still care about the NSW Police. I care about the force's reputation, I care about the uniform, I care about the men and women. I always will.

When they're hurting, I feel it. When they do well, I'm proud.

I think anyone who's been a cop would agree.

CHAPTER 24

The Red Line

2016

Unlike some who retire from the force, I had a purpose literally the next day. I had just a couple of weeks to pack up and head to The Hague. I was under pressure to start ASAP – 'We need you here yesterday,' I was told – and I was happy to get out of Sydney.

Natalie and I had decided at the beginning of our relationship that wherever I went, we were going to go together. I should point out that since we've been married, Natalie has given up her career on two separate occasions and followed me to some desperate situations. I feel blessed, because it just wouldn't work if we were apart. We've both found happiness again late in life, for which we're both grateful, so we never want to be separated for long.

I left for New York to go to the UN headquarters for briefings and to meet the senior team, then I went to The Hague. Shortly after, Natalie joined me there.

* * *

Like the Special Tribunal for Lebanon, the Joint Investigative Mechanism (JIM) had been established by a UN Security Council resolution. There was a leadership panel of three individuals at ambassador level – an Argentinian, a German and an Albanian – who would act like a board of directors. Then I, as Chief of Investigations, would carry out the work with my team.

I'm not a chemist, I'm an investigator, but I was happy to surround myself with a whole lot of people with really good expertise, people who understood the technicalities of chemistry and related matters. We would be working out of the headquarters of the Organisation for the Prohibition of Chemical Weapons (OPCW), in The Hague, with full use of their laboratories and other resources. They were extremely helpful and hospitable.

Chemical weapons are generally considered inhumane and nearly everyone is committed to locating and destroying all of the weapons that are still out there. I say 'nearly everyone' because there are rogue nations that are not on board with this, for their own reasons.

It appeared that Syria was one of them. For the previous five or six years, the country had been torn apart by a civil war. The Assad regime had been growing ever more desperate, resorting to increasingly extreme measures, both in military tactics, and in arresting, torturing and killing dissidents.

There had been dozens of allegations that chlorine, mustard gas and the nerve agent sarin had been employed against civilians, which was against all international protocols, treaties and laws. The Security Council had resolved that the allegations had to be investigated and, if possible, acted on.

My investigation into the assassination of Prime Minister Hariri in Lebanon had been tough, but this took things to a whole other level. All the alleged incidents had taken place in the Syrian hinterlands, which were either controlled by insurgents, or still contested between the Syrian Government and insurgents. We were not going to have access to the crime scenes, and there were people we weren't going to be able to interview, either as witnesses or as suspects. We couldn't do the usual door-knocking and canvassing of an area to ask who saw and heard what, when. We weren't going to get access to a lot of the victims' medical records or, in some cases, to the victims themselves.

Many victims had not survived, some had fled to other countries or were missing, or they simply feared reprisal from one or more parties and did not want to engage with us. This was a war zone, and battlefield investigations are always just plain harder.

We knew we would have to deal with a whole range of stakeholders. As in Iraq and Lebanon, we would need to listen, but always apply not just a grain of salt but a sack. Everybody had their own agenda and outcome that they wanted to achieve in Syria.

It was going to be a hard one.

In the beginning, we had a year to complete our investigation, and our resources were limited. By the time I landed, we only had nine months. It was obvious to everyone that we were never going to be able to look into every allegation. We had to have a transparent formula for which cases we looked at. So we came up with a set of criteria and trimmed down the list to just nine, based on the availability of evidence and therefore the probability of success. Ultimately, that number was further whittled down to five that we could pass judgement on. We hoped these five cases would be indicative of others and give us a clear idea of who had been behind the attacks.

The Assad regime were most definitely in the crosshairs. The delivery method for chemical attacks is always aerial. You drop the weapons from a great height then get away as fast as you can, because the impact is widespread. And at the time of the incidents we were investigating, the only airpower over Syria had been the Syrian Air Force.

We had teams go there and interview a number of people within the Assad regime. These people *had* to cooperate because of obligations under UN laws, but that didn't mean they would tell us the truth. Indeed, they were less than frank.

At one stage, they said it must have been the terrorist organisation Islamic State, but Islamic State didn't own planes. Then there was a suggestion that Islamic State must have cobbled together a helicopter using bits of ones they'd shot down. We had experts confirm that you can't cobble together a helicopter like that, even if you could have, and Islamic State certainly didn't have that level of technical ability, nor the expertise to fly one. It was ridiculous.

Next, they said that Islamic State must have used 'hell cannons', homemade, mortar-like cannons used by Syrian rebels. You can't fire a hell cannon more than about 100 metres, 200 at the very most. And if you tried to fire poisonous barrels, you'd be subject to the effects of the chemicals blowing back at you.

Even if any of these things was remotely possible, Islamic State simply didn't have the technology to mount successful chemical weapons attacks of the magnitude of the alleged incidents. Then there was motive. Some of the areas that had been hit were very clearly anti-Assad strongholds, held by radicals aligned with Islamic State. There's no way Islamic State would be hitting their own. It just wouldn't happen.

Then there were the major regional and international powers who each wanted to tell us their side of the story. At that time, Donald Trump looked like he was going to win the White House for the Republicans. He didn't take over until the following year, but there were a lot of people from the conservative side of politics in the West already talking about wanting to get rid of the Assad regime in Syria.

We also had to interview the victims of the attacks. Some of them were part of groups that were off limits to the UN and the international community. Then there were insurgent groups that the UN didn't deem to be terrorists. Victims were both civilians and insurgents, but the one common factor was that the attacks occurred in areas under the control of the regime's enemies. We met with the relevant UN officials in Geneva and ascertained whom we were allowed to approach and whom we were not. It was essential to get this right, otherwise the allegation could be made that our evidence had been tainted by groups that world bodies had decreed were untouchable.

We struggled to collect written statements from victims and witnesses, so we tried to interview some of them using Zoom or Skype, but their internet connections were often dreadful. It meant we had to rely on the help of groups who were active on the ground in Syria.

We also used social media mining – looking at social media posts relating to specific attacks in an attempt to verify when and where they had taken place. There was a plethora of information out there; a lot of random people had recorded eyewitness accounts with live commentary. They would say things like 'I'm walking down the street, there's been another chemical weapon attack', then they'd ask bystanders what they'd seen. Watching these, I found it was impossible not to be moved by the human tragedy playing out.

It was a battle to get the likes of Facebook, Twitter and YouTube to assist, but when they did cooperate, we could prove the times and locations of these recordings and check the metadata to determine whether it had been interfered with in any way. For me, it was a whole new way of carrying out an investigation.

* * *

Because a lot of my staff were not actually investigators, my contract specified that I was to help run training in interviewing and other investigative skills – how to ask questions to get the best outcome, how to collate evidence in a coherent way to formulate a brief. The teaching wasn't hard for me, and I had plenty of case studies to rely on. There's a British interrogation model often used in the English-speaking world called PEACE, an acronym of Planning; Engage and Explain; Account; Clarification, Challenge, Closure; and Evaluation. I found it helpful for the team.

These were incredibly bright people, from really diverse backgrounds: Europeans, North Americans, South Americans, Africans. A true league of nations – with very different world views. There were some clashes of personalities and very different opinions about the best way forward. We conducted a couple of retreats, where we talked not just about the investigation, but also about team building and how to get along with each other and respect each other, given our varied ways of looking at things. I tried to get everyone together for dinner once every couple of weeks to build our team spirit.

* * *

In October 2016, our leadership panel submitted our fourth and final report to the UN Security Council. It was *their* names that appeared on the reports, not mine or those of my staff, which suited us fine. Some of my investigators were worried about being publicly credited, especially those with an Arabic background, because of possible recriminations.

We had proven that the Assad regime had been responsible for the chemical attacks on the population in a number of instances. But it simply confirmed what the world already suspected: that the regime were dropping barrel bombs full of chlorine gas on civilians from planes and probably helicopters, causing injuries, fatalities and widespread devastation.

All we could do was ensure our report gave an account of exactly what had occurred. It was up to others what happened after that. Having said that, our scrupulousness meant we could not go as hard as we wished to. The evidence was there, but we were held to such a rigorously high standard regarding the burden of proof that it hamstrung us. And of course we had only looked at one-tenth of the total number of similar alleged attacks.

The following month, we concluded our duties in the JIM. It would be some months later, and following many more allegations of further chemical weapons use, that there was a reformation of the JIM, known as JIM II.

Barack Obama said when he was US President: 'We have been very clear to the Assad regime, but also to other players on the ground, that a red line for us is we start seeing a whole bunch of chemical weapons moving around or being utilised.' The red line had clearly been crossed. But no consequences followed.

Following our investigation, more allegations were made. More fact-finding missions were set up. The outcomes always incriminated the regime.

At the 25th Conference of the States Parties to the Chemical Weapons Convention (CWC) in April 2021, the members would suspend Syria's rights and privileges under the convention. It meant nothing to President Assad, who would be re-elected shortly after.

The red line had been crossed many times, and continues to be. The UN was never going to be the body that punishes the Syrian regime for the deployment of chemical weapons. I thought the Western powers might do so, but apart from sanctions, nothing has happened.

There were some similarities to the assassination investigation I led in Lebanon, in that people understandably asked: 'What's the point?' In Syria, my hope was not that President Assad would be punished – although that would have been more than appropriate – but that it would make him worried enough to cease the attacks.

The regime did do that for a while, but then later on, more allegations came in. It seemed he would be able to carry on with impunity. No one was going to do anything serious about it, especially with the Russians on his side.

* * *

But while President Assad has been found to have done terrible things in various forms, those waiting in the wings were probably worse. During our investigation, I met with some of the opposition leaders who would potentially take over if the Assad regime fell. We could only meet with opposition groups that had been determined by the UN to be acceptable, not aligned with Al-Qaeda or ISIS. Yet it seemed the only opposition that had been left standing after all those years of civil war were religious extremists, who would likely turn Syria into another Afghanistan under the Taliban.

For all Assad's faults, he has protected minorities. It's hard to admit, because he's done many evil things.

I thought those calling for a regime change really needed to think about what was going to happen if Assad was toppled. The lessons of Iraq and Libya were on my mind. The Americans said, 'Let's get rid of Saddam Hussein.' All right, how's *that* working out? Then it was, 'Let's get rid of Gaddafi in Libya.' There's still a civil war happening there.

It's not as simple as saying, 'Let's get rid of Assad.' Syria has strategic significance: it borders Israel, it has Mediterranean access. It is an attractive ally for Russia and others seeking a foothold in the region, and it has the support of the other Shi'a-aligned powers, Iran and Hezbollah.

Not for the first or the last time, those wanting to overthrow Assad weren't playing the tape through to the end. They didn't have a clear plan for what was going to happen afterwards, just like they didn't have a plan for Iraq, or Libya, or Afghanistan.

* * *

After the Leadership Panel delivered our October report, I had to return to Sydney for my official send-offs from the NSW Police. Things had moved so quickly before I headed to The Hague that I hadn't had time for the traditional celebratory dinner to mark my retirement. There would also be a number of other functions in my honour within the Arabic, multicultural and business communities.

Months earlier, all the non-government parties in the Parliament of NSW – Labor, the Greens, the Christian Democrats and the Shooters, Fishers and Farmers – had held a press conference. They said, 'We don't agree on anything else, but we are calling on the government to bring back Nick Kaldas as Commissioner.' I was flattered, but I'd moved on.

Meanwhile, the UN – confident that the mandate for the JIM was about to be renewed – asked me if I would return to The Hague and head the investigation into another series of of allegations of chemical attacks in Syria. I told them that for me to do that, I'd have to believe the work was worthwhile, that it would lead to some sort of meaningful outcome. I asked them what the UN had done with our last report. The silence was deafening. I politely declined. When the JIM came up for renewal again in November 2017, Russia – an ally of the Assad regime – vetoed any further extension, and JIM was shut down.

Besides, there was another UN job that appealed to me more. Earlier, on my way from New York to The Hague, I had flown to Jerusalem to meet the Commissioner General of the UN Relief and Works Agency for Palestine Refugees in the Near East (UNRWA). As a result of that meeting, I won the position of Director of Internal Oversight Services.

It would mean going back to the Middle East, this time to be based in Jordan, for three to five years. Neither Natalie nor I were ready to stay in Sydney; a stint in Jordan would suit us well, and, again, hopefully I would be doing something meaningful.

* * *

I was sad to leave The Hague and my colleagues after such an intense period of time together. I still keep in touch with a lot of those people. Some of them have gone on to bigger and better things in the UN system, though most of them have returned to their home countries.

So it was for me. In Sydney, my retirement celebrations awaited.

The main police function was held at Darling Harbour. It was hosted by 2GB radio host Ray Hadley and the guest list included over 850 people. Many of Sydney's legal fraternity were there, along with senior police from NSW, interstate and even New Zealand, politicians past and present, emergency services leaders, senior AFP figures as well as the Director of the Australian Criminal Intelligence Commission. I was humbled.

Did I go out with a bang, or a whimper? Well, the headline the next day in Sydney's *Daily Telegraph* read: 'Former Deputy Commissioner Nick Kaldas Fires Off at Top Cops in Farewell Speech'. I had a captive audience of powerful people that night and I *did* have a bit to say. I spoke about how leadership means doing what is right and looking after your troops, rather than doing what will please the powers that be. Some liked it, some didn't. But I felt I had sounded a positive note, one that was hopeful for a bright future.

Then, after all the send-offs – which my daughter cheekily called 'The Festival of Nick' – it was time to turn my attention back to the Middle East.

CHAPTER 25

16 Checkpoints

2016–2018

At the end of November 2016, in the dead of a snowy winter, Natalie and I arrived in Amman, the home of the UNRWA HQ. We rented an apartment across the road from the American Embassy, in a residential neighbourhood called Abdoun, home to many diplomatic missions and residences. With its restaurants and cafés, it was the vibrant heart of the city.

Both Natalie and I liked Jordan a great deal because we could enjoy all the benefits of the Western world – shopping centres, supermarkets, easy transport – as well as the Arabic culture and comforts that we both liked. The food was spectacular, the weather was not too bad and, once again, we travelled a fair bit.

But I was here to work, and not for the first time, it was a steep learning curve.

* * *

UNRWA was set up as a temporary body after the founding of the State of Israel led to the 1948 Arab–Israeli War – referred to by Palestinians as 'Al-Nakba', 'the catastrophe' – and the displacement of hundreds of thousands of Palestinians, who became homeless refugees. Later, it was mandated to assist their descendants, and give emergency help to those displaced by subsequent conflicts.

Over 75 years on from the 1948 war, UNRWA is still around because many of the displaced, who now number five and a half million, have nowhere to go. UNRWA provides them with accommodation, medical care, social services and education. They try to get them into university and give them employment, to help them shed their refugee status.

UNRWA has three headquarters – in Gaza, Amman, and the West Bank in Jerusalem where the Commissioner General and other staff are – as well as offices in the other two locations where the refugees are to be found: Syria and Lebanon. Most of its employees are Palestinian, and there are a number of international staff. UNRWA has a staff of over 30,000 and an annual budget of over US$2 billion.

The infrastructure required for UNRWA's more than five and a half million refugees is equivalent to that of a mini-country, split across the five different locations, each of which has its own particular problems. In Lebanon, for example, the Palestine refugees are not allowed out of the camps. They can't work, they can't hold a driver's licence and they don't have national identity papers. They struggle. In Jordan, refugees have been integrated in many ways, but there are still a lot of people in camps.

The camps sometimes sprawl over hectares, with populations often bigger than sizeable towns. While you may be picturing a sea of tents, there are actually mostly buildings, because people have been there for 75 years. An air of gloom permeates the camps, because even after 75 years, everything is temporary. It's a strange permanent–temporary situation, all day every day.

On many occasions I saw Palestine refugees wearing a chain with a key around their neck. It's the key to the front door of the house in Palestine that was once their family's home – the home they pray they are going back to one day but most likely never will.

* * *

In my oversight role, I had four divisions under my control. The Investigations division is about protecting the resources of UNWRA by investigating allegations of fraud, corruption, sexual exploitation and more. The Audit division is tasked with looking at UNRWA systems and processes to ensure they are effective. The highly specialised Evaluation division assesses programs, particularly aid programs, to see whether they were giving donors bang for their bucks, and generally whether systems and processes are effective or not. And the Ethics office – which was more or less independent of me because *I* could be complained about as well – answered to me administratively only. They examine systems and identify issues before they become problems and recommend improvements.

In some ways my role was similar to Internal Affairs in the police, in that I was looking into what everyone else was up to. But it was also a bit different from that. It was about ensuring integrity and accountability in an international body that was scrutinised very closely by critics and had to satisfy donors that all was well.

* * *

I went to Gaza quite a few times. I couldn't believe there were over two million people crammed into an area just 51 kilometres in length and 11 kilometres across at its widest point. At that stage, they'd been fenced in for over 15 years. There wasn't enough medicine, food and fuel going in. Needless to say, since the Israeli invasion of Gaza in October 2023, the situation has grown catastrophically worse.

Even back then, just getting in and out of Gaza was extraordinarily complex, encapsulating the problems between Israel and Palestine. The Israelis refused to deal with the militant group Hamas, yet Hamas were the governing authority of Gaza.

Gaza was a two-and-a-half-hour drive from Jerusalem. When you got to the first border post, staffed by Israeli border control, you couldn't see who you were talking to; there was just a speaker system and opaque, bulletproof glass. You had to pull out all your bags and put them through X-ray machines. They'd talk to you like you were a ten-year-old who'd dropped something on the floor and made a mess.

Then you'd get to the second barrier, staffed by the Palestinian Authority, which controlled Gaza before 2006 and was recognised by Israel. Because Israel wouldn't have any direct contact with Hamas, the Palestinian Authority was inserted in the middle.

Finally, you had to get through the *third* checkpoint, controlled by Hamas.

I had a bad experience one of the times I was trying to exit. I had driven to Gaza with a colleague, an Italian investigator, to conduct an inquiry. In the days leading up to our trip, it had been reported that Israeli special forces had assassinated a Hamas leader inside Gaza. Hamas were up in arms, trying to work out how the Israeli hit squad had got in and out. Everything was even more tense than normal.

Still, we went in and did what we had to do. We were there for three or four days, conducting interviews and carrying out our investigations. Then it was time to leave.

Normally the hardest part was getting through the Israeli checkpoint, but on this particular day, given what had been going on, the toughest part was trying to get through the Hamas border post.

At that checkpoint, officials were ferocious. 'We don't have a record of how you came in! When was it, before or after the murder? What do you know about the murder?'

I had my UN diplomatic passport, but that didn't seem to matter. I tried to placate them, explaining that I had come in through the usual official channels, but it seemed Hamas recordkeeping could not confirm any of this.

'You're not going anywhere, we've got to work out how you came in!' they shouted.

Suddenly I seemed to have become a murder suspect.

I took a deep breath and told them I'd driven in with my offsider, who confirmed that we had come in together. They had *him* logged in the system, so surely I must have been in there with him?

Eventually, an influential Palestinian member of UNRWA's security team came in at my request, and literally screamed at them to get their facts straight.

Still, it took a couple of hours before I was finally allowed to go. I was happy to exit Gaza, but I wasn't too fazed by the whole ordeal. It was simply part of the world I lived in at that stage.

* * *

Getting into Syria to visit our office there was a whole other story. You can't fly in directly so I used to fly into Beirut. I would be picked up from the airport by a UN driver, and security team depending on the situation at the time, then driven across to Damascus, which would take about two and a half hours. I once counted 16 checkpoints that we had to get through, all manned by trigger-happy personnel with guns pointed right at us.

In Damascus, the UN had taken over the Four Seasons Hotel, and the whole building was barricaded. The first time I stayed there, I was warned that the only people allowed into the hotel apart from the UN staff were mukhabarat agents – the Syrian secret police. I was told the agents regularly went through the rooms of UN staff while they were out.

As a result, I never travelled to Syria with any information I wouldn't want the regime to see. When I left my room, I would also set up a couple of 'traps', which would tell me if anyone had been in there while I was away. These traps were set off – often.

* * *

While I had my hands full with five and a half million Palestine refugees, back home, the wheels of 'justice' had been slowly turning.

On 20 December 2016, the NSW Ombudsman's report into Operation Prospect was finally handed down. What was supposed to be a 12-month investigation had gone on for almost five years and cost much more than expected.

All up, seven QCs were reported as criticising the Operation Prospect report and the way the Office of the Ombudsman had conducted the operation. Ian Temby QC, an eminent leader of the profession and the inaugural head of the Independent Commission Against Corruption, wrote in correspondence that Operation Prospect was 'the most grotesque abuse of justice, fairness and process' he'd seen in almost four decades at the Bar.

The report did recommend that the Premier and Government apologise to those, including me, who were wrongly targeted by the bugging operation. I am still waiting.

In my view, the report made little or no effort to get to the bottom of the bugging saga but attacked me and other complainants instead. At that point, I could have probably just sat quietly and taken it on the chin, but I decided to fight back. I went to the Supreme Court, suing the Office of the Ombudsman. We lost.

We could have gone to the Court of Appeal, but the legal bills were mounting up. I'd reached a point where my barrister told me: 'You can appeal, and the chances are 80 per cent you'll get up, versus 20 per cent you won't.' I asked how much I would be up for, as I would be wearing the entire cost. 'About $400,000,' was the reply.

I simply could not risk that kind of loss just to win the argument, so I withdrew. Given the feedback I'd received after the parliamentary inquiry, I knew at least I'd won a moral victory. It is sad that successive governments have sat on their hands when the evidence became clear, and been happy to fund legal processes from their bottomless pit to ensure the massive wrongs were never righted.

* * *

In June 2017, the NSW Crime Commission (NSWCC) made public its response to Operation Prospect:

> The Prospect investigation has taken over 4 years and the Report occupies 882 pages. Notwithstanding the time and effort involved, the NSWCC considers that the Report carries limited weight. The procedures adopted in the publication of the Report have been flawed and many of the findings and recommendations are based upon errors of fact and/or law.

In the NSWCC's opinion, the Ombudsman's investigation 'lacked procedural fairness' and the report was 'technically invalid and of no legal effect'.

I also received a letter from NSW Crime Commissioner Peter Hastings QC. He wrote:

> The Acting Ombudsman found that the conduct of officers of the New South Wales Police Force in naming you in affidavits supporting the issue of listening devices warrants ... [and] in obtaining a telephone interception warrant on the telephone number of your former home where you no longer lived, was unreasonable, and recommended that the Commission apologise for that.

I understood a similar letter went out to 14 other serving and former police detectives, and one went to my former wife. Peter Hastings had arrived at the NSWCC in 2012, so he had not been there when the bugging occurred. But he felt he had a moral obligation to send these letters. I shall always be grateful for his actions.

A month or so after the NSWCC response, following many complaints, the Police Integrity Commission, one of the three bodies involved in the bugging saga, was shut down. It had been established in 1996 on the recommendation of the Wood Royal Commission, but had barely struck a blow against police misconduct during its existence, and had been the subject of a long series of sustained complaints against it for having acted improperly or having denied people procedural fairness, among other sins. The irony of an integrity body being more guilty of misbehaviour than those they are monitoring was lost on successive governments for a couple of decades.

A replacement body, the Law Enforcement Conduct Commission, was established, supposedly with new staff and a new way of operating.

The NSWCC's response laid the blame for the bugging saga squarely at the feet of the NSW Police Force. To date, there has been no acknowledgement of the wrongdoing, or any apology from the NSW Police or NSW Government.

CHAPTER 26

'This We Will Do'

2018–2024

My mother passed away in early 2017, while Natalie and I were living in Jordan. Over the next year or so, I started yearning for home. We were both missing our friends and family, and I was especially missing my kids. Even though they were now grown up and living lives of their own, I wanted to spend time with them. Natalie would have been happy to stay longer, but eventually we reached a consensus and returned to Sydney.

We settled back in and I was happy in semi-retirement, doing short-term projects that suited me. I delved into the private sector, as well as taking on a number of positions that I felt were productive, positive roles. One of these was being on the Board of Commissioners of the Commission for International Justice and Accountability (CIJA), a body funded by European Union members and others. The purpose of CIJA was to fill a gap left by the United Nations' inability to adequately and quickly respond to crises around the world and gather the necessary evidence to hold people and governments to account. CIJA's early work revolved around the atrocities committed in the Syrian conflict then moved on to issues involving the Rohingya minority in Myanmar. It investigates war crimes, crimes against humanity, genocide, terrorism, human trafficking and migrant smuggling, placing a particular emphasis on gathering evidence that can 'assist in identifying those leaders of a group or criminal organisation that may order, direct or manage criminal activity'.

Many prosecutions have resulted from the work CIJA does, bringing numerous people and organisations to justice, and I'm proud and happy to be contributing to righting wrongs in the international sphere again.

I was also honoured to become a member of the independent steering group of the Scotland Yard investigation into historic IRA-related crimes, which has been an enlightening experience for me. Many murders and crimes committed during the Troubles remain unresolved, and the families of the deceased have taken legal and political action to force the cases to be investigated.

My positions with both CIJA and the independent steering group are honorary, with no salary or remuneration. I'm happy to be involved in these investigative bodies, and in a sense to be able to give a bit back.

In early 2019, a couple of politicians asked me to consider running for the Liberal Party at the next federal election. It wasn't the first time the suggestion had been put to me. I'd been approached a couple of years earlier, and also before the previous federal election in 2016. Regrettably it made the media, and, as I had both times in the past, I politely declined.

During this time, I conducted a couple of reviews. One was a health check of the planning and development approval process for the NSW Government. The second was an independent review of the police response to the 15 March 2019 mosque attacks in Christchurch, New Zealand – a 'lone wolf' armed attack carried out by an Australian citizen from the north coast of NSW. He killed 51 individuals and attempted to murder another 40 in a hate-filled frenzy.

I was asked to conduct this review alongside a former solicitor general of New Zealand and a leading academic. A royal commission had been established ten days after the shooting to look into whether anything could have been done to prevent it, but the New Zealand Police Commissioner Mike Bush felt a separate examination of the police force's actions was needed because this was not, strictly speaking, in the royal commission's terms of reference.

Our report was released on 9 December 2020, a day after the royal commission findings, and concluded that on the whole the police response had been excellent. The NZ Police had very effectively prepared for the so-called 'active armed-offender scenario'. While NZ police are renowned for being community minded and not necessarily armed, I learnt that all frontline or first-response police were in fact trained for just such an incident, facing a heavily armed offender, and they had access to weapons in an emergency. They acquitted themselves admirably in this incident, and the actions of the arresting police confronting the offender were nothing short of heroic.

* * *

In mid-2021 I received a call from the Federal Attorney-General's Department. The government were establishing a royal commission into suicides within the military and veteran communities, and I had been nominated as a person who might act as chair.

I'm not a lawyer, or a judge, and for a minute I thought they might have got hold of the wrong person. But the people at the department pointed out that I had run a number of major inquiries, and I had spent some time in conflict zones – real ones, not just the ones in the police executive offices! And at the same time I had never served in, nor had any allegiance to, the military, so I could bring an independent mind to the investigation.

As negotiations progressed, two other commissioners were named: Dr Peggy Brown, a prominent psychiatrist, and James Douglas QC, a former Queensland Supreme Court judge. I felt we were a good mix and would complement each other's skills and expertise. The Royal Commission into Defence and Veteran Suicide officially commenced on 8 July 2021.

We identified at least 57 previous inquiries that had looked at all aspects of military suicide and contributing factors. Some of them were significant Senate inquiries. Out of all those inquiries had come around 770 recommendations.

While many of these recommendations had been 'ticked off' by the relevant departments, it seemed no one had ever properly checked whether the intentions *behind* the recommendations had actually been achieved. Despite numerous inquiries, the plight of the men and women who serve in the Australian Defence Force (ADF) had not improved, and the figures for suicide and suicide risk had not been significantly affected.

We held 12 hearing blocks, each consisting of several weeks, around the country, in all State and territory capital cities, as well as major military centres such as Wagga Wagga in NSW and Townsville in North Queensland. We received nearly 6000 submissions, some of them quite lengthy, held 897 private sessions, took evidence from more than 350 witnesses and visited 26 military establishments. We also issued 1500 compulsory notices and received some 250,000 documents in response, comprising three million pages of information.

A couple of shocking statistics from the inquiry stood out. The first is that at least 20 times more veteran and defence personnel die from suicide than are killed in combat. The second is that, contrary to popular belief, 70 to 80 per cent of past or serving defence personnel who take their own lives have not been to a war zone.

So it appears that there are factors in play other than the trauma of serving in conflict zones. It seems it's as much about how men and women are treated in the ADF, how they feel, what their day-to-day working life is actually like and how the workplace culture impacts their mental health.

Our commission established beyond any reasonable doubt the alarming prevalence in the ADF of bullying, harassment and abuse, as well as the stubborn inability of our military apparatus to admit wrongdoing and simply look after those who wear the uniform.

A raft of other issues occur once men and women leave the military – whether due to 'transition' (as they call it), retirement, resignation or forced removal. These men and women then have to claim their various entitlements from the Department of Veterans' Affairs (DVA) and other agencies. The whole ecosystem of compensation, superannuation, pensions and medical expense claims has become so convoluted – almost impossible for the average person to navigate – that many veterans cannot see a light at the end of the tunnel. Worse, the months, and sometimes years, of delay in processing claims mean that many simply lose hope.

Compounding all of these problems is what can be described as a lack of curiosity, not only among the leadership of the ADF and the bureaucracy but also among successive government ministers and prime ministers and, just as importantly, the media and the public. It is this lack of curiosity that caused the problems we identified to fester and grow. We hope we have contributed to raising awareness and compelling interest and action.

Our terms of reference also required us to look at what was occurring in this space among Australia's allies in the Five Eyes nations: the USA, UK, Canada and New Zealand. My fellow commissioners and I visited all of these countries and looked at how they deal with these same issues. There was much commonality and many good ideas that we were able to take on board.

The work of our commission finally concluded with a ceremonial closing in Sydney on 28 August 2024. After such an exhaustive process, one would have to be inhuman not to feel some of the trauma that we heard about on an almost daily basis. The experience has profoundly affected me on a personal level, as I know it has others.

The commission's final report recommended a series of reforms that we hope will, for once, not just be implemented but also properly reviewed. To put them into a nutshell: we could not see any other option in the longer term than for a small entity with appropriate powers to monitor the situation, act independently of the various government departments and, most importantly, report publicly. There is no other overarching solution.

These men and women have done all we have asked of them. They've often gone where angels fear to tread, and they and their families have endured much. It is nothing short of a national disgrace that successive governments have failed to do all in their power to fix the problems within the system and decrease the rates of defence and veteran suicide. At a time when there are proposals for spending hundreds of billions of dollars on submarines and equipment, surely it's time to spend what is required to better care for our defence personnel and veterans. We hope that one of the things our royal commission has done is ensure that these problems can no longer be denied or ignored.

The DVA motto is 'For what they have done, this we will do.'

They also say sunshine is the best disinfectant. Our commission has poured light onto the issues; it is my fervent hope that our current and future governments will do the rest.

* * *

On 2 December 2024, the Australian Government handed down its response to the Royal Commission's recommendations. Of the 122 recommendations, 104 were accepted. Seventeen recommendations were noted, essentially as needing more research, and only one was rejected. The main recommendations regarding the establishment of bodies to monitor the issues were accepted, and that was heartening, as was the fairly rapid response by the government.

All of that is positive. We now need to see the implementation process and the funding and resourcing that will ensure its success. Bipartisanship and vigilance from our political leaders will be key. I remain cautiously optimistic, but the rates of suicides among our serving and veteran military community is something that will haunt me for some time and I will watch for further developments with great interest.

I Regret Nothing

2024

As I write, events in the Middle East are moving at an incredible pace, and much is dramatically changing and escalating. The Assad regime in Syria has fallen and it is unknown what direction the country will go in under its new government. In Gaza, the West Bank and Lebanon, the tragic conflict shows no sign of abatement. The places I've been and the people I've worked with and for are all under extreme stress and in danger at the moment. I wonder what has happened to the Syrian general I dealt with and if I will ever find out. I wonder how many of my former colleagues from the United Nations in Gaza have been killed. I can only join the many others hoping and praying for peace.

It is ironic that my family fled the Middle East with all its problems for safety in Australia, given I have spent a fair portion of my life heading towards it, often into the eye of the storm. I have found the magnet of those issues pulling on me again and again: to Iraq during the insurgency, to Lebanon to investigate Hezbollah and the various assassinations, to Syria to investigate the use of chemical weapons, and again to the Middle East to lead oversight efforts in UNRWA, the agency dealing with Palestine refugees.

Looking back, I can see the parallels between what my father stood for, and stood up against, and how I have lived my life. The way he responded to the injustice that caused him to uproot his family and leave his country has shaped my thinking in my career and my personal life. In some subconscious way, I have never been able to give in. I have never been able to resist fighting back, often at great personal cost.

An example of this is during the bugging saga and the decade following the Wood Royal Commission into corruption in NSW Police. It is clear to me that the oversight bodies operated without effective oversight, sometimes acting as rogue organisations, and were more guilty of 'noble cause corruption' than anyone they were investigating. What is also clear to me is that successive people in leadership positions in the police, judiciary and government knew what was happening but instinctively went into cover-up and brand-protection mode, extending no compassion to victims of that wrongdoing. Super-judicial oversight bodies in general have extraordinary powers. With those extraordinary powers there must be extraordinary accountability. In my view, that has not been the case.

I simply did not have it in me to look away and worry about my own progress and interests. I firmly believe that leadership is about moral courage above all, about standing up for what is right no matter the consequences.

One leader I greatly admired was US General Colin Powell. He was Chairman of the Joint Chiefs of Staff and he also served as Secretary of State under George W Bush. He made the point in his memoir that the world may have been very different if the top US military leadership during the Vietnam War had said to the president and the government that the war was unwinnable and that the country must change tack. True leadership should never be a popularity contest or about selfish aims.

I used to tell my staff in the Deputy Commissioner's office that we had to right one wrong a day. I don't know if I always achieved this, but I know I gave it my best shot. Despite having tried, hard, I don't feel I succeeded in righting all the wrongs. After 35 years, including ten as Deputy Commissioner, I reached a point where I knew it was time to move on. But it was a huge wrench to walk away.

There is something about police work that makes laughter all the more important. I learnt very early in my career not to take myself too seriously, and to relax and enjoy the moments of fun. I also learnt that black humour in policing, as it is in many other professions, is a way of coping with awful things.

By the time I got to the senior ranks, I had some stock sayings that my staff used to make fun of. One was that 'hope is not a plan'. Hoping all's well is never going to work. You have to have a plan in policing and be flexible enough to change that plan as the situation changes. I used to tell those I promoted to senior ranks that I had one main demand of them: 'treat others as you would like to be treated'.

I also stressed to all my staff that there was a difference between being in charge and taking charge. That is leadership. The failure of leaders, in whatever walk of life, to actually accept the responsibility of their role and do their best to get the job done has often been the cause of failure and harm. Too often, I have seen leaders who, at their core, are motivated by their own interests.

I stuck to those maxims throughout my career and they served me well.

When I look back over the decades, I reflect fondly on all the experiences I have had. Most importantly, I have been blessed with the people I've worked alongside, the people who worked for me and, mostly, the people I worked for. I'm proud of what we achieved in the numerous commands and operations we were involved in. I'm proud of the good we did.

When I retired from the police force, I was asked at a press conference if I would miss the job. Quoting an old friend, retired assistant commissioner Peter Dein, I said: 'I won't miss the circus, but I will miss the clowns.' It's the people; they are always the most important thing.

I also made a point of saying one final thing at that press conference that I truly meant. Despite friends saying to me I could have sat still and not fought the many battles I have taken on throughout my career, I said: 'I regret nothing.' That has never changed.

ACKNOWLEDGEMENTS

This book has been a labour of love for a couple of years. There are many people who have encouraged me, advised me and put up with me throughout the process. I want to thank them and ask for forgiveness if I have left anyone out.

I also want to make it clear that, while every effort has been made to be accurate in all aspects, human memory is fallible, and I accept any responsibility for errors.

I want to thank my former workmates from the various squads and units in NSW Police, whom I have worked alongside and sometimes led, and who have stood by me through thick and thin. Your loyalty and staunch support of me against the many adversaries we faced has meant more to me than you can know.

I would also like to thank Robert Ishak and the team at William Roberts Lawyers for your continuing support of what's right.

I want to thank my editors and the staff at HarperCollins Publishers, who have been outstanding, understanding and patient. My initial contact points at HarperCollins were Helen Littleton and Jude McGee, who were both welcoming and reassuring for a novice like me. I was and am lucky to have had your counsel. A number of editors and support staff then helped along the way, and I am very grateful to each and every one of you for your patience, insight and support through a somewhat torturous process, which was entirely new to me. So I must thank Georgia Frances King, Rachel Dennis, Emma Dowden, Sophie Ambrose, Madeleine James and Luiza Grinstein; without you I would have surely floundered.

I must also thank my agent, Nick Fordham, for your steady hand and advice on all aspects of this journey. I hope our journey together does not end with this book. My old mate Gary Jubelin encouraged me throughout – had it not been for you, perhaps this book may never have happened.

And, of course, I want to thank author Roger Joyce who spent countless hours with me, patiently teasing out pertinent facts and asking questions to make sure what I say is intelligible to the reader.

Most importantly, I want to thank my family. Thank you for your eternal support, love and encouragement, you are my world and will always be.

Finally, I want to thank my wife, Natalie, without whom I would be truly lost. You are my life and my sunshine.